A Sample of Reviews

Writing with strong conviction, in a clear and direct manner, Steve Kellmeyer captured and held my attention from the very first chapter in which he presents a dramatic, but realistic portrayal of the current crisis in Catholic education. I did not expect to agree with him, but his arguments are indisputable. Kellmeyer has written a powerfully enlightening and intriguing book which analyzes the historical factors behind the current crisis in the Catholic parochial system. This book will most certainly impact the way that American Catholics view parental responsibility for their children's religious education and, hopefully, will result in positive changes to bring about a solution to the crisis. Designed to Fail is a must read for all adult Catholic laity and Religious who are interested in the education and catechetical formation of both Catholic youth and adults in America.

**- Jean Heimann,
retired school psychologist and educator**

Kellmeyer provides hope that the "new Evangelization" called for by the late Pope John Paul II can be realized by parents reassuming their primordial and inherent responsibility as teachers of the Faith in the family.

**- Rev. C.J. McCloskey III,
Fellow at the *Faith and Reason Institute***

All homeschooling parents know in their hearts why they are doing what they are doing, but Kellmeyer has helped get that knowledge into our heads as well. His research is ground-breaking; his analysis, coherent. In the context of a wider culture that has launched a frontal assault on the moral formation of our children, Designed to Fail spells out both why and how we parents are to succeed in raising the next generation of Catholics nonetheless.

**- Helen M. Valois, MI
Lapis Crucifer Editorial Services**

DESIGNED TO
FAIL

Catholic Education
in America

DESIGNED TO
FAIL

Catholic Education
in America

Bridegroom Press   Peoria, IL

To obtain additional copies of this book, contact:
Bridegroom Press
2901 Country Place Dr.
Plano, TX 75075
www.bridegroompress.com

Printed in the U.S.A.

ISBN: **0-9767368-0-2**

Dedicated to the primary catechists
of every Catholic child,
often ignored on Catechetical Sunday
but honored here:

Catholic Parents

Contents

Acknowledgements

I would like to begin by thanking Kevin Murphy, who kept after me until I wrote the book we had discussed on so many occasions. My thanks also goes to Elaine Spencer and Debi Katy, who spent innumerable hours proofreading.

Jared Olar has been of enormous help in the production of most of my books, and this one is no exception. His careful analysis and wise comments were, as always, invaluable, as was his assistance in recommending readers.

If you ever have cause to use the most excellent index in the back of this volume, please thank Helen Valois as profusely as I do. She did yeoman's work on it.

My very deep appreciation and thanks likewise goes to Ben Nguyen. He graciously took time out of a very busy schedule to answer numerous questions on the canon law issues involved in Catholic education.

Similarly, Fr. McCloskey took time away from his own book to peruse the draft of mine. His comments and advice were both illuminating and very heartening.

I also thank my parents for having provided me with a sure grounding in Catholic Faith. Were it not for the foundation they laid at home through their instruction and example, the apostasy my own Catholic school experience helped bring about might have been permanent. Thanks as well to my siblings for their prayers.

Finally, I owe my greatest debt of thanks to my wife, Veronica, and our children. Together they are teaching me how to be a husband and a father.

But no matter how many people assist me in an endeavor, I am, and always have been, a cussed obstinate man. Thus, the reader can rest assured that every error in this work, right down to the smallest misplaced comma, is entirely my own.

Introduction

> The swollen and ulcerated condition of the State is to be
> attributed to the elder statesmen; for they have filled the
> city full of harbours and docks and walls and revenues and
> all that, and have left no room for justice and temperance.
> And when the crisis of the disorder comes, the people will
> blame the advisers of the hour, and applaud the [rulers of
> the past] who are the real authors of their calamities... [1]

In *Gorgias*, Plato points out to Callicles how irrational it is to
blame current leaders for current crises. Crises are merely the fruition
of a long chain of events, a chain that often begins years, even
centuries, before the current rulers are born. Typically, it is the revered
founders of a movement or school of thought who inadvertently lay
the necessary starting conditions which breed crisis.

Today, Catholic education in America is in crisis in the sense
that it has almost totally collapsed. Over 3,000 Catholic elementary
schools and roughly half the nation's Catholic high schools have
closed nationwide since the 1960's. We have returned to roughly
the same number of Catholic elementary schools and about four-
fifths the number of Catholic high schools we had in 1918. In those
by-gone days, over fifty percent of the nation's Catholic children
attended Catholic school; only twenty percent do today. In days past,
nearly all students at a Catholic school were Catholic. Today, it is not
unusual for the majority to be non-Catholic. Worse, the schools often
do not transmit the Faith in its fullness.

As we will discover, Plato's observations are as true for this
crisis as they were for the crises of his day. Thus, if the Catholic
educational crisis we currently face became apparent in the 1960's,
we can be sure the roots go much farther back. This book aims to
give the reader a sense of those roots, so that the solution to the
problem we face will be clear.

We must begin by recognizing a single fact: the Catholic Church
in America was in crisis well before Vatican II. In fact, the Church in
this country has never been doctrinally stable. Consider, for instance,

---

1   *Gorgias, Plato's Dialogues.*

how American Catholicism handled slavery. From Paul's letter to Philemon onward, Catholics have taken a dim view of the practice. Rome officially condemned it in 873, 1435, 1454, 1537, 1686, 1839, 1888 and 1889. However, despite the clear teaching of the Church, one looks in vain to see American bishops or priests before the Civil War publicly join Rome in her condemnations. Indeed, it was much more common for America's consecrated men to misinterpret Rome's statements. Our bishops, when they spoke on the subject at all, insisted that while trade in slaves was prohibited, owning slaves was acceptable. They were material heretics.[2]

American Catholic laity have historically been no better. For a variety of reasons, we have long had a habit of open defiance towards our bishops. It is not at all difficult to look through American history and find Catholic congregations that physically kept priests out of their own parishes, even bishops out of their own cathedrals. Like the Protestants we live among, American Catholic laity have always had a certain distrust of Catholic leaders.

As I hope this book makes clear, the collapse of Catholic education cannot be laid entirely at any one door. Each generation made decisions they thought were best given the circumstances, both non-Catholic and Catholic, consecrated and lay. Given the forces arrayed against the United States' bishops, the fact the Catholic Faith survived at all is something of a miracle. Still, we must face our history with a clear eye, so that we can address today's problems with a clear understanding. I do not promise you will like what is presented, but I do promise to adhere as closely to the facts as human frailty allows.

---

2   This isn't as bad as it sounds. All of us engage in material heresy. Material heresy is simply holding what you think is an accurate view of God and His design for us when that view is actually inaccurate. Formal heresy is the decision to hold to the falsehood even after the Church has presented you with the Truth. Material heresy is a problem of simple ignorance: education can easily overcome it. Formal heresy is a problem of pride, of attitude. It can be healed only through humility and confession.

Part I: How The First Cracks Appeared

As a product of Catholic school education myself, I can say Catholic schools made me an agnostic for seven years. - *email from California*

Chapter 1: Catholic Education - The Incarnation to Trent

The Example of Scripture

> Then were little children presented to him, that he should impose hands upon them and pray. And the disciples rebuked them. But Jesus said to them: "Suffer the little children, and forbid them not to come to me: for the kingdom of heaven is for such." And when he had imposed hands upon them, he departed from thence. [1]

Start a conversation on Catholic schools in America today and someone will invariably bring that passage up with a look of heartfelt passion. Many seem to assume it forms part of the divine mandate which authorizes the Church to teach children. It doesn't.[2] In fact, if the passage demonstrates anything, it demonstrates that Jesus didn't teach children. Instead, He focused like a laser on adults. The Gospel of Matthew describes the events in the third and last year of Jesus' ministry. He apparently focused so strongly on instructing adults in the Faith that when children were brought to His apostles, these same apostles - having had two full years of training with the Master - told the children to go away. They had never seen Jesus involve Himself with healthy children.

Imagine the apostolic shock when Jesus, apparently for the first time since they had met Him, took a few moments off from teaching adults to pray over children and impose His hands upon them. But notice something else: He did not teach those children. Matthew is very clear on this. Instead, as soon as He had finished praying over them, He left. In the very next verse, He has returned to teaching adults.

Many would consider the above interpretation of the Scripture passage absurd, but they fail to notice the context of the passage. To begin with, it is embedded in the Gospels. One may say many things about the Gospels, but one may not say that they are anything other than distinctly adult books.

---

1   Matthew 19:13-15.

2   The authority to teach actually comes from the Great Commission of Matthew 28:18-20.

Indeed, the same is true of every book of Scripture. The Pauline letters carry no children's illustrations. Peter's letter, written for adults, tells us Scripture is hard to understand and easily twisted: in short, not recommended for children. The Old Testament liturgies, laws and prophecies are complex, detailed and require a broad acquaintance with the whole of Scripture and adult life. Animals are slaughtered wholesale and retail, war and illicit sex abound, of a children's Passover there is no hint. We too easily forget that children's Bibles are created only through enormous expurgation. The divinely inspired prophets wrote for adults.

From all the historical evidence, the Apostles, personally trained by God Himself, seem as oblivious to teaching children as the divinely inspired prophets of old. Even the most cursory reading of the Acts of the Apostles demonstrates this. Not one of the men personally chosen, trained and ordained by God looked out on the vast pagan world that jostled about them and said, "Well, the adults around here are thoroughly pagan and definitely past saving. They won't come to hear our sermons. If we are to succeed in passing on the Faith, we must work on the next generation – the children. Let's start a parochial school." That alone is instructive.

The Examples of the Fathers and Doctors

But the divine example does not end there. Not only did the prophets never instruct children directly, not only does Jesus never instruct children directly, not only did the twelve apostles fail to start parochial schools, but the men personally trained by the Twelve also failed to see the instruction of children as the key to transmitting the Faith. None of the early bishops seemed to have directly involved themselves in the training of children. This is most remarkable, especially when we take into account another relevant fact, that of infant baptism:

> As to what pertains to the case of infants: You [Fidus] said that they ought not to be baptized within the second or third day after their birth, that the old law of circumcision must be taken into consideration, and that you did not think that one should be baptized and sanctified within the eighth day after his birth. In our council it seemed to us far otherwise. No one agreed to the course which you thought

should be taken. Rather, we all judge that the mercy and grace of God ought to be denied to no man born.[3]

Although Cyprian insists on the earliest possible baptism, this Father of the Church does not appear to have started a single school of instruction for the children he baptized. Irenaeus, Hippolytus, Origen, Gregory of Nazianzen, John Chrysostom, Augustine, the Fifth Council of Carthage and the Second Council of Mileum – all insisted on infant baptism, but not one appears to have started or even mentioned elementary schools.

At this point, the alert reader might reply that this is not entirely accurate. Did not St. John Chrysostom say, "What greater work is there than training the mind and forming the habits of the young?"[4] Indeed he did. But the Latin reads "Ouid maius quam animis moderari, quam *adolescentulorum* fingere mores?" (emphasis added). That is, Chrysostom was referring to the education of teenagers. This is quite clear from the context of the homily in which the sentence appears, a homily in which the saint is at pains to point out:

> The fathers are to blame. They require their horse-breakers to discipline their horses, they do not permit the colt to remain untamed. Instead, they put a rein and all the rest upon it from the beginnings. But their children? These they overlook. They allow their children to go about for a long season unbridled, and without temperance, disgracing themselves by fornications and gamings and attending the wicked theaters. Before the fornication began, they should have given their son to a wife, to a wife chaste, and highly endowed with wisdom. Such a wife will bring her husband away from this disorderly course of life, and will be instead a rein to the colt.... Do you not know that you can do no greater kindness to a youth than to keep him pure from whorish uncleanness?[5]

But Chrysostom does not stop there. In this same homily, he also points out that many people are giving the wrong reading to Matthew 18:10, and he intends to put them straight:

> [The Gospel says] take heed that ye despise not one of these little ones; for I say unto you, that their angels do

3   Cyprian of Carthage. *Letters* 64:2 [A.D. 253]).

4   Homily #59 on Matthew 18.

5   ibid.

always behold the face of my Father which is in Heaven"
(Matthew 18:10). By the phrase "little ones" He does
not mean those who are really little. Rather, He means
those who everyone considers useless: the poor, the
contemptible, the unknown – these are called little, but
they are equal in value to the whole world, they are called
little who are dear to God. But no one among us thinks of
them in this way. [6]

Chrysostom is not alone in this reading. Origen, Jerome, Hilary,
Remigius and even Aquinas, writing a millennium later, give
essentially identical interpretations of Matthew 18:10. Again, we may
hear the complaint that Aquinas, near the end of his life, loved best to
train children to receive the Eucharist. True, to a point. The reception
of First Eucharist during Aquinas' life was typically twelve to fifteen
years of age – Aquinas was training what we would consider teens,
but what he would consider young adults.

During Aquinas' life, marriage at the age of 16 was not
uncommon, death by 45, typical. As we shall see later in this book,
agrarian societies considered anyone twelve or older essentially
an adult. Such a person was expected to act like an adult and thus
generally did so. This puts rather a different perspective on things.
We are now beginning to see that none of these Fathers and Doctors
of the Church addressed the problem of elementary school education.
They poured all of their energies into teaching adults.

While the Church did establish schools in the first century, these
schools were almost invariably for adults, not children. They were
intended to train Christian philosophers to answer the objections
brought by pagan philosophers against Christian doctrine. No council
mentions the need to train children in the Faith until the Council
of Vaison in 529 A.D. – that's half a millennium after Jesus rose
from the dead. Even then, the directive was only towards the training
of boys in the liturgy and the Scriptures, that is, the Council was
primarily interested in training young men for the clerical life.

But how can this be? After all, once a person is baptized, that
person has the right to receive instruction in the Faith. The Church
has a duty to instruct the baptized in the Faith, a duty to impart all
and everything the Catholic Church knows to the baptized. Indeed,
the Church has only three missions in this world: to govern, to

---

6   ibid.

teach, and to sanctify. Baptism not only sanctifies, it creates the obligation to teach the one sanctified. Why would Apostles, Fathers, Doctors, even Councils of the Church insist on infant baptism yet be so marvelously, immovably silent concerning the establishment of schools of instruction for those same baptized youth?

How Christian children were trained

It may be hard to believe, but for at least the first five centuries Christian children were educated in the Faith exclusively at home. While none of the Fathers and Doctors of the Church mention elementary schools, many comment on the importance of mothers in passing on the Faith, beginning with Paul himself.[7] Mothers such as Macrina, Emmelia, Nonna, Anthusa, Monica, and Paula,[8] mothers of saints and scholars, show the success of Christian homeschooling against pagan influence and pagan schools.

For the first twelve centuries of Church history, the sacramental preparation of children was not an issue. Baptism, Confirmation and first Eucharist, via the Precious Blood, were all delivered to the infant in a single ceremony shortly after birth. Thus, sacramental preparation of children in today's sense of the word was both unnecessary and unknown. Pagan children who were very young were simply baptized, confirmed and given the Eucharist as any infant would be. If they were old enough to understand the content of adult instruction, they would be included with the adults who were being instructed in the Faith. These adults were also baptized, confirmed and given First Eucharist in that order in a single Easter Vigil ceremony. There were no separate instructional processes for children. Sacramental instruction was a unitive whole.

Every baptized child's education in the Faith was exclusively the task of the parent. This is why Jesus prays for the children, but does not teach them – that was the parents' duty. The Twelve preach to adults but not to children – that was the parents' duty. In the first millennium of the Church, schools were established primarily to train adults or to form priests, but they were generally not established to pass the Faith onto Christian children – that was the parents' duty.

True, by John Chrysostom's time (380's A.D.), parents were already beginning to fail in this duty. Chrysostom laments the fact

---

7   2 Timothy 1:5.

8   Catholic Encyclopedia, *Schools*, http://www.newadvent.org/cathen/13554b.htm

that parents no longer took seriously the task God had ordained them to do. But even though Chrysostom notes the fact, he does not take it upon himself to step into the breach and provide elementary schools, nor does he delegate any of his priests or deacons to do so. Instead, he simply continues to teach the parents, and exhort them to do their duty.

Early Mission Schools

This is, of course, not the entire story. There were a few attempts to set up elementary schools early on. In about 372 A.D., for instance, a Christian named Protogenes, who had been denounced for holding the Faith, was exiled to the town of Edessa, on the right bank of the Nile. Upon reaching the town, he discovered that most of the inhabitants were pagans. So, with the local bishop's permission, he set up a school for pagan children, teaching them to read the Psalms and the Gospels. When one boy fell sick, he healed him through prayer. As others fell sick, parents brought their children to him for healing. He refused to pray for the children unless the parents agreed to baptize them. While the school seems to have been successful, its existence also seems to have ended when his exile ended and he was allowed to return home.

Another recorded attempt to set up an elementary school did not go quite so well. After Julian the Apostate, the anti-Catholic Emperor of Rome, forced the bishop Saint Cassian to flee his episcopal see in 363 AD, Cassian established a school for training pagan boys. He wanted to teach them about Christ by first teaching them to read and write. Yet, within a year of the school's founding, his educational plan was interrupted when he was denounced as a Christian. His punishment? He was turned over to the pagan students he had been teaching. The students promptly showed their love of elementary education by stabbing the bishop with their iron styluses and breaking their slates over his head. None of the children proved able to deal a killing blow, however, so Cassian bled to death in his classroom over the course of hours.

The story of his martyrdom is not one of elementary education's success stories, but it is instructive. Notice that these elementary schools were set up exclusively to teach pagan children. They were mission schools. There is no mention of teaching the baptized in such schools. Notice also that the bishop with whom Protogenes worked had not been running even a mission school for pagan children and he does not seem to have been much interested in the enterprise.

Organization of the Christian School

Now, as time went on, schools to train young men for priesthood and for monastic life were established. The importance of the monasteries in reference to Christian learning cannot be overemphasized. There were no parishes in the early church. Each city had its own bishop and the cathedral was often the only church building in town. While the country-folk might be associated with a particular city, they would typically find their spiritual life most thoroughly satisfied through contact with the monastic communities in the countryside. They would hear the bells of the monastery calling the monks to prayer. The monks were the closest source of healing sacraments. Their manual labour made the surrounding area safe for human habitation as they cleared impenetrable forests and drained swamps. Since the vast majority of people in agrarian societies lived in the country, monasteries were key to the transmission of adult Catholic Faith.[9]

These adult monastic communities served the spiritual needs of their neighbors. Eventually, as adults inquired about living the monastic life, the monasteries found it useful to create schools of instruction for those who wanted to join the community. As these schools grew over the centuries, they began to take in other Christian students, students who clearly did not intend to take up religious life. Still, as we shall see, this latter tendency grew slowly. It isn't until the ninth and tenth centuries that we begin to see a reliable distinction being made between students who are being trained for religious life and students who are being trained for secular life.

In the monastic schools established for Christian instruction, the curriculum commonly revolved around seven subjects: the "trivium" of grammar, logic[10] and rhetoric, and the "quadrivium" of arithmetic, geometry, astronomy, and music. Both groupings were intended to serve a larger purpose. Grammar provided the introduction to literature, the study of how adults wrote to and about other adults

---

9   As Fr. Joseph Fessio pointed out at the 1996 Wanderer Forum, 14th century Europe had 15,000 monasteries in a population of 75 million. To reach a comparable density of monasteries today, each and every U.S. diocese would need roughly 300 monasteries.

10   Sometimes also called dialectic.

concerning adult issues. Logic studied how to construct formal arguments, how to build a set of concepts towards a coherent whole. It involved dialectic, the study of how to resolve disagreements that arose from logic. Rhetoric discussed basic law and history, necessary for the study of philosophical and metaphysical concepts.

So, grammar provided the basic vocabulary of the adult world. Logic/dialectic showed how those adult concepts and virtues tied together and had been lived out in the past. Rhetoric discussed the general theory of virtuous living. Together, the three described how man should live in the world.

The higher studies, that is, the disciplines suitable for "high school," included the quadrivium of arithmetic, geometry, music, and astronomy. Together, these described the physical world in much the same way the trivium described the life of the adult. Arithmetic was not just addition and subtraction, it included basic statistics, number theory and logic. Numbers were, in a sense, the grammar, the language, of the physical world. Geometry applied Euclid's elements, and thus could include things like geography and surveying. It was the logic of the physical world; it showed how the pieces of the physical world fit together. Astronomy laid the foundation for physics and advanced mathematics; it described the physical movement of the cosmos. Music discussed both theory and practice; since the planets were believed to produce music as the angels moved them, music was the language of the cosmos.[11] The quadrivium taught the student how to think of the earth beneath his feet and the sky above his head – the whole universe outside himself.

Together, the trivium and the quadrivium described every aspect of the known world, both spiritual and physical, the inner man and the world through which he moved. Once this training was completed, the student had a firm understanding both of the world and of his place in it. Christian education rounded these seven subjects out with theology, the eighth subject that suffused every subject. It was the goal for which the first seven subjects prepared a man. In short, theology, God's plan for man's salvation, tied it all together in a coherent whole.

---

11   Gustav Holst's symphony *The Planets* recalls this understanding.

> We sent our three children to Catholic grade school for three months. The textbooks were books used by the state schools (we are in Texas) and were very secular. We didn't feel that our children were receiving a Catholic education. In fact, at this point, we don't even know what a "Catholic education" truly means... We now home school our children to be certain they receive proper instruction and strong academics. We were very disappointed with our brief Catholic school experience because we do not feel that our school, which has been around for nearly 60 years, is Catholic in its fundamental teachings. Things must have changed. – *email from Texas*

The Problem of Literacy

As the schools grew, they needed regulation. The Third Lateran Council (1179) required "[I]n order that the opportunity of learning to read and progress in study is not withdrawn from poor children who cannot be helped by the support of their parents, in every cathedral church a master is to be assigned some proper benefice so that he may teach the clerics of that church and the poor scholars."[12] By that time, entire clerical communities, such as the Brothers of the Common Life, were being founded expressly to be educators. Schools continued to grow. By the late 1300's, the number and variety of schools was rather impressive: monastic schools, cathedral schools, canonicate schools, chantry schools, guild schools, hospital schools, city schools, and special educational institutions.

Even so, literacy was a skill as common to medieval populations as airplane piloting is a skill common to our own. The reason is simple. Flying a plane is a wonderfully useful skill if you can afford to own one. Before the advent of the printing press, books were as expensive as private planes are today. The vellum and parchment for the pages required calf, kid or lamb-skin – lots of it. A single book represented the slaughter of an entire herd, something only a wealthy man could afford. Once the skins were obtained, each skin had to go through long chemical preparation before being converted

---

12   Third Lateran Council, 18th decree.

by careful scraping. Once that was done, monastic scriveners could spend weeks, months or years copying out the complete work by hand and illustrating the pages. Finally, a suitably rich protective cover, not uncommonly embossed in gold or encrusted with jewels, had to be produced to protect the new and precious item. Covers were sometimes so rich that thieves would rip out and leave behind the vellum pages of a book just to get the cover.

So unless a king supported the training of literate men, there was little way to finance it. In a subsistence society, the time and energy it took for small communities to train large numbers of people in a little-used skill that didn't directly contribute to feeding and clothing that community was an expense few could afford. Thus, while schools grew in number, most schools were oriented towards producing the biggest bang for their buck: priests. Since priests mediated the sacraments of salvation, it was crucial that they understood what they were doing in the liturgy. Salvation came first.

Monks were trained to read and write because they had to know the Scriptures and the liturgy. They were supposed to guard and maintain these holy things as they assisted a person towards heaven. As the advantages of literacy to management became clear, kings who were themselves illiterate would employ monks to help them manage far-flung holdings, much in the same way that today's CEO's hire computer people, and for much the same reason. We may understand how rarely lay people were trained in literacy skills by simply considering the name we still give to management support staff. To this day, we hire "clerical" staff. Why? Because the secretaries to royalty were always men consecrated through the sacrament of Holy Orders. They were clerics.

When we consider the expense of books and thus the expense of education in general, we can see why so little attention was paid to specialized curricula for children. Even rich men could rarely afford to train themselves or their retinue in literacy skills. Children could not be secretaries and advisors to kings. A child who might one day rule would be trained in the art of literacy, but only because someone who had money sponsored the child.

Thus, when the Lateran Council insisted that even the poor be taught, it said this in reference to training for the priesthood – after all, the poor are as legitimately called to Holy Orders as the rich. No one who wished to discern the priesthood would be turned away simply on account of poverty. The Church provided the only real path for upward economic mobility in Europe if only because she made no distinction between peasants and princes. She assisted both on a daily basis.

During this time, the idea of children's books was, of course, completely absurd. Schools taught adults by lecture for the simple reason that the only one who might have a book was the teacher. If students had the vellum, the pen and the literacy skills, they were expected to create their own books by copying down what the lecturer said word for word as he read from and commented on his own book. At the end of the course, all the students would then have a text to keep and refer to for the remainder of their lives. It was a far cry from a modern publishing house, but given the circumstances, it was the best anyone could do.

Early Changes in Education

Two things changed the state of education. First, the rapidly growing Christian population quickly outstripped the number of bishops available to administer Confirmation. As a result, while infants could be baptized, they were not being confirmed. Indeed, Confirmation was often delayed for years at a time. Since the Church insisted that the sacraments should be received in order - Baptism, Confirmation, then Eucharist - reception of the Eucharist was also pushed back. By the time of Thomas Aquinas, the reception of these last two sacraments had been pushed so far back that the young needed to go through a specific post-baptismal instructional period.

The reason for this is simple: when we receive a sacrament, we must give everything we are to Christ. At baptism, the infant does this through the gift the parents make of him to God. The infant cannot choose for himself. He is under the authority of his parents, so his parents choose for him. But, once a person gains the use of reason, he must personally choose to give himself to God. Of course, in order to do that, the person has to know what it is he is choosing. Thus, a person who has the use of reason must be instructed before sacramental reception in a way that an infant need not be. Sacramental instruction of baptized youth was an innovation made necessary due to the relative absence of bishops.

The second change was more prosaic. In 1450, the printing press was invented.[13] Within a few short years, the price of a book dropped to two percent of its former value. Forty years after Gutenburg set ink to press, America was discovered. Twenty-five years after that discovery, Luther hammered 95 theses to the cathedral door in Wittenburg. America and Europe would together ride the crest of the explosion in books and literacy that Catholics had created.

The Council of Trent (1545-1563 A.D.)

The invention of cheap books changed education tremendously. It not only made literacy an affordable hobby, it changed the way the Faith was transmitted. Schooling children in large numbers had never before been possible. Now, while still not exactly common, creating schools that could teach the masses, both children and adults, became a possibility. If Luther got everything wrong theologically, he did understand one thing. He saw the possible ramifications of using schools to interpose himself between the parent and the child.

By 1529, Luther had created the first question-and-answer catechism, his Small Catechism. The Large Catechism would follow in 1530. Luther's theology survived because it suited the German princes in their contest with the Pope over secular authority. Luther's ideas gained ground among the population primarily where little adult instruction was taking place. Luther knew the ideas he was promoting were not popular in many areas, so he not only courted the support of the German princes, he also tried to gain control of the children. Sheldon Richman points out that Luther was the first Christian ever to advocate compulsory schooling.[14] "I maintain that

---

13   The Chinese invented paper in 200 BC, and its use spread to the Middle East by the 10th century. Unfortunately, the Middle East was controlled by Islam. Though paper was known to Christian Europe by the 12th century, it was not widely used, since it was seen as a Moslem invention and the Moslems had cut Christians off from the Holy Lands. The First Crusade had retaken Jerusalem and re-established the pilgrimage routes, but all the gains were lost by 1200. So, by 1221, Holy Roman Emperor Frederick II decreed that any legal document written on paper was invalid. It was not until the printing press created astronomical demand for printing materials that paper became common throughout Europe.

14   He was also an extraordinarily strong proponent of the separation of Church and state. Luther taught the prince did not need to consider morality when governing his kingdom, for faith alone saved. Thus, during Münzer's Peasants' War of 1525, Luther wrote the tract *Against the Murderous and Rapacious Hordes of Peasants*. In it, he urged ruling princes to "stab the [peasants] secretly and openly... as one would kill a

the civil authorities are under obligation to compel the people to send their children to school," he said.[15]

Luther tried to control the children because he found even badly taught adults often rejected his theology. Most adults in Europe were badly taught because their priests – when they had one – were still not the best quality. Despite the growth in schools, the quality of priests had been a hit or miss proposition for several hundred years.

Prior to the Council of Trent, priestly training was primarily by apprenticeship in an essentially illiterate culture. While a priest might receive some formal education in the schools, books were scarce. Literacy skills were often little used as the village priest came to rely on memorized liturgical formulae instead of the liturgical book he had copied out in his youth. The priesthood was often seen as a job, not much different than being a butcher or baker, rather than a sacred vocation. The problems this caused were not obvious in a thoroughly Catholic culture, but the attitude did not lend itself to answering the kinds of probing questions that Christianity had commonly encountered in the early years of its existence when it faced a pagan world. The habit of defending the Faith had grown stale.

In other words, as Catholic Faith and conformity to outward ritual had become ubiquitous, the perceived need for an adult grasp of the Faith among the general population dropped. As a result, when one man challenged the Faith by arguing in an essentially pagan fashion, when this man was supported by secular princes in questioning Catholic doctrine, the culture was not able to respond. Many adult Catholics fell away from the Faith precisely because they had not been trained to defend it in an adult fashion.

The Council fathers of Trent recognized this. The Council of Trent commanded that each bishop personally preach the Gospel to the adults because "it is the principal duty of bishops" and "the preaching of the Gospel is no less necessary to the Christian commonwealth than the reading thereof." All priests were required to "feed the people committed to them with wholesome words... on Sundays and solemn feasts." The instruction the priests provided should explain "the things which it is necessary for all to know unto

---

mad dog." His advocacy for the separation of Church and state was both heretical and decisive in the Germans' break with Rome.

15   Sheldon Richman, *Separating School & State: How to Liberate America's Families,* (Fairfax, Virginia: Future of Freedom Foundation, 1994), p. 40.

salvation" and clearly and concisely explain "the vices which they must avoid, and the virtues which they must follow after, that they may escape everlasting punishment, and obtain the glory of heaven." Anyone who neglected these duties was to be rigorously punished or entirely dismissed from his office.[16]

In addition to teaching adults the Faith, the Council required all pastors to preach on the Scripture passages read at Mass, and "explain some mystery of this most holy sacrifice, especially on the Lord's days and festivals."[17] Likewise, all preachers had to "announce the sacred Scriptures and the divine law." This was to be done not only "on all Lord's Days and solemn festivals; but [also], during the season of the fasts, of Lent and of the Advent of the Lord, daily, or at least on three days in the week, if the said bishop shall deem it needful."[18]

All of these decrees spoke of the need to teach adults. What of the children? On that subject, the Council said something very interesting: "[B]ishops shall also take care, that, at least on the Lord's Days and other festivals, the children in every parish be carefully taught the rudiments of the faith, and obedience towards God and their parents, *by those whose duty it is*" (emphasis added). Further, all pastors were required to assure the sacraments were received with reverence by first explaining "in a manner suited to the capacity of those who receive them, the efficacy and use of those sacraments." This should be done through the use of the catechism of the Council of Trent. During Mass or the celebration of the divine office, they were also to "explain... on all festivals, or solemnities, the sacred oracles, and the maxims of salvation; and that ... they endeavour to impress them on the hearts of all, and to instruct them in the law of the Lord."[19]

Now, as even a perfunctory reading of these passages show, the Council directed the great thrust of instruction towards Catholic adults. It is interesting to note that in the commands concerning the instruction of adults, the Council always names exactly who is to provide the teaching. Whether it be bishops, priests, or those who "have the cure of souls," the catechists for adults are always

---

16 Council of Trent, Session Five, Chapter 2.

17 ibid., Session 22, Chapter 8.

18 ibid., Session 24, On the Reformation, Chapter 4.

19 ibid, Chapter 7.

clearly designated. But when it comes to the teaching of children it is different. The Council exhorts the bishop to make sure children are taught "by those whose duty it is." The teachers of the children are not explicitly identified.

The Importance of Trent

The Council of Trent is critical for several reasons. First, Trent is the guide for seventeenth and eighteenth-century American bishops as they consider how to shepherd their flocks. Second, Trent's enormous emphasis on teaching adults will become a point of contention in the Church by the beginning of the twentieth century. Third, it is at Trent that we see the compulsory school first established. While the first and second points will be developed in the pages that follow, we will spend a moment here to discuss the third point.

In its twenty-third session, Trent established the first compulsory schools in Christendom: the seminaries.[20] While there had been many kinds of schools up to this point, none had required any segment of the population to attend. But, with the creation of the seminary, that changed. No one could receive the sacrament of Holy Orders, no one could enter the priesthood, without first passing through seminary formation. The creation of this compulsory school turned out to be an excellent way to form priests.[21]

---

20   The success of the seminary would have been impossible without the printed book. To enter seminary, applicants had to be at least twelve years of age and already literate, that is, applicants had to be literate adults.

21   Few remember that the Confraternity of Christian Doctrine (CCD), established in Rome (1562) in response to the Council of Trent's call for education of the faithful, was originally designed to teach both adults and children. Operating in much the same spirit as the Legion of Mary, and backed by such luminaries as St. Charles Borromeo, it taught in streets, schools, and homes. It was comprised of two branches: one for priests and the other for laity. While it was recommended to every parish as early as 1571 and grew relatively quickly over the years, it was only Pope Pius X's 1905 encyclical *Acerbo Nimis* that required the establishment of CCD in every parish throughout the world (more on *Acerbo Nimis* in Chapter 2). Despite the papal command, the United States would not officially recognize and establish CCD until 1934. It didn't become operational until 1935, after Pius XI reiterated the command in *Provido Sane Consilio* (1935), which re-iterates CCD's adult emphasis in article #25: "In every parish, besides the Confraternity of the Blessed Sacrament, the Confraternity of Christian Doctrine, as the most important of all others, must be established in accordance with Canon 711:2, and it should embrace all who are capable of teaching and promoting catechetical instruction, especially teachers in the schools and all who are skilled in the science of teaching children." America's CCD was dissolved by 1974. The closest modern equivalent is the National Conference of Catechetical Leadership (NCCL).

The Church had the power to require this formation because Holy Orders is unique among the sacraments. It is a privilege, not a right. For every other sacrament, the baptized have a right to the graces of the sacrament in question; when requested by someone with the appropriate disposition, the sacrament cannot be withheld. A sacrament can, perhaps, be delayed for good reason, but never withheld. Even baptism, while not a right in the absolute sense, can only be delayed in order to assure that the catechumen who desires it truly has a full knowledge of what the sacrament does and is truly willing to accept the responsibilities it entails.

With Holy Orders, it is different. The standard for proper disposition is much more stringent. Thus, the Church has a unique ability to require formation for this sacrament, an ability to require certain proofs from the candidate that have no parallel in reference to the other sacraments. Further, those who subject themselves to this process are adults who choose to undergo the preparation themselves.

Thus, while seminary formation is compulsory, it is not compulsory on everyone, rather, it is compulsory only on those male adults who freely choose to discern for themselves and the Church whether God calls them to receive the gift of Holy Orders. While the seminaries were an admirable solution to a difficult problem, anyone who failed to keep in mind the special status of Holy Orders might well draw the wrong conclusion. The success of the seminaries might cause some to consider that compulsory schools should be established in a different, less appropriate context.

> The thought has crossed our mind before about closing down the parish schools for a year or two to focus on adult education and then reopening with a more solid adult foundation in place. A practical solution? Absolutely not. Something that will ever happen? Unlikely. Yet at the same time, to even have that thought crossing our minds is an indication of the desperate straits Catholic education finds itself in. - *email from Illinois*

Chapter 2: Catholic Schools in America

It is worthwhile to pause a moment and consider what we have learned. For roughly one and a half millennia, children were largely educated in the Faith at home. Those compulsory schools that existed were strictly for adults. In fact, although most schools were reserved to adults, the majority of adults could not afford to attend. Europe was, therefore, largely illiterate even centuries after the printing press was developed.

This would not be the case in America, however. While Catholics can practice the Faith regardless of literacy level, Protestantism cannot exist apart from books and literacy. America was populated after the invention of the printing press. The Protestants who emigrated to her shores tended to be literate before they boarded ship. As a result, America's eastern seaboard would see education in an entirely different light.

The First Century

By the time America was discovered and settled, the Catholic tradition of schools was firmly established in Europe. Nearly all of the European schools, from the smallest parish school to the largest universities, were founded by the Catholic Church. In America, this was not true. While some early colleges and universities were Catholic, beginning with Georgetown in 1789, and Baltimore's St. Mary's Seminary in 1791, many more colleges were Protestant. And, as in the early Church, Catholic elementary schools were slow off the mark.

The Spanish and French colonies in what would become California, New Mexico, and Florida had established Catholic schools in the early 1600's. These, however, were mission schools intended primarily for the conversion and education of the pagan native American population. In these areas, as in Europe, a few literate priests ministered to a largely illiterate native society.

On the British Eastern seaboard, the story was quite different. Due to Henry VIII's heresy, England had been Protestant for roughly a century prior to the settling of Jamestown. The rift Henry caused and the ensuing struggle over the throne reduced Catholics to a minority in England and created an unyielding anti-Catholic bigotry in the hearts of most English colonists. Thus, while the Catholic colony of Maryland had established a school in about 1640, Catholics soon formed a minority even in that colony.

The British did not love Catholics. In the seventy-five years prior to the American Revolution, the British colonies mimicked the laws of their English homeland. Thus, it was not uncommon for Catholic colonists to suffer a double taxation or to be deprived of the right to vote or hold office. Though begun as a Catholic colony, Maryland had closed all Catholic missions and schools before 1700. From that year forward, New York did not see a publicly celebrated Mass until French troops, with their French priests, arrived to assist Washington during the Revolution. In 1756, the colonies contained 7000 Catholics and six Jesuit priests in a largely literate population of two million. Thirty years later, Catholics still made up only one percent of the population in the thirteen colonies, and there were but twenty-four Jesuit priests.

The French and Indian war fought during those years was widely viewed as a religious war, pitting Protestant British colonists against French and Indian Catholics, the latter having been evangelized by French Jesuits.[1] For American colonists, the Indian was not just nature's savage, but a religious savage as well, someone who exchanged heathen paganism for idolatrous Catholicism at the behest of scheming Jesuits. Anti-Catholic fervor in America during the war was high, and was only slightly moderated by the Protestant victory in 1763.

While America's Protestants found it necessary to enlist French Catholic help in their battle for independence, the core of American anti-Catholicism was not much altered. Its expression simply became politically unwise and was therefore, as a rule, not publicly encouraged. For instance, after the French joined the war on the side of the American rebels, Washington had to advise his troops to stop burning the Pope in effigy on Guy Fawkes' Day, the anniversary which celebrated the Protestant foiling of a Catholic plot to blow up Parliament.

---

1   See Francis Northcote Parkman's remarkable history, *The Jesuits in North America* (1867). Though virulently anti-Catholic himself, Parkinson admitted that his own primary-document research showed how Jesuit influence tamed the cannibalistic, predatory habits of the native Americans.

Given these attitudes and the extremely small Catholic population, Catholic schools were extremely uncommon in the British colonies and would remain so for quite some time.[2] There was a further problem. Because America was mission territory with virtually no priests, Catholics who did congregate had no clerical guidance. They often bought land, built a church and then corresponded for months or years with European priests in an attempt to get someone to come to serve. The priests who did come were often essentially vagrants on the run from problems in their home country. One of the first priests appointed to New York, for example, later turned out to have forged his documents so that no one would realize he had been stripped of his priestly faculties by his Dublin bishop.

> Catholic students who visited a Catholic high school teacher at his apartment were well aware that he used cocaine and had regular sexual liaisons with one of his seventeen-year old female students. The school principal, a former high school football coach, dealt with the problem by asking the teacher if he was indeed having sex with a student. When the teacher denied it, the matter was dropped. The young girl continued to have sex with her teacher. - *email from Illinois*

Given these circumstances, Bishop Carroll's first pastoral letter in 1792 was perfectly logical. He called on Catholic parents to homeschool their children in the Faith:

> I have considered the virtuous and Christian instruction of youth as a principal object of pastoral solicitude. Now who can contribute so much to lighten this burden... and who can have so great an interest and special duty in the forming of youthful minds to habits of virtue and religion, as their parents themselves?... Wherefore, fathers and mothers, be mindful of the words of the Apostles, and bring up your children in the discipline and correction of

---

2   Indeed, early Catholic schools were a form of non-violent resistance established to combat overwhelming Protestant influence in public life.

the Lord. In doing this, you not only render an acceptable
service to God, and acquit yourselves of a most important
duty, but you labour for the preservation and increase of
true religion...[3]

While he did recommend newly-established Georgetown as a
place of instruction, he did so in a specific context. He hoped some
of the graduates would return to their communities and help with
instruction, but he also hoped some of its graduates would go on for
seminary formation. The bishop saw Georgetown at least in part as
a pre-seminary.

Thus, as it had been throughout most of Catholic history,
homeschooling in the Faith continued to be the rule for Catholics in
America.[4] But, while homeschooling formed the children, Bishop
Carroll had no corresponding way to form adults. Unlike Europe,
America had no monastaries, no stable community life through
which Catholic adults could receive formation or regulate their
lives in accordance with an adult Catholic culture. Far from having
monastic communities, many American Catholics were lucky to have
even an itinerant priest minister to them. Consequently, the mutual
enrichment that monastic communities and Catholic families blessed
each other with throughout European history was simply not present
in the United States. Despite the Church's best efforts, Catholics in
America were orphans both spiritually and culturally, awash in a
Protestant sea of individualism that soaked into their bones.

Staunching the Protestant Tide

Despite these difficulties, St. Peter's Catholic School in New
York had, by 1806, been established and successfully managed to
petition the state for public aid. But, more important, Saint Elizabeth
Ann Seton began her own system of schools. Mrs. Seton had always
felt an attraction towards the Church, and the time she spent in

---

3   Bishop Carroll's first pastoral letter. http://www.ewtn.com/library/BISHOPS/
BC1792.HTM

4   It could hardly be otherwise. The diocese of Baltimore established under Bishop
Carroll in 1789 had only 36 priests for the 35,000 Catholics spread through essentially
all the land east of the Mississippi. Even by 1818, Archbishop Ambrose Maréchal of
Baltimore had only fifty-two priests to serve 100,000 in that same territory. Worse,
only twelve of those priests were American; the archbishop himself was French. Rome
considered the U.S. mission territory until 1908.

Italy following her husband's death solidified her desire to become Catholic.

Returning to the United States, she started a school in New York in order to support her family and assure the proper education of her own children. Though it was a private, secular institution, she ran it along the lines of a religious community. The archbishop of Baltimore heard of her work and invited her to set up a Catholic girls' school in Baltimore. She agreed, and the school flourished. Other women were attracted to the religious life she had established for herself, her family and her school. In 1809, she founded the order of the Daughters of Charity to run her school in Emmitsburg, thereby establishing both the first native American religious community for women and the seed for the parochial school system in America. But the seed required feeding in order to grow. Events soon supplied the necessary fodder.

Though St. Patrick's School in New York had applied for and received state aid in 1816, the state had refused further aid by 1824. Instead, all state money was thrown towards the Public School Society, a society dedicated to making the public schools adamantly Protestant. The resulting bitter dispute between Catholics and Protestants reached the state legislature, becoming so intense that it arguably sparked the Catholic episcopal push for an independent parochial school system. In 1829, the First Provincial Council of Baltimore announced: "We judge it absolutely necessary that schools should be established, in which the young may be taught the principles of faith and morality, while being instructed in letters."[5]

The wave of Irish immigration in the 1830's raised the Catholic percentage of the American population to roughly five percent by 1850, but this was still too little to wield any real political power. However, when combined with the second wave of Irish immigration in the 1850's, it was sufficient to touch off a political backlash.[6]

Between 1840 and 1860, legislation banned state aid to Catholic parochial schools in New Jersey, Wisconsin, Michigan, Ohio, Indiana,

---

5   First Provincial Council of Baltimore, Decretal #33.

6   The Eighth Provincial Council (1855) recommended establishing the American College in Rome (Decretal #8) and the Tenth Provincial Council (1869) recommended "the establishment of missions and schools for negroes" (Decretal #5), that is, it recommended setting up mission schools for populations that were not Catholic. Other than this, the provincial councils were silent on education.

Massachusetts, Iowa, Minnesota, and Kansas.[7] Massachusetts and Maine passed laws that required the reading of the King James Bible in public schools. In 1852, the same year the First Plenary Council of Baltimore met, Massachusetts passed the nation's first compulsory education law, aimed at all children in the state. It ordered that every child between the ages of 8 and 14 attend public school at least twelve weeks per year, six of which had to be continuous. In response to these legal setbacks, Baltimore's First Plenary Council exhorted pastors to teach Christian doctrine "to the young and ignorant," while bishops were exhorted to create a Catholic school in every parish, with teachers' pay coming out of parochial funds.[8]

A decade later, the Second Plenary Council (1866) provided a few more guidelines. Title XI's decree, *Of the Education of Youth,* declared that religious orders should run any schools established, and reiterated that a school be established in every parish. Attendance was not compulsory, however, as the council specifically indicated that catechism classes should be established "for children who attend the public schools." Industrial schools and reformatories were encouraged in large cities, and a desire was also expressed for a Catholic university.

As the drumbeat for compulsory education began in the secular world, the American bishops began to address the lack of adult formation. Unfortunately, while the Second Plenary Council warned adult faithful against errors like transcendentalism, spiritism and religious indifferentism, it laid out no formal criteria for adult formation or evangelization. Instead, part of its decrees inadvertently created the conditions for a new heresy, now widely accepted by America's Catholics: the heresy of Americanism.

Separating Church and State

When Bishop Carroll was appointed as the first bishop to the United States, he faced an American population that was over ninety-nine percent Protestant. Nearly every Catholic was poor and about an eighth of them were slaves or Indians. In many states, it had been illegal for Catholics to participate in politics. The separation of Church and state was not so much something he advocated as it

---

7   Until 1877, New Hampshire permitted only Protestants to be public officials or school teachers.

8   First Plenary Council of Baltimore, Decretals #12 and #13.

was a fact of life. Catholic Faith was separate from the state because the state was thoroughly Protestant and would not permit Catholics to participate politically. While the Church had always taught the importance of making the Faith part of the public culture, there was in America not enough Catholic presence numerically, financially or politically to accomplish what the Church required. Apart from Bishop Carroll's own uniquely wealthy family, there were very few Catholics in a position of any power at all.

Unfortunately, while Bishop Carroll could do little about the separation of Church and state, many of his successors in the priesthood and the episcopacy would take a different view. Bishop John England, an otherwise excellent bishop and the first Catholic prelate to address Congress, made a stunning assertion during his 1826 address:

> I would not allow to the Pope, or to any bishop of our church, outside this Union, the smallest interference with the humblest vote at our most insignificant balloting box. He has no right to such interference... (There is) a plain distinction between spiritual authority and a right to interfere in the regulations of government... [If Congress attempted to pass a law prohibiting the Catholic Faith] I would not obey it, because it would be no law; for you have no such power in such a case . . . You (the Congress) have no power to interfere with my religious rights; the tribunal of the church has no power to interfere with my civil rights.[9]

Bishop England's phrasing was, at best, wrong.[10] When he said, "the Pope has not the right to [political] interference," he could only mean the Pope cannot cast the ballot for the individual Catholic. He could not mean Catholic Faith may not influence the public square nor could he mean the Pope's authority does not extend to secular or political matters. Indeed, the authority of the Church extends to every matter involving the welfare of any human being. Thus, his conclusion was simply erroneous. The Church has every right to forbid the faithful to cast votes in favor of a Hitler, a Stalin, a Pol Pot or any other politician, political movement or law that opposes God or His teachings.

---

9   As quoted at http://cyberfaith.com/examining/roots14.html

10   Archbishop Fulton Sheen once called the separation of Church and state "a shibboleth of doctrinaire secularism."

All any orthodox bishop could mean by statements as badly phrased as Bishop England's is that the state must make sure every citizen has the ability to exercise the rights given him by God. The state must recognize the divine image in man. If the state fails to maintain or promote such a government, the Pope is within his rights, indeed -- the Pope has the divine obligation -- to inform the state of its errors and help that state correct those errors. He does this through the work of the bishops who teach in union with Him, that is, through episcopal instruction that directly reminds Catholic citizens they may not vote in ways that assist an attack on the Faith or on its transmission.[11]

As Bishop England was no doubt aware, the Church cannot be separated from the state. To attempt this is a heresy, a complete misunderstanding of Christ's teaching. True, Christ did insist on rendering unto Caesar that which is Caesar's (Mark 12:17), but this must be understood in context. As theologian Christopher Spiller pointed out:

> Christ is in no way implying the equality of the sacred and the secular. The Gospel shows Jesus being tested regarding the morality of paying taxes to the Romans. The coin produced bears the likeness of Caesar and so may be given to Caesar. But Jesus' answer regarding giving to God what is God's refers to man's creation in the image and likeness of God (Gen 1:26-27). While one pays taxes to the state, one's very life is owed to God. Given the universal scope of the creation accounts in Genesis, Caesar himself is bound by this same responsibility. These passages also present an implicit ruling against the state religion of the Romans, which deified the Emperor.[12]

In short, Christ means this: any state that attempts to make itself the supreme authority is in error. The Church He established is alone the supreme authority on earth. She is subject to the divine law She guards and hands down. She has the solemn obligation to instruct the politicians of the state in their proper duties. She has the

---

11   In 1962, for instance, the Church in Malta warned that any Catholic who voted for the Labor Party would face interdict, losing access to all the sacraments. The Church was aware of communism's bloody past and did not want it in Malta.

12   Christopher Spiller, *Church and State: The Sacred, the Profane, and the First Amendment,* presentation at Duquesne University's 11th Annual *GSO Conference: The Academy and the Polis* (2005).

solemn obligation to instruct the faithful so that they can see to it the politicians of the state carry out their proper duties. Insofar as the members of the Church do not involve themselves in establishing the true, that is to say, the Catholic, understanding of human law, the nation and the world will suffer.

Unfortunately, in a nation whose Catholic adults were almost wholly untaught and were actively marinated in Protestant misunderstanding of correct Church-state relations, this would be misunderstood. The decrees of the Second Plenary Council forty years later were no better understood:

> While explaining the Church's doctrine, preachers should also treat fully of points denied by heretics or unbelievers. Their style, however, is not to be controversial but explanatory. In their method they should follow the Roman Catechism and make a careful study of the writings of the Fathers of the Church. Let them accommodate themselves to the capacity of their auditors. In reprehending vices, let them never become personal; neither should they be influenced in their preaching by human motives but declare the truth fearlessly. *They are not to mingle political and civil matters with religious doctrines in their sermons or attack public magistrates. (emphasis added).*[13]

The last sentence in the quote was just as incomplete as Bishop England's statement forty years before. Public magistrates often need Catholic guidance. Unfortunately, the Second Plenary Council failed to insist that religion belonged in the public sphere. Instead, it seemed to require that priests act as if religion was irrelevant to the public sphere.

Given the lack of adult formation in America, it is understandable that bishops would want to emphasize that people should learn first about the Kingdom of God. Unfortunately, the emphasis on this laudable goal meant the bishops were not emphasizing the Catholic duty to see that divine justice is implemented in the law. Put another way, the bishops of the Second Council inadvertently encouraged the faithful to believe a heresy: the idea that the power of the state can be separated from that of the Church. The state has its own proper sphere of authority, but that authority is based in its accordance with the divinely revealed Truth. If the state is separate from the Truth the

---

13   Second Plenary Council of Baltimore, Title III (v).

Church guards and promulgates, then every manner of state assault upon the human person is permissible.

Unfortunately, the error Bishop Carroll was forced to live with, that Bishop England failed to correct and that the Second Plenary Council seemed to confirm was becoming more and more common. By 1888, Pope Leo XIII would call this attitude "the fatal theory of the need of separation between Church and State" and remark "the absurdity of such a position is manifest."[14] Sadly, the absurdity would only be manifest to well-taught adults. In America, most of the lay faithful and not a few of the clergy lacked an adult grasp of Catholic Faith.

The consequence was ironic. While the Second Plenary Council exhorted the faithful to be on guard against both Protestantism and religious indifferentism,[15] its own decrees effectively countermanded the order.[16] By requiring the clergy to slice religion out of the public sphere and the public sphere out of religion, the decree inadvertently enshrined the dominance of exactly the Protestant culture it opposed.

> When faced with the scandal of a divorced Catholic man dating a Catholic high school teacher, the pastor announced that couples who had received a civil divorce but no annulment could licitly date as long as no sexual relations were involved. One wag, a married man, pointed out that this meant all the married men and women in the parish could date as long as they didn't have sex. - *email from Nebraska*

Episcopal Errors

Some have argued that the Council's warning not to speak on current political events was based on the Council's timing: it was held one short year after the close of the Civil War. While we must read the situation with as much charity as we can, we cannot ignore the facts. It is nearly impossible to find any Catholic priest or bishop

---

14   Leo XIII, *Libertas*, #18.

15   Second Plenary Council of Baltimore, Title I (b).

16   See the wording in the previously quoted Title III (v).

in America prior to the Civil War who taught accurately concerning the Catholic opposition to the American slave trade. Instead, several American prelates, either through ignorance or deliberation, actually *distorted* Rome's position on slavery, claiming it was acceptable for Catholics to own slaves as long as they did not trade in them.

The level of American episcopal error in this regard was breathtaking. The American Catholic failure to hold and teach the abolitionist position arguably made a significant contribution to the enormous cataclysm that was the Civil War. In short, if the Civil War influenced the decision to forbid priestly commentary on politics, that influence was driven entirely by the fact that America's consecrated men had been on the wrong side of both the war and Catholic teaching.

But that was not the only point the Council Fathers had mistaken. The sense of the American conciliar documents demonstrates a fundamental misunderstanding of the decrees of the Council of Trent. The American conciliar discussion of preaching, for instance, clearly indicated that the priests were to give homilies that focused on delivering doctrine and that this doctrinal series could be broken only occasionally and only to comment on the Gospel reading and/ or the current feast. That is, the American bishops considered the homily not only the appropriate means of adult instruction, but the sole, or at the very least primary, means of adult instruction.

To be fair, this was not entirely their fault. Trent had insisted on regular adult instruction outside of Mass. But the American bishops, having no well-established monastic communities to form the faithful and having far too few priests, had no effective way of carrying out Trent's commands. The Church was used to mission territory in which illiterate inhabitants were relatively fixed in stable pagan communities. Even in nomadic societies, tribes generally migrated as a coherent whole. In these settings, Catholic mission territory could be grown into parishes and dioceses by steady instruction and accretion.

In America, the population was not stable; it was highly fluid and it scattered Catholics across daunting geographical obstacles. This alone might have been overcome, but there was another problem. Protestant examples of worship were everywhere while Catholic opportunities to participate in liturgy were much less prevalent. This competing Christian vision damaged the bishops' ability to impart the Faith and it skewed everyone's understanding of Catholic Faith.

By de-emphasizing liturgical Scripture readings, the American bishops inadvertently demonstrated a tendency to consider the homily extraneous to the liturgy. That is, the Second Plenary Council unintentionally treated the Mass as the carrot that drove Catholic adults into the building so the homily could teach them. This incorrect understanding of the homily was something of a parallel to the Protestant understanding of worship. For most non-Catholic Christians, worship is primarily a teaching service, not a liturgical service.

Of course, if the "Mass as carrot" concept had been described so bluntly to the bishops, they would have immediately repudiated the concept as grievous error. But the point remains that the Second Plenary Council, both in its refusal to engage the political culture and in its emphasis on the homily as the primary mode of adult catechesis, had swerved significantly from Catholic understanding.

The problem was not unique to America. Many of America's bishops were from Europe, where the wars of religion had also skewed their understanding of the Faith. The problems exemplified in the Second Plenary Council eventually became so widespread that Pius X wrote a 1905 encyclical, *Acerbo Nimis*, which directly addresses the episcopal misunderstanding of the relationship between homiletics and catechetics, that is, the difference between giving a homily and teaching the Faith:

> For this reason the Council of Trent, treating of the duties of pastors of souls, decreed that their first and most important work is the instruction of the faithful. It therefore prescribes that they shall teach the truths of religion on Sundays and on the more solemn feast days; moreover during the holy seasons of Advent and Lent they are to give such instruction every day or at least three times a week.[17]

Pius had to remind the world's bishops that Trent existed and still applied. Adults were supposed to be taught, and taught frequently. The American bishops, hobbled for most of their history by a far-flung, very thinly spread flock and burdened by an incredible lack of priests, had fallen into very bad habits. In explicitly reiterating Trent,

---

17   Piux X, *On Teaching Christian Doctrine (Acerbo Nimis)*, #11.

Pius reminded the bishops that they were all supposed to use Trent as their guide. But Pius X was not finished:

> This, however, was not considered enough. The Council provided for the instruction of youth by adding that the pastors, either personally or through others, must explain the truths of religion at least on Sundays and feast days to the children of the parish, and inculcate obedience to God and to their parents. When the Sacraments are to be administered, it enjoins upon pastors the duty to explain their efficacy in plain and simple language.

> …Perhaps there are some who, wishing to lessen their labors, would believe that the homily on the Gospel can take the place of catechetical instruction. But for one who reflects a moment, such is obviously impossible. The sermon on the holy Gospel is addressed to those who should have already received knowledge of the elements of faith. It is, so to speak, bread broken for adults. Catechetical instruction, on the other hand, is that milk which the Apostle Peter wished the faithful to desire in all simplicity like newborn babes. [18]

As had been true for the whole of Church history, Pope Pius X was reminding bishops that adult instruction was of pre-eminent importance. True, it also mentions the importance of teaching children. We should, however, keep in mind that this encyclical was written at a time when the sacraments of First Confession, Confirmation and First Eucharist were being administered to adolescents of twelve through fourteen years of age. The decree that changed the age of First Eucharist to about the age of seven, *Quad Singulari*, would not be issued for another five years. Thus, when *Acerbo Nimis* speaks of explaining the sacraments, it is *not* describing a discussion with second-graders; it is describing a discussion with teenagers. As we will see in the next chapter, this is an enormously important distinction. In short, Pope Pius X meant to emphasize the importance of teaching adults. As the decrees of the Second Plenary Council show, the American bishops, by and large, had not the same emphasis.

It should now be clear the American bishops' failure to teach the Faith accurately and at an adult level, was systemic. They had far too

---

18   ibid., #11-12.

few priests. Their flocks were spread over thousands of square miles. Travel and communications were terrible. Their own understanding of Catholic teaching, both from Rome and in the Council of Trent, was not fully correct. As Bishop England's remarks demonstrate, when America's bishops taught, they frequently fell into either error or the appearance of it. They had not properly engaged the issue of slavery, they now refused to engage the political culture, and they had failed to properly teach the adult faithful. As a result of these difficulties, America's bishops fell into habits of teaching that would be expressly denounced by Rome.

Indeed, the weight of these episcopal mistakes would slowly curve the backbone of American Catholicism. But America's bishops would soon commit an even more serious set of errors, errors that would result in an even more immense bloodletting than the Civil War from which America had just emerged. Oddly enough, it would begin in what would seem to be a stroke of brilliance: the Third Plenary Council's demand for the compulsory parochial school system.

Part II: The Smashing Blow

[As a former Catholic school religion teacher, can I say the author is] right about the state of things in Catholic schools? I sadly agree that he very much is. It isn't that the teachers aren't lovely, kind people for the most part. It isn't that they don't want a certain level of cultural Catholicism to be held by the students. The problem is deeper than that.

These teachers were trained in systems that didn't really hold to the full message of the Faith. They were trained in places that were encouraging people to mistrust the teachings of the past and remake the Church in some new guise. Consequently, the teachers themselves don't know the faith in a way that they can faithfully transmit it. The truly sad thing is that they believe that they are transmitting the faith. - *email from the Midwest*

Chapter 3: Secular Schools in America

The State of Education

When we study the secular model today's Catholic schools are built on, it is much easier to understand why they fail. Between the First Provincial Council in 1829 and the Third Plenary Council of 1884, America industrialized. The original public compulsory school system was intended to produce neither Catholics nor Protestants, but only factory employees. John Gatto's remarkable book, *The Underground History of American Education,* explains what happened in the interval and beyond in fascinating detail. Much of the material in Part II discussing this social change is drawn from his research.

Due to her peculiar post-printing press history, America had universal literacy and a high standard of education without much recourse to schools. Parents taught children to read as part of their home life; it was part of their religious education.

Thus, in 1812, Pierre Dupont claimed less than one in four thousand Americans could not read well. In 1820, five million copies of James Fenimore Cooper's *Leatherstocking Tales* were sold to a population of 20 million unschooled but highly self-educated farmers.[1] In 1840, Alexander de Tocqueville testified to a literacy rate approaching 100 percent as he marvelled at a country where every farmer balanced a book on the plow. According to the 1840 Connecticut census, one in 579 adults was illiterate.[2] While most Americans had attended an elementary school of some sort prior to 1900, they spent no more than two to three years in it, if that – perhaps forty weeks total.[3] While in school, they were generally not learning to read, write or do arithmetic.[4] Instead, students read voraciously.

1   John Taylor Gatto, *The Underground History of American Education,* p. 57.

2   ibid, p. 52.

3   The first compulsory school law was passed in Massachusetts in 1852. The second law would not be passed until 1864, in Washington D.C. In 1860, one-third of the 300 high schools in the country were located in Massachusetts, where the school year was twelve weeks long, and only six of those weeks were consecutive. Even by 1890, the school year was only twelve to twenty weeks. Attendance fluctuated between 26 and 42 percent nationwide. The higher figure was rare.

4   Indeed, private schools tended not to admit a student who had not already mastered these basic skills, skills that could be learned in a few months at home through parental instruction.

Fifth grade readers included works by William Shakespeare, Henry Thoreau, George Washington, Sir Walter Scott, Mark Twain, Benjamin Franklin, Oliver Wendell Holmes, John Bunyan, Daniel Webster, Samuel Johnson, Lewis Carroll, Thomas Jefferson, and Ralph Waldo Emerson.

Schools were simply not necessary for gaining an education. America's Constitution was designed by men who were all, for all intents and purposes, homeschooled or self-taught. In fact, *everyone* in America was home-schooled or self-taught. Even by 1900, only six percent of American teenagers had graduated high school; only two percent of Americans 18 through 24 were enrolled in a college.[5] Elementary schools were not much used, high schools and colleges were essentially unused, yet literacy was stratospheric and the general population of the United States was commonly acknowledged to be among the best-educated in the world. These facts apply to the entire American population, not just to the fifteen percent who were Catholic in 1870. Thus, when we read about the establishment of American Catholic elementary schools, high schools, colleges and universities in the centuries leading up to the twentieth, we should keep these numbers in mind. These schools were pleasant but not particularly relevant to gaining an education.

We should also keep something else in mind. When we look at the number of innovations in Asimov's *Chronology of Science and Discovery* (1994), and chart those innovations against total world population for each year, we discover something very odd. The highest rate of per capita innovation in the history of mankind rose sharply to peak in the period 1891 to 1908, right before the compulsory school system really started working. Today, the rate of innovation has dropped back to the level of the 1640s.[6] It raises an obvious question. Why?

---

5   *Historical Statistics of the United States: Colonial Times to 1970*, Washington: US Dept of Commerce, 1976.

6   Bruce L. Gary, *A New Time-Scale for Placing Human Events, Derivation of Per Capita Rate of Innovation and a Speculation on the Timing of the Demise of Humanity*, August 9, 1993. http://reductionism.net.seanic.net/brucegary3/Speculations/innovations(t).html.

America Looks to Prussia

The Civil War (1860-1864) forced enormous technological advancement and regimentation upon the United States. Roughly ten percent of the population had been mobilized for combat. Railroad and telegraph lines had sprouted everywhere the army had reason to travel. The railroads needed iron, the burgeoning iron mills needed coal, the steel mills that followed needed more coal. The discovery of ways to extract and use oil not only increased the demand for energy, it allowed the mills to grow all the faster. Industrialization had begun serious growth in America, and it required a whole new kind of citizen.

America's pre-industrial population was made up largely of self-employed small businessmen: primarily farmers and a few merchants. These were highly individualistic and independent men who innovated at a tremendous rate. Worse, American communities were mostly self-sufficient because American families were mostly self-sufficient. Whatever they needed, they grew or created themselves.

These were exactly the kind of men who could not be easily forced or fit into a factory job, even if they desired such a job, which they generally did not. Given a choice between family and factory, they consistently chose family.[7] These were also not the kind of men who would consume an enormous amount of new products just because the products were new. For the most part, they had what they needed and they were too smart and self-reliant to want more.

In short, the citizens of agrarian America did not have the qualities an industrialized society needs. By the 1860's and 1870's, these farmers had begun to produce so much food they were shipping to world markets. The men who were building the coal industry, the iron industry, the steel industry and the railroad industry wanted that kind of market as well, but in order to produce their goods in great quantities, they needed a large pool of factory men, men who were satisfied to punch a clock and do rote, mindless tasks for hours on end with perfect precision. Factories required not only men to work them, but also men who would consume the enormous amounts of material a factory can produce.

---

7   As late as the 1840s, for instance, we know employers in the Connecticut Valley had a highly unstable labor pool because laborers fit factory jobs in around their family concerns as time permitted, not vice versa.

America's industrialists saw England, which had successfully begun industrialization a century prior, and realized they needed to emulate that system. For a number of reasons, industrialists came to believe America's egalitarian population had to be forced into a caste system. American men had to become less literate and less intelligent in order to work the factories more efficiently. They had to become more consumer-oriented, that is, more needy, less self-reliant, less competent. But by 1870, American industrialists realized something else. While the English were good at creating this kind of man, the Prussians were even better at it.

Where Prussia Got the Idea

Prussia, always a resource-poor country, was not an industrial giant. Like the Swiss before them, the Prussians made their living largely through their remarkable military skill. So, when Napoleon crushed the Prussians during his conquest of Europe, Prussian livelihood was put at risk. The problem had to be fixed. Prussian leaders laid the blame for their defeat on an insufficiently malleable infantry. Prussian civilians and soldiers had to become better at blindly following orders. The Prussian leadership stole their solution from the English.

Between 1755 and 1800, England had begun to industrialize. While many histories concentrate on the geography, the machines, and the banking habits that made the event happen, they tend to neglect the human factors. England had a clear-cut class system and an educational model stolen from India. Her industrialization was grounded not only in her geography, her money, and her skill at harnessing the power of coal, but also in her ability to produce docile men to work the new machines.

In England's class system, men knew their place. This made it easier to implement a manager-worker relationship. The systematic enclosure of small farm holdings created a large class of ex-farmers who needed work. By the 1790's, the English had discovered and adapted a Hindu method for making men docile: mass schooling. England, you see, had discovered the Eastern secret to cutting the heart out of a man.

India's Hindu society is composed of four castes. The top five percent of the population, the Brahmins, warriors and shopkeepers, ran society while the bottom caste of servants and the caste-less untouchables composed the other ninety-five percent. Hindu schooling was designed for one purpose: to preserve the caste system. In India, five hundred or a thousand children would be crammed into one large hall and divided into groups of ten, where each group was taught by a group leader. Group leaders were just a year or two advanced from the groups they taught. In these small groups, students were taught to be docile and conform to ritual and routine.

In 1789, Anglican clergyman Andrew Bell tried their techniques on the members of a male orphanage he ran in Madras. He discovered that the system accomplished two marvelous goals. First, the routine of the thing kept the orphans quiet and organized. Second, it kept them from learning to read. Bell saw this as a distinct advantage, since reading led to independence of thought and difficulty maintaining control. By 1797, he had returned to England and published a book about his methods. By the time of Bell's death in 1832, more than 12,000 of these "monitorial" schools for the poor were established around the world.[8]

As Charles Dickens would later describe in *Oliver Twist* (1837), orphans and other young children flooded the streets of London and other large English cities. The British upper class hoped that mass schooling based on the Hindu model might sweep the streets clean of the little beggars. Better, it would teach them discipline and allow them to be more easily controlled. As it turned out, it also supplied exactly the kind of factory men that England needed in order to industrialize.

How Prussia Used the Idea

When the Prussians heard of the new English schooling method, they were ecstatic. This was precisely the tool they needed to rebuild their army. Begun in 1819, the Prussian system of mass schooling would become the wonder of the world. Over the course of the next century, the Prussians would add several refinements of their own to the system to improve its effectiveness.

The Prussian system of compulsory schooling consisted of three parts. The "academy" was for the top one-half of one percent of students. This school trained the leaders of the nation, the Brahmins. The second part, the "real" school, diluted education somewhat; it was meant for the five to seven percent of students who would

---

8   ibis. Gatto, p. 20.

become trained professionals in law or business. The "people's" school, where over ninety percent of the students ended up, was for everyone else.

> As a former president of our own Catholic school I know first-hand the challenges we faced. Today our schools are more of a business than they are a formation entity. Making sure that the best and brightest teachers are sought and maintained is paramount to the product delivered. Assuring that we could compete compensation package-wise with our public school competitors was paramount even to the detriment of a sound budget and fiscal management.
>
> Where is the solution to this issue? How I wish I knew. For our 20-year old daughter I today truly question the value of her four year Catholic high school experience. Educationally, it was sound and she was certainly challenged by several educators. From a Catholic perspective it was questionable at best.
>
> Once again our archdiocesan school board of which I was a member as well was proud of the percentage of non-Catholics. Once again the affluence of our population was more important than our responsibilities to the Catholic students and our responsibility to bring them up in the true values of our faith. I wonder how those who began our Catholic schools across our country would feel about where we have gone with the gift, the sacrifice they struggled to begin. We no longer seek to educate, we seek to profit. It is all about the bottom line. - *email from Western United States*

Basic literacy, enough to follow written orders, was sufficient for the Prussian purpose. Beyond that, the students of the "people's" school were not encouraged to go. The Prussians agreed with the English: literacy breeds discontentment. Knowledge was artificially split into discrete individual subject areas whose subject matters were not allowed to overlap. This prevented the future servant class from making connections and seeing how individual parts made up the whole. Prussian teachers were sent through certification processes that screened candidates for correct attitudes towards the state. As with the English and the Hindus, the whole point of the Prussian school system was not education, but caste, conformity, obedience and efficiency.

It worked. Throughout the 1800's, the Prussian elite grew rapidly dominant in chemistry and philosophy while the malleable masses perfected their military strength. Their school system was the key – the Prussians demonstrated an ability to control their industrial workers to a far greater extent than any other industrializing country had managed.[9] Ironically, by 1870, the United States and Prussia were the only countries that could boast a 100 percent literacy rate. At the time, American literacy was still attained through classless self-education, where each individual strove to build himself up by personal study to be self-sufficient. Prussian literacy was attained through ruthless imposition of classes and mass schools, it was oriented towards social conformity and state socialism.

1870 was notable for several events, not least among them the Franco-Prussian war and the anticipated publication of Darwin's *Descent of Man*. His 1859 publication of *The Origin of the Species* had already become required reading in all the finest clubs and salons of Europe and America. His new work was an even greater sensation: the best thinkers believed it pointed the way towards completely restructuring society into utopia. When the Prussian army, now built from the finest compulsory school students available, ran through France in six weeks during the 1870 Franco-Prussian war, everyone viewed the results as the triumph of Darwinian theory, a demonstration of the superiority of the German race over the French race. Intellectuals on both sides of the Atlantic concluded that the

---

9   Gatto points out a paradox. A corporate culture requires a large mass of people with mediocre intellectual skills, people who will not start their own businesses and are content with mindless detail work. Thus, an inefficient school system, as long as it is inefficient in the right way, is actually the key to corporate success. The slow accretion of individually small successes that such a corporate structure builds can and does replace the need for individual genius. Indeed, too much genius simply creates a hyper-competitive environment, wherein wealth is difficult to to amass. Who needs that? The US Bueau of Education's *Circular of Information* (April 1872) points out that "inculcating knowledge" makes workers "more redoubtable foes" and "is bound to retard the growth of industry." (Gatto, pp. 151-153). More on the role of the corporation will be said later.

Prussian methods of socialization and control were a necessary step in the evolution of the human race.

Hungary and Austria had already begun programs of compulsory schooling in 1868 and 1869, respectively. The Franco-Prussian war provided the key to the 1871 unification of Germany, and the Prussian system was thereby extended to every corner of the new German nation by 1872. Switzerland followed in 1874, the newly-unified Italy began the practice in 1877; Holland followed in 1878 and Belgium in 1879. Britain made their existing system of mass schools compulsory in 1880 and France completed their system in 1882. Thus, by 1882, the United States could officially view itself as being on the trailing skirt of educational fashion and Darwinian eugenics.

Chapter 4: The Purpose of Mass Schools

Invent Adolescence

> In 1909 a factory inspector did an informal survey of 500 working children in 20 factories. She found that 412 of them would rather work in the terrible conditions of the factories than return to school.[1]

> In one experiment in Milwaukee [circa 1980], for example, 8,000 youth...were asked if they would return full-time to school if they were paid about the same wages as they earned at work; only 16 said they would.[2]

In an agrarian society, children are producers. They work the farm side-by-side with their parents, thereby both putting food on the table and learning adult methods of thought and speech. Children in such a society are expected to pull their own weight and help provide for the family. In such a setting, the example of adult habits and interactions, specifically the habits of their parents, are constantly before them: such children are socialized by adults. Prior to about 1820, essentially the whole world was agrarian except for England, which had only just begun industrialization – this was how children had always been raised.

This expectation that children should be treated like adults because they had spent the first decade of their life working side-by-side with adults was so common as to merit no discussion at all. Precisely because they were treated as adults, children were expected to master adult subjects.

At the age of nine, Samuel Johnson was, according to his own testimony, reading and enjoying Hamlet. At the age of ten, David Farragut, the U.S. Navy's first admiral, was commissioned midshipman on the warship Essex while Benjamin Franklin was helping his father in the chandler business. At the age of eleven, the fatherless George Washington started school. Though judged an absolutely ordinary intellect by everyone who ever knew him, he was already as literate and well-read as today's college graduates before he crossed the threshold.

---

1   Helen Todd, "Why Children Work," *McClure's Magazine* (April 1913), as quoted in Gatto, p. 303.

2   David Tyack, *Managers of Virtue* (1982), as quoted in Gatto, p. 303.

At the age of twelve, John Paul Jones began working at sea as a cabin boy, while twelve-year old Farragut – who now had two years of experience at sea under his belt – was already in command of a prize ship captured during a fierce battle in which he actively participated. At this age, Thomas Edison, judged feebleminded by the school, was working on a train, and had started his own newspaper using cast-off type from a printer. Before his thirteenth birthday, his newspaper had five hundred subscribers.

Likewise, at age twelve, Benjamin Franklin was apprenticed to his brother, James, the printer. He was also reading Bunyan, Burton, Mather, Defoe, Plutarch, and works of "polemic divinity" or what we would today call Christian apologetics. At this age, Andrew Carnegie was a bobbin boy in a textile factory, and a delivery boy a year later. Abraham Cowley was taking infinite delight in Spenser's epic poem, The Faerie Queene. In colonial Mexico, young girls were able to marry by age twelve.

By thirteen or fourteen, Southern women in colonial America could marry. Compare this to ancient Rome, where a fourteen-year old was given his sword and shield and could legally take a wife. At the age of fifteen, Farragut was hunting pirates in the Mediterranean.

Between the ages of sixteen and nineteen, many young men and women in America were getting married. At the age of seventeen, George Washington was Virginia's surveyor general.

At the age of nineteen, Lafayette was a major general in the French army and a member of George Washington's general staff. At the age of twenty, Alexander Hamilton was leading the retreat from New York. By this age, roughly half of the colonial population was married. At the age of twenty-one, Aaron Burr and Light Horse Harry Lee were leading troops into battle.

One might argue that since adult life expectancy was only about forty-five to fifty years, children in pre-industrial society had to grow up fast. Indeed, this is true. But given that children had done this throughout the entirety of human history, save for the last century, it might be more accurate to say that industrialization forces children to grow up slowly.

Agrarian America, prior to the advent of "professional" education, had an essentially one hundred percent literacy rate, as Alexis de Tocqueville witnessed. An adult was prized for his sound judgement, not his technical skills. Samuel Pepys, president of the

Royal Society, the most prestigious intellectual body in Europe, and Secretary of the Admiralty, only learned how to multiply and divide after he assumed the latter office. As the British knew, skill at math is pleasant but not a prerequisite for sound judgement.[3]

Washington, Franklin, Edison, Carnegie, Farragut – their childhoods were not exceptions to the rule. Their lives are examples of the rule that existed for all of human history. They were doing neither more nor less than any other boy their age had ever done. By the age of twelve, boys were expected to be doing adult work in every aspect of their lives: reading, writing, working – it was all the same. There was no such thing as adolescence because these gentlemen and their colleagues had, by the age of twelve, already entered into manhood. They entered into manhood through apprenticeships. Apprenticeship was the weak link that the mass schools were meant to attack.

Break the Spirit

Today, biologists tell us that brain development in adolescents is enormously more complex than we first imagined. Due to the teenage surge of hormones, the teenage brain is subject to fundamental structural changes that affect how teens think and behave. Their brain is being sculpted.

In an agrarian society, teens living through this extremely malleable period live in an apprenticeship, they live in the midst of adult supervision and guidance. They perform concrete tasks with concrete rewards. The shopkeeper or farmer to whom they are apprenticed models adult standards in his daily life for the impressionable youth and continues to require of his charge high standards of moral behavior and a strong work ethic.

The young man whose pubescent brain is being transformed throughout these teenage years already has a solid foundation of prior adult work experience and habit. He also has a mentor to emulate. These steady him as his biology catches up with his lived experience. The ever-present adult mentors keep the young man in line and on track while his hands continue the work they have always done and his brain becomes accustomed to seeing the world through the newly-formed eyes of an adult. The apprenticeship system both

---

3   I am indebted to John Taylor Gatto for collecting most of this information on individual careers.

contained and trained young men as they learned to become what they already were – men.

When agrarian society began to move towards industrialization, the agrarian model of apprenticing youth at first attempted to follow. Children who had worked in the barn and the fields now began to work in the mines and the factories. Experience soon demonstrated problems with this solution. While the farm had many dangers for an unwary child, the mine and the factory had more. But, more important, factory work required a caste system. Yankee farmers abhorred caste systems. They had to be broken to obey the new culture.

To break a man, first break his family. To break the family, physically separate the members from one another. Agitation for child labor laws insisted children had to be removed from the workplace for their own safety.[4] The law soon required the segregation of adults and youth, with the youth being thrown entirely out of work. Now the youth were idle. As was noted earlier, compulsory mass schools answered the problem of idle youth. Industrialization had already begun to tear at the agrarian model, but with the advent of mass schooling, the last traces of the agrarian system were wiped out.

Now young men were no longer under the personal tutelage of adult mentors, rather, they were grouped *en masse* with dozens of other young men going through exactly the same unsettling changes they themselves experienced. Whereas the number of adults to apprentices in a trade shop would generally be roughly comparable, or might in certain situations even provide more than one adult per apprentice, this was most certainly untrue of the school. Here, the youth always outnumbered the adults. As a result, the culture young people lived in was no longer controlled by the biologically stable adults, it was controlled by biologically unstable young people. This is the mass school environment.

Worse, the young man in the mass school environment no longer has a fixed concrete purpose in his work. It is often noted that young people are not good at abstractions. The agrarian society

---

4   Gatto notes the law did *not* require the workplace to become humane. Adults continued to work in atrocious conditions. The child labor laws simply separated the children from their parents. In *Faith of the Fatherless*, Paul Vitz points out that while mothers teach the Faith, fathers model it. His study of famous atheists shows every one had fathers who were dead, abusive, weak, or had abandoned them (Paul Vitz, *Faith of the Fatherless*, (Spence, 1999). Legal separation of father and child arguably contributes to the rise of atheism.

remedied that by making sure the apprentice dealt in concrete things; concrete work recompensed with cash payment for the adult work done, payment that fed the family. The twelve-year old knew his worth because the family needed his income. Indeed, in an agrarian society, women and children often generated about half of a family's income.

In the new mass school system, not only was the income the youth formerly generated now lost, the young man was forced to abstract his formerly concrete life during precisely the time he was least able to manage it.[5] What he was doing today would pay off at some nebulous, unknown future date, according to persons unnamed. He did not know he was useful today, instead he knew he was not useful today, and would not be useful for at least some unspecified period of time. He was made to feel like a wastrel.

This plays to weakness, not strength. This situation creates adolescence. Adolescence is nothing more or less than enforced idleness. It is the artificial removal of responsibility from those properly old enough to bear responsibility. It tears the heart out of a young man, breaks him in the core of his being. In short, mass schooling works. It works in more ways than one.

Emasculate the Body

As a result of mass schooling, children were, from an economic perspective, transformed from useful family members into artificially over-schooled wastrels: children started being expensive to keep. They provided an extra mouth to feed but the extra income to feed it with was now being put off for several additional years. Those extra years were enough to break the camel's back. Until the 1870s, most European nations maintained relatively high levels of fertility.

---

5   Watch how the game is played. Ellis Island began operation in 1892. In 1920, an estimated 75% of the 18.6 million Catholics then living in America were immigrants. The youth thrown out of work and forced into idleness and the streets by the child labor laws were considered "delinquents." These young men and women, almost always the children of Catholic and Jewish immigrants, were also considered mentally inferior. Thus, as Dr. Pedro Noguera points out, public schools were consciously modeled on insane asylums, they were detention centers for mentally deficient deliquents. Dr. Pedro Noguera, "Preventing Violence in Schools Through the Production of Docile Bodies," *In Motion Magazine*, January 12, 1997, available at http://www.inmotinomagazine. com/pedro31.html.) He refers to *Discovery of the Asylum*, David Rothman (Boston: Little, Brown and Company, 1971) pp. 83-84, and *The One Best System,* David Tyack (Cambridge, MA: Harvard University Press, 1974) pp. 51-58.

Between 1870 and 1920, demographers note a "demographic transition," a dramatic drop in fertility rates. The crude birth rate during these years declined by 44% in England, 37% in Germany, 32% in Sweden and Finland, 30% in the United States, and 26% in France.

The United States, which in the eighteenth century had experienced a fertility rate higher than that of Europe, also saw its fertility rate begin to decline steadily from the 1830's onward, dropping by 50 per cent between 1800 and 1900. most of that decline coming after 1870. The lead was taken in the northeast. "In Utica, New York, for example, native-born middle-class women who had begun their childbearing in the 1820s had on average 5.8 children; those who began ten years later had only 3.6 children."[6] This was, of course, precisely the geographical region in which American factories first began to spring up, starting with Eli Whitney's Armory in New Haven, Connecticut in 1798. The weapon his factory produced pioneered the idea of interchangeable parts.

Darwinian eugenics required not just control of the intellect. It required control of the gonads, population control. The masses not only had to be stripped of their individuality, taught to follow orders and made needy, they literally had to be emasculated. The unfit could not be allowed to breed. Reproduction was a privilege that should be permitted only for the highest classes.

Edward Thorndike, founder of educational psychology and professor at Columbia Teachers College, intended schools to establish conditions for "selective breeding before the masses take things into their own hands." H.H. Goddard, head of the Psychology Deparment of Princeton and a major architect of standardized testing, agreed. His book *Human Efficiency* (1920) described government schooling as "the perfect organization of the hive," and standardized testing as a necessary means of identifying and labeling the genetically unfit.[7]

By the turn of the century, scientific studies demonstrated that extending the duration and intensity of schooling caused sharp

6   Angus MacLaren, *History of Contraception from Antiquity to the Present Day*, (1990), pp. 178-179.

7   The Carnegie Institute's Cold Spring Harbor lab promoted the eugenic attempt to create a master Nordic race as early as 1913; at least one of its founding members, Harvard graduate Dr. Katzen-Ellenbogen, would eventually work for the Germans as a doctor at Buchenwald during WWII.

drops in fertility. This was desirable – it kept the unwashed masses from reproducing. The first forced sterilization laws in the world were passed in Indiana in 1907 in order to prevent those "unfit to breed" from having children.[8] By 1930, thirty states and Puerto Rico would follow Indiana's lead and pass similar laws.[9]

The Struggle over the Family

But breaking the spirit and emasculating the body was not enough. Every tie had to be destroyed so that dependence on the state was total. There was a backlash, of course. Given the scarcity of American labor to begin with, it is not surprising to find the power of unions grew fairly quickly. The National Labor Union, formed in 1866, had managed to force an eight-hour workday for government employees. The Knights of Labor, formed three years later, grew rapidly from its inception throughout the 1870's and 1880's. They agitated for all kinds of thing – better wages, better working conditions, more say in the operation of the work. Their bosses were not amused. Violence at factories was escalating. Something had to be done.

American coal and steel magnates could not stand idly by and let the 19th century equivalent of the Sputnik space gap open up on their watch. Deeply influenced by their own need for docile factory workers and voracious consumers, by the philosophy of Darwinian eugenics, by perceived German superiority and by their own need to stay on top, America's millionaires began pouring money into compulsory schooling.

Child labor laws not only threw children out of apprenticeships and out of work, it also reduced family incomes and closed small businesses that could not afford to hire adults as shop assistants. This forced more men into the factories where they could get a "steady

---

8   Gatto notes that Gary, Indiana was, coincidentally, the home of William Wirt, a student of John Dewey. It was Wirt who introduced to Indiana both departmentalization of subject matter and the system of bells that are used in every school today. When this method was introduced into the New York City schools in 1915, it was considered so outrageous parents eventually staged several days of somewhat violent riots in protest. The man who imposed this system on the children of New York immigrants was the New York City Superintendent of Schools, William Wirt.

9   In *Buck vs. Bell* (1927), the U.S. Supreme Court ruled, 8 to 1, that the state had a right to sterilize whomever it deemed a threat to society in whatever capacity. That ruling, though slightly modified by *Skinner v. Oklahoma* (1942), has never been overturned. Nazi eugenics programs were explicitly modeled on US law and medical practice.

job" and a regular paycheck. As idle children began to fill the streets, movements to place them in schools gained momentum. Magazine articles suddenly began appearing. Books, lecture series, government investigations considered the "problems" inherent in a school system that consistently produced literacy rates above 95%. "Book-ish" literacy was too high, it deformed the mind. Just two years after the Haymarket Square Riots, the 1888 Report of the Senate Committee on Education asserted: "We believe that education is one of the principal causes of discontent of late years manifesting itself among the laboring classes."[10]

Newspapers, magazines, circuit speakers all described the cure for that discontent. The passage of mass schooling laws accelerated. The laws requiring compulsory schooling were essentially in place throughout the United States by 1890, with the Prussian curriculum of dissected subjects providing the dry bones for students to chew. In 1901, Edward A. Ross published *Social Control*, a book that had enormous impact on the science of sociology. He pointed out "[p]lans are underway to replace community, family, and church with propaganda, education, and mass media.... the State shakes loose from Church, reaches out to School.... People are only little plastic lumps of human dough." He approved.

But all was not quiet on the Western front. Parents could see that these schools were not accomplishing the superlative education claimed. In Massachusetts, where the first compulsory school laws had passed in 1852, an estimated eighty percent of the population was in open revolt against the law. It took over thirty years to subdue the population and force the children into the schools, sometimes at the point of a gun. The town of Barnstable being the last to surrender. In that town, armed troops marched the children to class.[11] As parents rose in opposition to the results coming out of the enforced schools, fall guys were created. School management, in the form of required teacher certification plus the invention of an administrative class to handle both the schools and the teachers, was established by the 1930's.

---

10   1888 Report of the Senate Committee on Education, p. 1382.

11   Sheldon Richman, *Separating School & State: How to Liberate America's Families* (Fairfax, Virginia: Future of Freedom Foundation, 1994), p. 44, quoted at http://anti-politics.net/school/

Teachers had once been clearly the servants of the parents. The new administrative class and the new certification requirements combined with compulsory schools to transform teachers into replacements for the parents. As was soon discovered, the key to avoiding riots was gradualism. In 1919, Ellwood P. Cubberley described the process:

> *At first the laws were optional*...later the law was made state-wide but the compulsory period was short (ten to twelve weeks) and the age limits low, nine to twelve years. After this, struggle came to extend the time, often little by little...to extend the age limits downward to eight and seven and upwards to fourteen, fifteen or sixteen; to make the law apply to children attending private and parochial schools, and to *require cooperation* from such schools for the proper handling of cases; to institute state supervision of local enforcement; to connect school attendance enforcement with the child-labor legislation of the State through a system of working permits....(emphasis added).[12]

Even as late as 1901, compulsory school in America was only 20 weeks long, with only 12 weeks consecutive attendance, while truancy laws were acknowledged a "dead letter." The parents of the children being forced into the school would not swallow any more than that. Not yet, anyway.[13]

The Sacrifices of the Masses

For the industrialists and their fellow travelers, compulsory schooling was never about education. It was about applying Darwinian eugenics to perfect a social situation. Only a few people, the industrialists and the intellectuals, were worthy enough to reproduce. The rest, especially the poor, were little better than animals. They interfered with the plans of the worthy through their silly attachment to their own families, their own sense of self-worth and their God. If society were to reach perfection, they would have to do their part and give these things up.

---

12   Ellwood P. Cubberley, *Public Education in the United States* (1919, revised edition 1934) as quoted in Gatto, p. 101.

13   Again, I am indebted to John Taylor Gatto for the quotes and the analysis in the preceding sections.

As a professional with over 20 years experience with adult improvement and change, I have seldom seen a program succeed that does not possess some element of intrinsic motivation and desire by the participants. The majority of our feel-good, watered down parishes with their equally capitulatory homilies create a mindset among most parishioners that say, "Hey, as a Catholic, I'm doing okay…" This position not only fails to light that intrinsic fire, but further substantiates a sense that any advancement of knowledge beyond grade school is not necessary.

Imagine the impact if our priests were to just do a consistent job of stating the truths about our faith - and holding their flock accountable for said knowledge. How many Catholics would be surprised (or at least cajoled), by a proclamation of Church teachings on any number of topics (contraception, morality, the true meaning of marriage, any teaching from the *Catechism of the Catholic Church*), and wanting to be good Catholics - sought out more information? Unless our shepherds are pushing and inspiring their flock to possess this knowledge, instilling in them an intrinsic desire to know more, no adult formation program will accomplish the goals we seek.

Sadly, this fix is no easier than resolving the education morass we find ourselves in. Many of the dynamics in place that have created these challenges have affected several generations of priests - creating a dilemma where the heretical content of textbooks is often not all that different from that delivered via the pulpit. Our Church in general - and especially here in the U.S. - is in need of strong leadership to right this ship. How comforting it is to know that it is guaranteed that He will deliver this to us, leaving us only to ponder and pray about when. - *email from New Mexico*

So school had several goals. It was meant to sever the ties between family members. Loyalty to family could not be permitted to interfere with loyalty to the corporation. "Ask not what your company can do for you, ask what you can do for your company." Similarly, the ties between the individual and religion had to be severed. Religion provided a sense of worth, worth that did not derive from the company – it was a rival that had to be destroyed.

Likewise, the solidarity between common people had to be severed. Unions were ruthlessly put down. Adults and youth were already separated by the child labor laws and the very fact of the compulsory school. The youth were further separated and categorized. Whereas older children assisted younger children in the one-room schoolhouse, grades and class ranks were now strictly enforced, each group separated from the others on the basis of age. Within each group, natural rivalries, achievement, grade ranks and the establishment of a physical pecking order would further estrange each from the other. Spiritually, emotionally, intellectually, the inhabitants of the mass school had to become dependent on the supervisor, made needy, made to know their place.[14] They had to understand the importance of following orders and doing what they were told.

Even Pavlov contributed his bit. His 1903 work showing dogs could be trained to salivate at certain sounds rang a bell in the Prussian mind. Their school systems soon incorporated this technique, forcing children to drop whatever they were engaged in every hour at the sound of a bell. The point was not to teach them to think, the point was to teach them to respond to bells – a marvelous attribute for a military or factory man. American school systems soon adopted the technique themselves. Between 1896 and 1920, American industrialists – men notorious for the spendthrift ways they ran their factories – would spend more money promoting forced schooling than the government did.

Annihilate the Real Person

But any history of Catholic education would be incomplete without considering a specific assault on Catholic ideas, an assault so subtle to the modern mind that we don't even realize its impact: the assault on personhood itself. Though almost never told, this story

---

14   Thus demonstrating that the first thing to be outsourced in an industrial society is parenting.

contains a key to understanding how society justifies treating men, women and children like cogs in a wheel.

The word "person" has ancient origins, origins rather important to our story if only to see how pagan thought became Christian and has again returned to paganism. The word "person" is derived from the Greek *prosopon*. *Prosopon* means "to sound in all directions." It refers to the mask worn by an actor during the performance of a play. The mask not only hid the actor's face, it also made his voice resonate. Thus, the word not only referred to the mask, it also became associated with whatever character was being presented during the play itself. If you have ever seen the happy/sad masks that sometimes adorn the posters advertising stage festivals, you have seen *prosopa*.[15]

When Tertullian (d. 220 AD) was trying to describe the inner life of God, he took the Greek term and used it in a specific and theologically technical sense. He said God is Three Persons. He did not mean that God wore different "masks" as He acted in the world, rather: Tertullian intended to express the way in which Father, Son and Spirit were distinct in both action and relation even though there is but one God. His work, *De Trinitas*, was one of the earliest attempts at providing a thorough theological explanation for how the Trinity operated and how God could take on human flesh in the Incarnation.

Over time, the word was Latinized, becoming *persona* and through the impact of Christian theology, it became associated with what we now call the individual human person. As the understanding of each generation grew and deepened, the theological description of the word's meaning became more technical still. Augustine's fifth century understanding essentially ruled Western civilization for over a millennium.

Everyone agreed the divine nature, that is, the divine intellect and the divine will, is God. With St. Augustine's new technical understanding of the word "person," we could now begin to see how the doctrine of Trinity worked. As he described it, God has a perfect knowledge of Himself. Since existence is more perfect than non-

---

15 The plural form of the word. Some think the word *person* was derived from the term *phersu*, the Etruscan image of a masked dance. It doesn't matter for purposes of this discussion. All the pagan usages, refer to the part/role played or the mask worn, not to the substance of the actor. Even the pagan Roman law usage of *persona* follows this abstract understanding.

existence, God's perfect knowledge must have His own existence. He does. We call Him God the Son. He is the Logos, the Word breathed forth from the Father, "God from God, Light from Light, True God from True God, begotten not made, one in being with the Father." In a certain sense, God the Father pours out all that He is into His self-revealing Logos. Since this happens without reference to the created thing we call "time," we can say God the Father eternally begets God the Son.

The Son, seeing what the Father does, imitates Him. He pours Himself out completely into the Father, everything that He is. This is called the divine exchange of Persons, and it is a perfect exchange. This exchange of Persons, each giving Himself totally to the Other in perfect service to the other, is what we mean when we say "God is love." Love is the way one divine Person gives Himself totally to another Divine Person, in perfect service.

But if this exchange is perfect, then He must also have His own existence. He does. He is God the Holy Spirit. He is the Person who is the divine love between the Father and the Son. So, since this Person is Love, we can say the Father pours Himself out into Son through Spirit, and the Son pours Himself out into Father through Spirit. The word used to describe how the Father and the Son generate the Person of the Spirit is "spirate" or "breathe." Even today, we hear young lovers tell one another, "You are the air I breathe." This terminology is understandable to us because it is actually a description of God's inner life. For God, the Spirit is the air He breathes.

So, the Father eternally begets the Son, the Son is eternally begotten. The Father and the Son breathe forth the Spirit, the Spirit is breathed forth. These relations, begetting-begotten and spirating-spirated, are the only things that distinguish the three Persons of the Trinity. Were it not for these divine relations, the three Persons would not exist.

Earlier generations of Christians understood that this relationship-based definition of person is incredibly important for us. We are made in God's image and likeness. If God is three Persons only because of the divine relations, then we are human persons only because of divine relations. Put another way, we are only persons because God calls us into relationship with Himself. If He did not do this, if He did not give us the tools of intellect and will necessary for us to respond to His call to enter into divine relationship with Him, we would not be human persons. We would be human animals. Our personhood depends on divine relationship.[16]

Invent New Persons

For roughly 1500 years, this was the meaning of the word "person." It was a purely religious term denoting the relationship of a specific set of created entities (humans, in this case) to God. When we look at law, for instance, this was the meaning that always obtained. English law always began with the phrase: "No person shall…" In other words, no one who is called into divine relationship with God shall attack that divine relationship using method X.

By the 16th and 17th century, however, men began to unite themselves into small formal bodies. They named these bodies after the Latin word for body, *corpus*. These *corporations* soon attempted to exploit what they thought were loopholes in English law. Certainly no person shall do X, but a corporation is not a person, so a corporation can do X with impunity. English courts responded that this was not a valid line of reasoning. Corporations were "artificial persons," that is, they were called into existence not through a divine call, nor through an entering into relationship with divinity, but through a human call. Corporations embodied purely human relationships. Thus, though they were like persons in some respects, they did not have the rights of persons.

Corporations, it was decided, could be sued, taxed and otherwise hobbled just as normal persons could be, but since they were artificial, they had no civil rights. This was an important distinction. You see, if I am a human person in the original religious sense of the word, I have to be paid a certain amount of respect if only because God found me important enough to call me into relationship with Himself. If God, the Creator of the Universe, finds me important enough to respect me this way, then it is rather important for everyone else to treat me with respect as well. This is the basis for the concept of civil rights. My civil rights are based in the idea that God has granted me a certain amount of autonomy, a certain set of rights by virtue of my relationship with Him. These might even be called divine rights. Since corporations are not called into existence directly by

---

16   This discussion of divine personhood is drawn from my theology of the body book, *Sex and the Sacred City* (Bridegroom Press, 2003).

God, since they have no relationship directly with Him, they are not worthy of divine rights.[17]

Unhappily for corporate owners, this definition of personhood made corporations subject to all sorts of legal controls and restrictions that simply would never be permitted towards a human person with divine civil rights. But the founders of the new American nation loved these restrictions. Jefferson, Madison and the rest detested corporations. Though there were few corporations in the New World, those that had occupied the territory had run virtually everything. New York, the Virginias and the Carolinas were all controlled by the Dutch West Indies Company, for instance. Throwing off the shackles of King and Corporation lay at the heart of the American Revolution.

The only corporations that survived the Revolution were non-profits like Dartmouth College; the rest were destroyed. Jefferson and Madison even attempted to pass an eleventh amendment to the Constitution that would have severely restricted corporate power, but they were, sadly, unsuccessful.[18]

Despite the slow start, corporation building began to increase in the early 1800's. Jefferson was not pleased: "I hope we shall crush in its birth the aristocracy of our moneyed corporations which dare already to challenge our government in a trial of strength, and bid defiance to the laws of our country." His desires were not granted. Instead, as the American economy grew, the corporation grew with it, always champing at the bit to be released from "artificial personhood."

As we have seen, the close of the Civil War brought things to a head. Coal, iron and especially railroad interests sent legions of lawyers into the courts in an attempt to redefine corporate personhood. Even though the judges were drawn mainly from the ranks of these same corporate lawyers, they could not issue a public opinion in favor of corporate personhood without risking enormous public outcry. It was a terrible problem. In the end, the solution was finally found. Everyone simply lied.

---

17   Corporations were, in that respect, something like the earliest legal definition of what we might now call a robot or an artificial intelligence.

18   Even so, the United States had not a single bank until 1780, and that bank's charter was revoked in 1785. Four more banks were commissioned by states in 1790, but they were not held by private individuals, they were run by the states that chartered them.

As Thom Hartmann demonstrates, the railroads got around the consistent court refusals to permit corporate personhood through a friendly court reporter, Harvard Law School graduate and former railroad president John Chandler Bancroft Davis.[19] Mr. Davis deliberately lied in a summary of one of the Supreme Court cases he reported. Even though the 1886 Supreme Court decision in *Santa Clara County v. the Southern Pacific Railroad* said not a word about corporate personhood, Davis wrote a summary of the opinion which included the statement, "The defendant Corporations are persons within the intent of the clause in section 1 of the Fourteenth Amendment...which forbids a State to deny to any person within its jurisdiction the equal protection of the laws."

What was the basis for this statement? Before oral argument took place, Chief Justice Waite announced: "The court does not wish to hear argument on the question whether the provision in the Fourteenth Amendment to the Constitution, which forbids a State to deny to any person within its jurisdiction the equal protection of the laws, applies to these corporations. We are all of the opinion that it does." Knowing full well that lawyers often depend more on case summaries to find what they need rather than the case law itself, Davis accomplished his task by adding to the trial summary a pre-trial comment that had nothing to do with the trial itself. It was good enough. Judges and lawyers could now act as if corporate persons were due the divine rights that had formerly been recognized only in human relationships. It was now settled case law and no public decision needed to be made. Twenty-three years after Lincoln's Gettysburg Address, "government of the people, by the people, for the people" took on a whole new meaning.

Make Persons Into Parts

At that moment, the connection between personhood and religion was severed. Personhood was no longer dependent on divine relationship, it was now redefined to mean whatever the state determined it to mean. Put another way, if corporations could be given full personhood, human beings could be stripped of it. Even better, if the state could define persons, it had no need of divinity. Schools could now be stripped of religion because society had no more use

---

19   Thom Hartmann, *Unequal Protection: the Rise of Corporate Dominance and the Theft of Human Rights* (Rodale Books, 2002).

for it. Prior to the legalization of this lie, corporations were objects, things with no rights. The state could revoke corporate charters, seize corporate books, search corporate factories without warrant or warning, even arbitrarily forbid corporate stores or factories from being established.

But, once the corporation legally acquired the same rights as a human person, things changed. Now the corporation has the same rights any human person has, constitutional rights. Objects have become persons. Conversely, persons are now objects. Listen to William Torrey Harris, U.S. Commissioner of Education from 1886 to 1906:

> Ninety-nine [students] out of a hundred are automata, careful to walk in prescribed paths, careful to follow the prescribed custom. This is not an accident but the result of substantial education, which, scientifically defined, is the subsumption of the individual.[20]

A key brick in the foundation of the modern state had been laid. If the law no longer recognized the divine relationship between God and man, then anything was permissible. Man and thing were interchangeable. The irony was enormous: corporate rights were being protected under the same Fourteenth Amendment that courts – staffed by judges who had once been corporate lawyers – found impossible to apply to children, women and blacks. Children could be compelled to attend state schools, a man one part slave by ancestry and seven parts white European descent could be segregated, but the corporation was sacrosanct. Again, listen to Harris:

> The great purpose of school can be realized better in dark, airless, ugly places.... It is to master the physical self, to transcend the beauty of nature. School should develop the power to withdraw from the external world.[21]

The fight had been long and subtle, but it had been won. Personhood was now subject to state definition. If the state said you were a person, you had rights. If the state said you were not a person, you had none.

---

20   William Torey Harris, *The Philosophy of Education* (1906), as quoted in Gatto, p. 105.

21   ibid.

In the 1600's, when the Spanish attempted to define American Indians as non-persons in order to enslave them, the Church protested loudly and vigorously. Two hundred years later, when Americans attempted to argue that blacks were inferiors with no rights, Rome pronounced the idea absurd. But by 1886, the United States had insulated itself from such criticism. The separation of Church and state advocated by the American bishops assured that no such outcry would arise in late-nineteenth century America, even if the Catholic bishops had noticed what had happened in the courts.

Like the rest of America, they hadn't.

Part III: The Shattering Impact

> Catholic schools worked very well when coupled with parents who were loyal to the Church and the Faith. Catholic schools do not work well when the parents aren't going to Mass on Sundays or don't believe in the Church. It's even worse when secularism and heresy get into our Catholic schools - a state too often seen. – *email from Missouri priest*

Chapter 5: The Theological Context

As we have seen, the agrarian system created master artisans, while the compulsory mass school created life-long apprentices. It created a social caste system artificially stratified by age and test grades. It took the youth out of the workforce, eliminated their income contribution to the family, separated them from their parents, made them dependent on non-familial authority, reduced their ability to read and learn, and eliminated both early marriage and large families. America's industrialists intended to quietly transform society into a Utopia, what Aldous Huxley would call a Brave New World.

But, as the American drumbeat for compulsory schooling suddenly increased in the 1870's, the American bishops had no real way of knowing all the reasons behind the noise. They knew that Congregational, Presbyterian and Baptist clergy had been staunchly behind the establishment of public schools since 1830. The Irish Catholic immigration of the mid-1800's had stirred enormous unrest and anti-Catholic violence among the dominant American Protestant population. The bishops likewise knew this bigotry infested most of the public schools. If schooling was to be compulsory, and it was clear that Protestant legislatures were going to make it so, then the bishops felt they had a duty to protect Catholic children from the incredibly virulent bigotry present in public schools.

One of the major Protestant complaints against Catholics was precisely that Catholic laity were Rome's slaves, ready to overthrow American government at a word from the Eternal City. Catholic bishops, it was said, sternly opposed public education lest their weak-minded Catholic subjects suddenly discover their own power and throw off the shackles of papal tyranny.[1] Even if the bishops had reason to rouse the lay population against compulsory schooling – and they knew of none – how would they do it? What good would it do? They had sworn off political commentary. Their opposition would simply use such a campaign to reinforce prevailing stereotypes,. It would accomplish little politically, since Catholics were a minority in

---

1   The Protestants had proof: many of America's Catholic immigrants were illiterate. No one stopped to consider that America began the printing-press era with a small population that was largely literate while Europe had to slowly educate a huge population that was largely illiterate.

the country. What is wrong with providing a high-quality education for every child?

There is, of course, nothing wrong with doing this. But that was not the correct question. The real question was much more subtle – to what extent had the State or the Church the right to require parents to school their children?[2]

The Principle of Subsidiarity

As we can see from the evidence presented so far, the Catholic Church had always left the education of Christian youth primarily to the parents. This was not just done for reasons of convenience. Catholic theology required it.

> Those in society who are in charge of schools must never forget that the parents have been appointed by God Himself as the first and principal educators of their children and that their right is completely inalienable.[3]

It took an absolutely unique set of events to destroy this understanding. In order to see what happened in 1884's Third Plenary Council, we must review the principle of subsidiarity.

Subsidiarity means "to help" or "to support." Specifically, it refers to the way in which a larger organization or community must help or support a smaller organization or community. Though this principle was first formally described by Pius XI in his 1931 encyclical *Quadragesimo Anno*, it has been recognized as a guiding principle within the Church from Her beginning.

> Still, that most weighty principle, which cannot be set aside or changed, remains fixed and unshaken in social philosophy: Just as it is gravely wrong to take from individuals what they can accomplish by their own initiative and industry and give it to the community, so also it is an injustice and at the same time a grave evil and disturbance of right order to assign to a greater and higher association what lesser and subordinate organizations can do. For every social activity ought of its very nature to

---

2   Certainly every child has a right to education, but as we all know, schooling and education are two entirely different things.

3   John Paul II, *Family in the Modern World (Familiaris Consortio)*, #40.

furnish help to the members of the body social, and never destroy and absorb them.[4]

The "principle of subsidiarity" must be respected: "A community of a higher order should not interfere with the life of a community of a lower order, taking over its functions." In case of need it should, rather, support the smaller community and help to coordinate its activity with activities in the rest of society for the sake of the common good.[5]

Origins in Scripture

The earliest example of the principle may be found in Scripture itself. Adam, as the patriarch of the human race, definitively rejected God's grace at the Fall. This created the problem of subsidiarity that only Christ could solve. You see, God respects the principle of subsidiarity. Adam was patriarch of the whole human race. He had the responsibility to accept or reject the inheritance of grace that God offered. If he refused God's gift of grace, the only way God could give to mankind the full gift while still respecting the principle of subsidiarity was to ask a human person who had greater authority than Adam to accept the gift. But Adam was the eldest, the father of the family of man: no human being could overrule his authority. The only one who had more authority than Adam was God Himself. Unfortunately, though God was the creator of human nature, He did not possess it. In Adam, He had given mankind the right to accept or reject the divine gift of grace, and what God gives, He preserves. He would not take that right away from mankind. What could He do?

God solved the problem by taking on human nature, flesh and blood. Jesus is both God and man. As both a member of the human race and God, He thereby had the authority to accept the gifts of grace Adam had rejected.

However, because God-made-man held greater authority than even Adam, He thereby not only took on the joy of again making sanctifying grace available to the human race. He also took on responsibility for the consequences of the errors Adam had committed. Thus, the new Adam bore in His body the penalty

---

4   Pius XI, *The Fortieth Year (Quadragesimo Anno)*, #79.

5   John Paul II, *The Hundredth Year (Centesimus Annus)*, #48.

incurred by the first Adam and all Adam's descendants. This is the principle of subsidiarity in action. When the higher body takes on the lower body's task, it also takes on all the consequences, good or bad, the lower body incurred by failing to fulfill those tasks.

The principle of subsidiarity runs throughout Jesus' life and ministry. Though He is God and has the power to create a human body from nothing, He consents to be born of a woman. It is the woman's responsibility to bear children, and God will not take it from her. However, the woman, in consenting to become the mother of God, thereby also consents to having her heart pierced by swords of sorrow. That is part of the responsibility, and God will not take that from her either.

Though Jesus is the one with the power to baptize, John the Baptist is the one who baptizes. He allows this apparent reversal of roles because He seeks to "fulfill all righteousness."[6] God gave to John the mission of baptizing, and God will not take it from him. John, in accepting this role, simultaneously accepts the consequence of imprisonment and beheading that will follow from that role.

Jesus healed the lepers. He could have pronounced them clean Himself. Instead, He orders them to show themselves to the priests as the law of Moses required, again fulfilling the law of subsidiarity. God gave to the Levitical priests the duty to make the judgement of ritual cleanliness, and God will not take the work from them. However, the priests with whom Christ interacted, in accepting this office, also had a duty to accept the Pure One who performed the cleansing. They refused to accept the humiliating aspect of their office, and the grievous error of crucifying God therefore followed.

Christ's apostles imitated His example of subsidiarity. In Paul's letter to Philemon, Paul admits he could order Philemon to release the slave Onesimus,[7] but he doesn't give the order. Instead, he "prefers nothing be done without your (Philemon's) consent."[8] That is, he gives Philemon a chance to exercise Christian charity and release the slave himself, an act he should have undertaken even without

---

6   Matthew 3:13

7   Philemon 8.

8   Philemon 14.

Onesimus' baptism.[9] As part of the request, Paul insists on taking on every one of Onesimus' debts.[10]

Paul knows and respects the principle of subsidiarity. When he sees the incorrect relationship between Philemon and Onesimus, he doesn't intervene in the relationship directly, rather he formally warns Philemon on the nature of his error and then exhorts him to correct the error. Philemon has authority in the relationship. Paul does not tell Onesimus to abandon Philemon, rather Onesimus is returned to Philemon. Paul gives them both a chance to heal the relationship, and he does so in part by taking on all of Onesimus' debts. When Paul sends Onesimus back to Philemon, he allows Philemon to correct injustice, exercise God's grace and prove himself a true child of God. Paul exercises the principle of subsidiarity.

Subsidiarity: Secular versus Ecclesial Applications

Unfortunately, while the principle has been with the Church since the beginning, the principle was not clearly explained until 1931. Fortunately, we can study the writings since that time in order to discover the formal principles. When we do this, we discover that there is but one principle with two entirely distinct applications: the application in the civil sphere and the application in the spiritual sphere.

> Leo XIII... in the Encyclicals *Immortale Dei* and *Sapientiae Christianae*...writes as follows: God has divided the government of the human race between two authorities, ecclesiastical and civil, establishing one over things divine, the other over things human. Both are supreme, each in its own domain; each has its own fixed boundaries which limit its activities. These boundaries are determined by the peculiar nature and the proximate end of each, and describe as it were a sphere within which, with exclusive right, each may develop its influence. As however the same subjects are under the two authorities, it may happen that the same matter, though from a different point of view, may come under the competence and jurisdiction of each of them. If follows that divine Providence, whence both authorities have their origin,

---

9   Philemon 11.

10   Philemon 18.

must have traced with due order the proper line of action
for each. The powers that are, are ordained of God.[11]

The distinction between the applications in human law and
divine law is necessary precisely because man is a fallen creature,
but he is not totally corrupt. He is injured, damaged by the Fall in
a way that only God can heal, but he still retains some measure of
grace, he retains the call to be in intimate communion with God,
that is, he retains his personhood. The damage to the person must be
recognized and healed, the grace of personhood must be recognized
and respected. This dual application has serious implications for the
family and therefore for both secular society and the Church, for the
family is the foundation of both.

> Education is essentially a social and not a mere individual
> activity. Now there are three necessary societies, distinct
> from one another and yet harmoniously combined by God,
> into which man is born: two, namely the family and civil
> society, belong to the natural order; the third, the Church,
> to the supernatural order. [12]

As we will soon see, education is an intrinsic part of the family's
function. The state and the Church are both larger organizations,
the family is definitely the smallest of the three. The family is the
organization that requires support from the other two in carrying out
its work. But, because of the different natures of state and Church,
those two societies have entirely different ways of applying the
principle of subsidiarity. Civil society, that is, the government, assists
men by recognizing and respecting the inherent dignity of man before
God, the grace that retains from the Fall. Ecclesial society, that is, the
Church, assists men by recognizing and healing the inherent infirmity
of man before God, the damage that he carries from the Fall.

The Responsibilities of the State
    In the relationship between the individual and the state, the
state is required to recognize the divine presence of grace inherent
in the individual person. Indeed, as we have seen, the very concept
of "person" is a religious concept. As Aquinas would say, "Person
signifies what is most perfect in all nature." Why would he say this?
Because "person" describes the inner life of the Trinity. It describes

11   Pope Pius XI, *On Christian Education (Rappresentanti in Terra)*, #51.

12   John Paul II, *Catechesis in Our Time (Catechesi Tradendae)*, #11.

the relationships within the Trinity. It recognizes that we are persons because we are called into relationship to God by God Himself.

Thus, when the state faces any human person, the state must recognize that its relationship to the person is secondary to God's relationship to the person. Put another way, the state must consider and implement whatever policy is most likely to bring each person into more perfect relationship with God. The state works from below, as it were. It must act in such a way that each person is encouraged to allow God to solidify the divine relationship, grace, in his life. The state must recognize the image of God in each person, it does this through recognition of each person's human rights, the power each person has to choose to embrace God's gifts of grace.

Unfortunately, the state is neither the source nor the mediator of the sanctifying grace that establishes divine relationship, so it can accomplish its work only through adjustment of physical circumstances. For example, if the state sees a child abused or a parent incompetent, it has the right to adjust the physical circumstances only insofar as that adjustment honors and assists each person in perfecting their relationship with God. That is the secular application of subsidiarity. Similarly, persons have a right to change the secular state so that it recognizes the inherent and paramount dignity of the person. But with the Church it is different.

The Responsibilities of the Church

The Church, being the supreme authority on earth, must recognize both the relationship between the state and the person and the relationship between the state and God. She must do all She can to heal and strengthen both relationships.

In 1946, as he addressed newly installed cardinals, Pope Pius XII simultaneously confirmed the universal principle of subsidiarity and attacked the centralization of socialist imperialism. But most important, he outlined this understanding:

> Our Predecessor of happy memory, Pius XI, in his Encyclical on the social order *Quadragesimo Anno*, drew from this line of thought a practical conclusion and enunciated a principle of universal validity: what single individuals, using their own resources, can do of themselves, must not be removed and given to the community. This principle is equally valid for smaller

and lesser communities in relationship to larger or more powerful communities. And the wise pope [i.e., Pius XI] goes on to explain, "This is true because all social activity by its nature is subsidiary; it should serve as a support for the members of the social body and never destroy them or absorb them." These words are indeed illuminating. *They apply to all levels of life in society as well as to the life of the Church, without prejudice to her hierarchical structure* (emphasis added).[13]

"The life of the Church" is, of course, the liturgy and the sacraments. Pope Pius XII is pointing out that the Church lives the principle of subsidiarity through application of the sacraments. Eleven years later, he pointed this principle out again using very similar words:

> The *consecratio mundi* (consecration of the world) is essentially the work of the laymen themselves, of men who are intimately a part of economic and social life and who participate in the government and in legislative assemblies. In the same way, only the workers themselves can establish the Catholic cells which must be created among workers in every factory and bring back to the Church those who have strayed from her.
>
> In this matter ecclesiastical authorities should apply the general principle of subsidiarity and complementarity. They should entrust the layman with tasks that he can perform as well or even better than the priest and allow him to act freely and exercise personal responsibility within the limits set for his work or demanded by the common welfare of the Church.... *[This] supposes that one has learned self-control and self-sacrifice, and has learned to draw constant light and strength from the sources of salvation which the Church offers.* (emphasis added).[14]

For the Church, subsidiarity is honored by recognizing the divine establishment of the hierarchical Church, the Divine Body through whom the power of the sacraments is applied to the world. Sacramental grace is the lens through which the principle and power

---

13 Pius XII, 20 February 1946 Address to newly installed cardinals.

14 Pius XII, 5 October 1957 Address to Lay Apostolates..

of subsidiarity is focused into each man's individual life. Man cannot heal himself, so the healing function of the sacraments properly comes only from the Church.

While the state is established by man, the Church is established by God. Just as a corporation cannot be accorded the same respect due a person, so secular society has not the same right to respect that the Church has. Neither the state nor her members have the right to tell the Church how to do what God established Her to do. No individual human being has a right to interfere with the sacraments, the conduits of grace, or the liturgy, the guard of sacramental grace, or the teachings, the guard of both the liturgy and the sacraments.[15]

Earlier, we saw how American law confused the establishment of man-made organizations with man himself. Those who invoke the principle of subsidiarity in order to agitate for a change in the form of sacraments (e.g. women's ordination) or a change in the hierarchy of the Church (e.g. making popular vote necessary to consecrate bishops) have likewise completely misunderstood the situation. Just as many today confuse human persons and corporations, so many likewise confuse Church and state.

But as we shall see, the nineteenth century American episcopal hierarchy had already begun to make this confusion. Grace is power. We are given sacramental power in order to use it. The bishops of the Third Plenary Council didn't understand exactly how this power worked in regards to marriage. As a result, they made an extraordinary error concerning their role in regards to Catholic education and the family.

---

15 In June 1967 the Pontifical Commission for the Revision of the Code of Canon Law made subsidiarity one of ten guiding principles in its work. The 1969 synod voted to apply subsidiarity to episcopal conferences. Pope Paul VI promoted the theme both in his opening address to the 1969 synod and in the 1974 synod. The official preface to the revised 1983 Code of Canon Law says subsidiarity "must all the more be applied in the church since the office of the bishops and their powers are of divine law." Pope John Paul II vigorously backed its application in civil society, and in a 1999 homily given at the national synod in Poland, he encouraged application of the principle of subsidiarity within the Church.

My husband and I have chosen to homeschool our son, but if there was a true Catholic school near my home, we would enroll him there in a heartbeat. The nearest one is 25 miles away and, last I heard, had a Protestant teaching First Communion preparation ("Oh, it's all right, she's Lutheran!" Huh?) – *email from Arizona*

Subsidiarity and the Catholic Family

By virtue of their ministry of educating, [parents]... become fully parents, in that they are begetters not only of bodily life but also of the life that through the Spirit's renewal flows from the Cross and Resurrection of Christ.[16]

In a very real sense, the quote from the Gospel of Matthew that opened the first chapter of this book reflects Jesus' application of the above principle. Though Christ blessed the children and prayed over them, He did not teach them. Now we can begin to see why.

The very fact that a man and a woman are biological parents creates in them the duty to become spiritual parents, i.e., to teach their children about the God who is Father. As we saw, the agrarian system of apprenticeship allowed young men to become what they already are. Similarly, in order for parents to become what they already are, they must realize and act on the divine duty to become spiritual parents.

God knows this. So, even though He is God, Jesus leaves to the parents the tasks that He established for them, He allows them to instruct their own children in the truth about Himself. He teaches the parents, the parents teach their own children. In this way, the parents gain the tools necessary to live out the divine task they are called to perform. They become parents. Pope John Paul II summarizes and describes the source and nature of parental authority very clearly:

For Christian parents the mission to educate... has a new specific source in the sacrament of marriage, which consecrates them for the strictly Christian education of their children... the sacrament of marriage gives to the

---

16   John Paul II, *Family in the Modern World (Familiaris Consortio), #39.*

educational role the dignity and vocation of being really
and truly a 'ministry' of the Church… Saint Thomas has no
hesitation in comparing it with the ministry of priests.[17]

The Church has long considered the family "the domestic church."
That is, within the family structure, the parents can be considered
the priests and the children the congregation. As the above quote
shows, the teaching authority a parent has towards his own children
is not given him by the priest, the bishop or the Pope. Rather, this
authority is invested in the parent directly by God Himself through
the sacrament of marriage. But if this is true, what is the relationship
between the family and the state, or the family and the Church?

> It also belongs to the State to protect the rights of the child
> itself when the parents are found wanting either physically
> or morally in this respect, whether by default, incapacity
> or misconduct, since, as has been shown, their right to
> educate is not an absolute and despotic one, but dependent
> on the natural and divine law, and therefore subject alike
> to the authority and jurisdiction of the Church, and to the
> vigilance and administrative care of the State in view of the
> common good. Besides, the family is not a perfect society,
> that is, it has not in itself all the means necessary for its
> full development. In such cases, exceptional no doubt, the
> State does not put itself in the place of the family, but
> merely supplies deficiencies, and provides suitable means,
> always in conformity with the natural rights of the child
> and the supernatural rights of the Church.[18]

So, when the parents cannot fulfill their physical or spiritual
duties towards their own children, others may step in to redress
the problem. After all, this kind of parental failure is precisely the
difficulty we saw lived out in the relationship between Adam, mankind
and Christ. Adam, as the first parent, had divinely-ordained duties
to pass on an inheritance of grace to his children, an inheritance he
had firmly rejected. But, though he had rejected the means by which
his duty could be fulfilled, he could not reject the duty itself. That
is, even though he had fallen from grace, he was still responsible for
handing on grace, something he no longer possessed, something he

---

17   John Paul II, *Family in the Modern World (Familiaris Consortio)*, #38.

18   Pius XI, *On Christian Education (Rappresentanti in Terra)*, #45.

could therefore no longer hand on. Though he had squandered his inheritance, the bill was still due.

Thus, he found himself incapacitated, unable to carry out that which he was made to accomplish. God-made-man entered into the situation to assist. However, He did so by actually becoming part of the family of man so that the authority of man was not broken. He actually assumed full responsibility for every consequence of Adam's original failure, so that the responsibility of man was not broken.

This is how subsidiarity is maintained. If you would act *in loco parentis*, in the place of the parents, you must take on every aspect of the parents' failed task. Pope Pius IX understood all of this, but it was a lesson the American bishops would not fully grasp.[19]

---

19 In the event, the relationship between Pope Pius IX and the American bishops would be strikingly similar to the situation between Christ and the apostles. Christ would often tell or live out a parable, but His apostles simply couldn't seem to understand the meaning.

Chapter 6: The Impact of Events in Europe

...[S]o jealous is [the Church] of the family's inviolable natural right to educate the children, that she never consents, save under peculiar circumstances and with special cautions, to baptize the children of infidels, or provide for their education against the will of the parents, till such time as the children can choose for themselves and freely embrace the Faith.[1]

Pope Pius IX and Edgardo Mortara

Even as the American bishops of the Second Plenary Council attempted to finesse the secular situation by bowing out of the public sphere, two events in Europe would convince them to make up for the lack by tightening their authority over the family. In 1858 and again in 1870, Catholics throughout the world saw their Faith attacked, but in two very different ways. Different as these events were, however, both seriously affected how American bishops viewed education and the rights of parents.

The first involved Pope Pius IX and Edgardo Mortara, a six-year-old Jewish boy who lived in Bologna, Italy. Bologna was, at the time, part of the Papal States. On the evening of June 24th, 1858, Momolo and Marianna Mortara opened their door to find the police chief and several deputies waiting outside. The chief announced he had been ordered to take their son, Edgardo, away.

A few years before, the Mortara family had violated state law by employing a teenaged Catholic girl, Anna Morisi, as a maid. When, at the age of sixteen months, Edgardo fell ill with neuritis and exhibited a high fever, the parents became gravely concerned and asked their rabbi and their friends to pray for his recovery. The young Catholic girl, seeing the boy's illness, afraid that the boy would die unbaptized and go to hell, secretly baptized him, but told no one. When he recovered, she realized the terrible situation she had created.

Every baptized person has a right to be taught the Catholic Faith, but the boy's Jewish parents, who knew nothing of the baptism, were

---

1   Pius XI, *On Christian Education (Rappresentanti in Terra), #39.*

certainly not going to do this. Four years later, one of Edgardo's six siblings, Aristide, likewise fell seriously ill. When someone suggested to Anna that she secretly baptize him, the older and wiser Anna refused, pointing out that she had done so for Edgardo and he had recovered. The comment was electrifying. A priest was told of Edgardo's situation and the priest notified the bishop. State law forbad a Christian child to be raised by non-Christian parents. The bishop passed the problem onto the Curia, and Pius IX ordered the child to be taken to Rome for a Christian upbringing.

As a result, Edgardo was removed from his family by the police and sent to live in Rome. Pope Pius IX, realizing that he bore responsibility for the child's situation, became the adoptive father. The Mortaras appealed first to the Inquisitor of Bologna, then to the international community and Pope Pius IX in order to recover Edgardo. Despite the resulting storm of international protest demanding that he send Edgardo back to his parents, the Pope stood firm. The child was not sent back.

International outcry over the event continued to build. Atheistic rationalists took the opportunity to highlight the medieval cruelty of Christian Faith. Italian nationalists used it as an argument to invade Rome and complete the political unification of the peninsula. By 1870, in part as a result of Edgardo's transfer to Rome, the Papal States were, in fact, invaded and papal holdings on the Italian peninsula were reduced to Vatican City.

Reports on Edgardo's disposition varied tremendously according to who told the tale. Catholic sources insisted he was happy in Rome. The family, who had regular supervised visits with Edgardo, insisted he hated it there. Edgardo's own testimony as an adult agrees with the Catholic version of events. As the first witness in Pope Pius IX's beatification process, Edgardo explicitly stated that he clearly recalls the events and he felt no desire to return to his family – a reaction he himself explained as a result of the action of supernatural grace. When given the opportunity as an adolescent to stay with his family, he did so for only a month, then returned to Rome and Pius IX. As he grew older, his relations with his family were good, if sporadic. He had a vocation to the priesthood and pursued it. Upon ordination, he took the name Pio, after his adoptive father, and his parents became reconciled to the situation.

This episode may seem offensive to modern sensibilities. That's simply because we aren't used to granting spiritual issues any value. Consider, for instance, a young boy whose parents are Christian Scientists. If the boy grew seriously ill and the parents refused medical treatment, most would agree that government authorities have the right to intervene, the right to hold and treat the child apart from the parents until he had been restored to health.

A very similar principle was at work here, the major difference being only in the nature of the illness. As a baptized but untaught child, Edgardo suffered from a lack of knowledge concerning Christ. His parents, being unbaptized, were unable to provide the necessary balm, they were incapacitated. Just as Christ stepped in to assist Adam, so the government – which, in this case, happened to be the Pope and the Curia – stepped in to provide the treatment the parents could not. Nothing else could be done. As has already been pointed out, the principle of subsidiarity required the Church to consider the child through the perspective of the sacraments.

We must remember that baptism changes who we are. Baptism not only granted Edgardo the right to know Christ, it joined him perfectly to Christ. Thus, it also imposed on the Church a duty to provide Edgardo with knowledge of the Jewish Messiah to whom he had been joined.

Momolo and Marianna Mortara made a grievous error in judgment by intentionally breaking the law and hiring a teenage Catholic girl. The young girl made an even more grievous error in judgement by baptizing the child without first obtaining the parents' consent. All of this is clear. But it is likewise clear that once the child was baptized, little else could be done from either a legal or a spiritual perspective. The law forbidding non-Christians from employing Christians as house servants was designed to protect against exactly this situation. The Mortaras had gambled, broken the civil law, but then repudiated the legal consequences their own deliberate negligence had in part created. The Pope, though not personally responsible for the child's baptism, recognized the responsibility the baptism imposed on him and unflinchingly accepted every consequence, up to and including the loss of a secular kingdom.

But the invasion and loss of the Papal States for the sake of a single Christian child was not the only loss the Pope and the Church suffered. There was a second, much more grievous loss to the entire Church as well.

The Vatican Council

In December, 1864, six years after Edgardo had been moved to Rome, two years before Baltimore's Second Plenary Council and two days before the promulgation of *Quanta Cura* (*Against Common Errors*), Pope Pius IX began to investigate the possibility of an ecumenical council to be held at the Vatican. His inquiries with cardinals and bishops were well met, and the council opened on December 8, 1869. The Council planned to compose three great dogmatic drafts: 1) On the Christian response to rationalism, 2) On the Church and 3) On Christian Marriage. In addition, there were a host of less important items to consider. Unfortunately, while it had much on its agenda, the only dogma the council was able to define was that of papal infallibility.[2] The next day, the Franco-Prussian war broke out.

The war created enormous pressure on the Vatican Council. The Papal States were protected from neighboring Italian states by French troops. Because the Prussians were winning incredible victories on the battlefield, Napoleon III was forced to call every soldier he had into service in France. By September, the French troops protecting Rome had withdrawn due to the collapse of the French government.

The northern Italian states that had been clamoring for the unification of Italy under their domination saw their chance. Piedmontese troops immediately threatened the city. By September 20, they had entered Rome. On October 19ᵗʰ, the Papal States were organized as a Roman province of a re-united Italy. The pope prorogated the Council the next day: council sessions were indefinitely suspended; the council was never called back into session. As a result, the dogmatic drafts the Vatican Council had intended to consider would wait almost a century before being taken up by another council, Vatican II.

Since this invasion and seizure of the Papal States had been predicated in part on returning Edgardo to his family, a search was made for him when Rome was taken. Though he was found, he was now eighteen. Despite enormous secular pressure to return to his family and his Jewish faith, he insisted that he wanted to remain a

---

2   July 18, 1870.

Catholic. In order to avoid the new Italian authorities, he and a friend secretly fled to France and entered a monastery where, five years later, he was ordained a priest and took the name Pio.

The Crucible Year

1870 is the crucible year. In that year, Darwin published his *Descent of Man* and started what would become the eugenics movement. The Franco-Prussian war seemed to confirm Darwin's theories. The industrialists began making their move to impose forced schooling on America at the same time that Edgardo's removal from his own family was forcibly returned to the front page of every newspaper in the world, but this time in the context of an ecumenical council's declaration of papal infallibility.

Under the pressure of events, Catholics throughout the world, bishops included, drew an incorrect conclusion. They concluded that the Pope had the infallible right to educate children, a right that superseded the right of the parents. Everyone had forgotten the relevant sacramental circumstances. As was pointed out by Aquinas, as is pointed out by both Pope John Paul II and the *Catechism of the Catholic Church (CCC):*

> The right and duty of parents to give education is essential, since it is connected with the transmission of human life; it is original and primary with regard to the educational role of others on account of the uniqueness of the loving relationship between parents and children; and it is irreplaceable and inalienable and therefore incapable of being entirely delegated to others or usurped by others.[3]

> The right and the duty of parents to educate their children are primordial and inalienable.[4]

But if the right to educate children is primordial to parents and inalienable from them, as Pope John Paul II asserts and the Catechism confirms, then on what grounds did Pope Pius IX order Edgardo removed from his home and transferred to the Vatican? The key here is to remember the context: sacrament.

> For Christian parents the mission to educate... has a new specific source in the sacrament of marriage, which

---

3   John Paul II, *Family in the Modern World (Familiaris Consortio)*, #36.

4   *Catechism of the Catholic Church*, #2221.

consecrates them for the strictly Christian education of
their children... the sacrament of marriage gives to the
educational role the dignity and vocation of being really
and truly a 'ministry' of the Church at the service of the
building up of her members. So great and splendid is
the educational ministry of Christian parents that Saint
Thomas has no hesitation in comparing it with the ministry
of priests. "Some only propagate and guard spiritual life
by a spiritual ministry: this is the role of the sacrament of
Orders; others do this for both corporal and spiritual life,
and this is brought about by the sacrament of marriage, by
which a man and a woman join in order to beget offspring
and bring them up to worship God.[5]

The baptized (and therefore Christian) Edgardo had non-
Christian parents. At the moment he was baptized, his parents
became spiritually incompetent to raise him. He needed something
they did not have to give: instruction concerning his Jewish Saviour.
In short, the Church had to step in precisely because the parents had
a natural marriage but not a sacramental marriage. As the passage
above testifies, the mission to educate others concerning Christ, the
power necessary to do so, derives from the power of the sacraments:
baptism, confirmation, holy orders, marriage. Since the Mortaras
had not these sacraments, they had not the power to hand on the
necessary instruction.

Pope Pius IX said exactly this. He expressly told the Mortaras
that if they received the sacraments, if they became Christians,
Edgardo would certainly be returned. With their acceptance of the
Jewish Saviour, they would gain the power to live out their duty and
their responsibility towards their baptized child. When they refused
to accept the power, the Pope was left with no alternative. The child
could not be un-baptized. What God had joined, no man could break
asunder. God had joined Himself to Edgardo. Edgardo had to be
taught about Christ.

The American bishops not only missed this distinction, they
missed a second and much more telling aspect of the situation,
even though that aspect had twice been splashed across the pages
of every newspaper, once in 1858 and again in 1870: Pius IX took
total personal responsibility for the boy. Just as Christ stepped in to

---

5   Thomas Aquinas, *Summa Contra Gentiles*, 4:58, as quoted by John Paul II, *Family in the Modern World (Familiaris Consortio)*, #38.

take on both the responsibility and the consequences that Adam had declined, so Pius stepped in to take on all the responsibility and all the consequences the Mortaras declined. As a result, the Papal States were lost, Rome was lost, the Vatican Council was suspended and the Pope became a prisoner in the Vatican. But the baptized child learned about Jesus from his adoptive father, the Pope. The child's gain was worth the father's losses.

When he took over the boy's education, Pius became a parent, taking on every responsibility, every consequence. It was the only way to respect the principle of subsidiarity and assure the boy his Christian rights. But this nuance was not immediately obvious in the turmoil of events. And it was precisely this turmoil which created the circumstances for the erroneous conclusion.

> The Protestant principal of a Catholic high school happily announced the engagement of one of the teachers. She was to marry a Catholic man who had received a civil divorce but no annulment. His non-custodial Catholic daughter was in class when the announcement was made. The pastors said nothing. - *email from Nebraska*

Because the Vatican Council had been interrupted, it never had a chance to discuss Christian marriage. If the Council had completed its business, the issue of the proper relationship between bishop, sacramentally married couple and children would have been defined and clarified. The principle of subsidiarity would have been explained in 1870, not 1931.

But this did not happen. Due to world events, the Council was only able to complete the business of defining papal infallibility. Worse, the infallibility declaration was accomplished only after a hotly contested, well-publicized debate over whether this was truly the appropriate time to clarify this doctrine, a debate that would focus attention away from the original conciliar agenda. Thus, the premature closing of the Council meant the world would come away with an unbalanced view of both the Church and her authority. The world would inevitably, if unconsciously, conclude that the Vatican Council meant only to declare papal infallibility.

Now, we should be very clear on this point. The dogma of papal infallibility defined by the Vatican Council was certainly correct in every particular. The problem is not with the dogma, it is with the context, or lack thereof, for the dogma. This dogma was originally intended to be but one among many definitions, and not the pre-eminent definition at that. Indeed, the great definitions of the Council were meant to concern rationalism, the Church and Christian marriage. But no other dogmatic definition was made. Thus, the relationship between infallibility and the Church or between papal authority and Christian marriage was never examined.

The American Catholic bishops were men who shared in the exercise of infallible authority through ecumenical councils and their own ability to teach in union with the Pope and their brother bishops. They got from the prorogated Council a certain exaggerated understanding of their own position in relation to the rest of the Church.

Considering how critical the role of the bishop is to the proper functioning of the Church, such an exaggeration would be easy to assume. After all, the four marks of the Church are her unity, holiness, universality and apostolicity. Since the bishops carry the burden of the last mark, they have enormous authority to begin with. The other three marks depend upon this last mark to avoid collapse as surely as a human body depends upon the spine. It would not be immediately obvious if a bishop were to claim more apostolic authority than he actually had.

So, taken together, the two events brought to the unwary a relatively straightforward conclusion. Since the bishop of Rome was right to remove a child from his spiritually incompetent parents in order to instruct that child in the Faith, and since the bishop of Rome had the charism of infallibility, it must be the case that bishops everywhere have the right to do the same.

The statement, as it is presented, is clearly in error, of course, and if it had been put this bluntly to any bishop, he would have recognized the errors immediately. First, the charism of infallibility has no bearing on whether Pius IX did the right thing in Edgardo's case. Second, the Mortaras were incompetent only in the sacramental sense, and sacramental incompetence would certainly not apply to a married Catholic couple. Indeed, the principle of subsidiarity required the bishop to assist parents who have a sacramental marriage, not to replace them. The bishop's task is to follow the example of the earliest bishops and make sure the parents are well-instructed, not skip over the parents and address themselves to the children directly. Third, even if a bishop could find grounds to completely take over a child's education despite the presence of a sacramental marriage, he would be required by the principle of subsidiarity to do as Pope Pius IX did – become an adoptive parent in every sense of the word.

But all of this was lost on the American bishops. They were faced with three facts that had to be dealt with immediately. First, their own plenary council decision concerning the appropriate level of Church involvement in politics meant they could not fight the compulsory education laws, even if they wanted to, and for cultural reasons they didn't want to. Second, the fact that they had done no formation of Catholic adults meant parents were not prepared to deal with the issues the compulsory Protestant public schools would raise. Third, the certainty that Catholic school children would soon be forced to attend virulently anti-Catholic schools meant something had to be done immediately. Local conditions in America and the unexamined examples Rome provided combined to create an inevitably distorted understanding of sacramental authority and of Catholic culture. This was the context for Baltimore's Third Plenary Council.

Chapter 7: Subsidiarity Violated

The Third Plenary Council

In 1884, just fourteen years after the close of the Vatican Council, the Third Plenary Council of Baltimore met. This council declared that every parish was obligated to establish a parochial school, preferably one requiring no tuition. With this obligation would eventually come the requirement, under pain of mortal sin, for every Catholic to send his child to a Catholic school.[1] The establishment of institutions of higher education was encouraged. The establishment of an obligatory catechism was ordered. The wheels were set in motion.

Ironically, the council highlighted its failure to understand the proper relationship between bishop, parent and child by producing not an adult catechism, as had the Council of Trent, but rather a children's catechism. For a third time, an American plenary council had essentially ignored the need to form adults, but this time it had done so emphatically. To ice the cake they had made, the bishops confirmed all the decrees of the Second Plenary Council: the clergy were again forbidden to mix religion and politics.

While the bishops were wrong in their suppositions, the logic they now followed was impeccable. According to the 1912 edition of the Catholic Encyclopedia, a reference which carries the nihil obstat and imprimatur from John Cardinal Farley, Archbishop of New York, "From the interaction and conflict of these fundamental rights arise the following more particular principles... The Church has the exclusive right to teach religion to Catholic children. Neither the parents nor the State can exercise this right except they do so with the consent (as parents do) and under the supervision and control of the ecclesiastical authorities."[2]

Canon 1374 of the new 1917 edition of canon law seemed to confirm this opinion: "Catholic children should not frequent non-Catholic, neutral, or mixed schools, namely, those that allow non-Catholics to attend. Only local Ordinaries can make decisions in accord with instructive norms from the Apostolic See concerning circumstances of things and any necessary precautions that will prevent the danger of perversion, [and] whether these things can

---

1   Third Plenary Council of Baltimore, Title VI (i).

2   Catholic Encyclopedia, *Schools.* (The Encyclopedia Press Inc., 1912), http://www. newadvent.org/cathen/13554b.htm.

be tolerated and such schools used." In many countries throughout the world, countries like America, Ireland, and Australia, bishops concluded that any Catholic parent who, without permission from the bishop, sent their children to a secular or otherwise non-Catholic school when a Catholic school was available violated a grave law of the Church. In short, such a parent committed mortal sin.[3]

It is difficult to overstate the enormity of the break this understanding constituted with the traditions of the Catholic Faith. In 1884, for the first time in the two-thousand year history of the Church, Catholic bishops began to compel Catholic children to attend Catholic schools regardless of their parents' wishes. Bishops replaced sacramentally married parents. It would not be obvious for another seventy years, but at that moment, all hell broke loose.

Mother Seton Revisited

It was noted earlier that Mother Seton's work in 1809 became, with the help of the Second Plenary Council decree on religious orders, the backbone for the parochial school system established by the Third Plenary Council. It is worthwhile, at this point, to analyze exactly what Mother Seton did, for this system is precisely what became the centerpiece of nearly every problem the Church in America has had since 1884.

We will begin by considering the reason Mother Seton founded a school at all. She did so to support her family economically and to educate her own children. Put bluntly, Elizabeth Ann Seton homeschooled her own children spiritually and intellectually; she took in other people's children in order to feed her own children physically. The school began as a job that kept her family going. In this, she did what many homeschooling mothers do today. Her attention to the grace of her sacramental marriage and her own family's needs formed the foundation for her success. Now, this is not to say that she did not care about the other children she taught. Her sanctity and her personal witness attest to her extraordinary love for them as well. But the core of her love for other children began in her desire to fulfill the duties Christ had placed on her to care for her own. And, as it turned out, she began her school in an area and a time very conducive to success.

---

3   *Radio Replies*, Volume 3, Rumble and Carty, 1941, Question #1335.

As has been noted, public schools had a long history of bigotry towards Catholics. While anti-Catholic sentiment waxed and waned throughout the 1800's aaccording to the number of Catholics immigrating from Europe, it was always a significant factor in American culture.

States routinely banned the establishment of Catholic parochial schools. Catholic families and institutions were frequently attacked. Schools and churches were not uncommonly burned to the ground. During the construction of the Washington Monument, an anti-Catholic group of Freemasons even threw the Vatican's donation of a marble block into the Potomac river. America was a thoroughly Protestant country in every sense of the word. Thus, Mother Seton's schools provided a safe haven for Catholic children whose parents had no other means to provide education.

But the seed Mother Seton planted did not grow exactly as envisioned. A century later, Catholic schools had begun to follow the curricula implemented in the newly compulsory schools of secular America, the schools built upon the "factory man" system that had been perfected in Prussia, a system that intentionally fragmented knowledge into discrete, unrelated subjects. That is, the newly established parochial schools generally did not implement the trivium and quadrivium of old, and where they did, they eventually abandoned it in favor of the new secular system of learning.

This Catholic adoption of the Prussian model whose embryo had been advocated by Martin Luther three hundred years before would have been an immediately deadly wound to Catholic Faith except for one thing: the American bishops. While they had done many things wrong, they had done a few things right. Though they could not stop the educational anarchy compulsory schools were intended to create, the decisions of the Second and Third Baltimore Plenary Councils managed to delay it for decades, long enough for the Church to realize the business of the First Vatican Council had to be finished. This is how it happened.

Holding Back the Flood

The decrees of the Second and Third Plenary Councils required Catholic schools to be staffed by religious orders. The councils had little choice. American Catholic adults were not well-formed in the Faith. The monastic orders that historically formed adults were almost unknown in America. Apart from priests, who were still in short supply, non-monastic religious were the only adults who could teach reliably in any capacity.

Fortunately, at least in the beginning, these religious had received their formation in non-Prussian settings. Thus, though the Catholic schools mimicked the Prussian system of the public schools in many respects, the teachers weren't formed in the Prussian methods. Instead, the religious who ran the schools adhered to Catholic principles and a Catholic worldview. And, while the compulsory public schools were being slowly, deliberately drained of all Christian influence, Catholic religious innately recognized the weaknesses of the Prussian curriculum and consciously strove to infuse Catholic doctrine into every subject. They fought the secularization.

Thus, the fragmentation of knowledge that the Prussian curriculum demanded was partially overcome by the unifying vision which Catholic philosophy and theology provided. This harmonizing influence was assisted all the more by the fact that the schools were closed to non-Catholics. It is interesting to note that the word "religion" is composed of two roots *re* and *ligare*. That is, the word "religion" means, "to bind back together." While this "binding back together" refers to the way in which Christ's cross binds back together our broken human nature, "religion" in the parochial school also bound something back together. It bound together the unified vision of the world that the Prussian system of fragmentation and marginal literacy had imposed on education.

Unfortunately, the inherent Catholic ability to salvage real education from the wreckage proved to be a double-edged sword. While the establishment of the parochial school system admirably addressed the pressing safety problem in Catholic culture, it also created a host of educational problems that went virtually unnoticed for over a century, if only because they were so very nearly solved.

To begin with, the new compulsion to attend parochial school inevitably separated parents and children, adults and adolescents. Mother Seton established a school in order to teach her own family, so her school firmly reinforced the familial connections between herself and her own biological children. However, the relationship was far more tenuous for the children she took in. For them, Mother Seton's school carried the capacity to weaken the parent-child bond.

When a child is presented with a tutor, he is also presented with an alternate source of authority. This is both good and bad. If the new source of authority agrees with the parents and reinforces the authority of the parents, then the child's sense of the world, a sense first instilled by the parents, is confirmed and renewed. But, if the new source of authority disagrees with the parents, the child is forced to choose: should he believe his parents or his teacher? What if the teacher is backed up by a textbook, by a principal, by other teachers? And the child knew he had been entrusted by his parents to these people, exhorted to listen to them carefully and to do as they say.

When parents instruct their own children, they have the opportunity to present opposing points of view in a way that does not demean their own relationship with their child. Even when the parent is in error, he has the opportunity to correct himself and thus enter a shared new understanding of the world with the child. But, if the parent is not present when the child is taught this new and contradictory thing, the child is the one who challenges the authority of his own parents. If the parent is wrong, the child becomes the one who corrects the parent.

As other sources of authority combine to support the child, the parent becomes an object of scorn. As Mark Twain noted, "When I was a boy of fourteen, my father was so ignorant I could hardly stand to have the old man around. But when I got to be twenty-one, I was astonished at how much he had learned." Since his own father died of pneumonia when he was eleven, it was unlikely that he spoke from personal experience. Rather, he was expressing the sentiment of his age. His age, that is, his literary career, began in 1867 and ended with his death in 1910. Twain's writing career almost completely encapsulates the years when American schools became compulsory.

Now, the advantages to Mother Seton's school were its voluntary nature and its short duration. No authority forced the parents to send the child to Mother Seton and the child knew that. The school year was counted in weeks rather than months. Further, because of her sanctity, Mother Seton worked in harmony with the parents, never undermining their authority. So, while the potential for difficulty was present, the actual difficulties never presented themselves.

But with the establishment of the parochial schools by the Third Plenary Council, things changed. To be fair, the bishops had been backed into a corner, even if it was a corner they had inadvertently helped to construct. They did not clearly perceive the host of purposes that drove the compulsory schools they were now forced to administer. Thus, their attempt to ward off the impact of Protestant society on American Catholics served only to delay an inevitable collapse. While they could create what appeared to be a separate school system impervious to the ravages of the culture, they could not, in fact, wall themselves off from the Protestant and secular society they inhabited. Besides their continued failure to provide adult formation, the bishops inadvertently left open two chinks in the armor of the parochial schools: textbooks and teacher accreditation.

Gaming the System

As was noted earlier, teacher and administrator accreditation was part of the buffer established to prevent the public schools from teaching efficiently. The degree coursework and accreditation necessary to become a teacher in the United States today are peculiar for one quality: all the oldest and best of such programs were originally established either by someone personally trained in Germany or by a student of someone personally trained in Germany. Take, for example, Russell's Teachers College of New York City. By 1950, this college, sponsored by the Rockefellers, had trained one-third of all presidents of teacher-training institutions, one-fifth of all American public schoolteachers, one-quarter of all superintendents. That's clout.

The clout served its purpose. Catholic students increasingly found they could not get on in the world unless their Catholic schools were accredited. Catholic schools could only be accredited if their teachers, members of religious orders, were accredited. The religious orders could only get accredited by passing courses taught by Prussian-inspired professors and administrators. Part of that accreditation meant exposure to, and at least tacit acceptance of, textbooks and methods produced by these self-same Prussian-inspired professors and administrators.

Worse, the bishops were trapped by this process. While nearly every diocese of that time had its own major and minor seminaries, schools whose course curricula were closely overseen by the bishop, none of them produced enough priests to staff an entire school – that's why the Second Plenary Council recommended religious orders be brought in. But, from the bishop's point of view, the great difficulty of a teaching order lies precisely in the fact that he ultimately has *no control* over a religious order that he has not specifically founded.

Religious orders have their own regulations and formation processes, their own discipline systems. A bishop might negotiate with the head of an order to alter the formation process or to send only specifically chosen individuals to his diocese, but the head of the order can ignore the bishop. If the bishop doesn't like that response, too bad. The only recourse a bishop has is to kick the order entirely out of his diocese. Religious orders have good reason to avoid getting themselves into this position, of course, but bishops also have good reasons not to kick orders out. When a situation deteriorates to that point, neither side comes out looking very good. Worse, if every parish is required to have a school, he can hardly kick an entire religious order out, for if he does, where will he get the staff to run the schools he has agreed to maintain?

And this gets to the heart of a false argument often brought forward. Many people like to argue that parochial schools are the key to passing on the Faith to the next generation. Let us ignore the fact that parochial schools, as they currently exist, are only a century old. Let us focus purely on the logic.

If this assertion is true, then we must simultaneously admit that the bishop, by the very fact of having created a parochial school system, instantly gives away his status as primary catechist in the diocese. After all, if parochial schools are the true key to passing on the Faith and if they are run by a religious order not under his direct control, in what sense is he the primary catechist? Parents are ordained by God to be catechists, but what of school sisters?

Remember, religious orders are difficult to reform. If the formation process used by the order becomes systemically unstable, the bishop is placed into a terribly serious position – kick the order out and thereby destroy the very school system the Plenary Council demands, or accept serious error in the formation of his flock while he enters into possibly fruitless negotiations with the head of the order.

It is useful at this point to remember that the only order in the two-thousand-year history of the Church that has *not* required reform at some point is the Carthusians. Every other Catholic religious order in history has either had to reform itself from serious doctrinal error at least once during its history (sometimes several times, as with the Franciscans), or it has entirely disappeared due to its lack of faithfulness.

> Students in a third grade class are told to use condoms to protect themselves from AIDS. Both the Dominican nun who runs the school and the third grade teacher, an ex-nun, argued that such instruction was necessary since the population of the school was mostly black and Hispanic. The Catholic religion teacher for the middle school is Jewish. - *email from California*

Monastic orders have historically had their share of problems, but they tend to eliminate many of these problems by intentionally limiting contact with the secular world. These orders do not seek out secular formation. Religious teaching orders have not this luxury. While the teaching orders attempted to functionally replace the monastic orders in the formation of America's Catholics, they were oriented towards the wrong group – children – and they were forced to absorb the errors of the world in a way the monastic orders never were. The religious orders running the Catholic parochial schools were almost all relatively new orders. Given these pressures, the odds they would sail along for decades without falling into serious error at some point were tremendously low. The bishops had no good way to deal with that contingency.

In effect, with the formation of the compulsory parochial school system, the bishops had created a double-edged sword. The system would not only allow doctrine to be efficiently disseminated, it would also allow heresy to sweep unchecked through their flocks if, or more likely when, the religious teaching orders became heterodox. Furthermore, these religious taught children, that segment of the population that is least able to resist the blandishments of error and heresy.[4] Finally, when it happened, the bishops had virtually no way

---

4   [The Church confers] valuable assistance in the right ordering and well-being of families and of civil society; for it keeps far away from youth the moral poison which at that inexperienced and changeable age more easily penetrates the mind and more rapidly spreads its baneful effects. For it is true, as Leo XIII has wisely pointed out, that without proper religious and moral instruction "every form of intellectual culture will be injurious; for young people not accustomed to respect God, will be unable to bear the restraint of a virtuous life, and never having learned to deny themselves anything, they will easily be incited to disturb the public order. – Pope Pius XI, *On Christian Education, #24*

to pull the plug. After all, they had poured all their resources into the school system. The bishops still weren't forming the parents. If the parochial schools were to be treated as the backbone of Catholic Faith transmission, then the religious orders, not the episcopacy, had become the spine. As it turned out, these orders had not the grace, the power, to bear the load.

The religious and priests who sought accreditation were aware of the problem. They entered the necessary secular accreditation processes with eyes wide open for the most part. But, as the bishops of the Second and Third Plenary Councils had already demonstrated, constant exposure to subtly skewed data will eventually and subtly skew any individual's outlook.

It is often asserted that Vatican II caused an enormous dislocation in the life of the Church. In fact, at least in the Church that existed in America, Vatican II merely highlighted a pre-existing problem. As we have seen, adult catachesis, as described by the Council of Trent, had never been implemented in the United States.[5] Instead, the bishops of America divorced Catholic Faith from political culture, substituted homiletics for adult formation, and were forced by cultural circumstances into focusing on children instead of adults.

As Protestant American culture increasingly attacked the principle of subsidiarity by tearing at family bonds, especially the family bonds of immigrants, the bishops consciously worked to fend off the obvious attacks. Episcopal denunciations of marriages between Catholics and non-Catholics, for instance, were frequent and thunderous. But, after repeated rebuffs in the public sphere, bishops also consciously attempted to make a ghetto of Catholic Faith and life, construct a Catholic enclave within which Catholics would be safe from the depredations of the culture they inhabited. While their concern was laudable, their technique was not.

Catholics are baptized in order to be crucified. Like Peter, who acknowledged the Christ but then insisted that He not go to Jerusalem lest He suffer Passion and Death, the bishops attempted to shield Catholic America from an American Golgotha. But, like Peter,

---

5   Witness the fact that the growth of Catholicism in America was almost entirely due to immigration, not conversion. Even by 1920, an estimated 75% of the 18.6 million Catholics then living in America were first-generation immigrants. Today, Hispanic immigration, whether legal or illegal, is the only thing keeping the American Catholic population roughly stable at about 24% of the population.

they soon found that the Cross cannot be avoided without enormous consequences.

With the establishment of compulsory Catholic parochial schools, the Catholic Church in America began to depend on a system designed to fail. Modeled on a foreign system that had been consciously founded to transform persons into tools, it was held back from the abyss only by the strong arm of well-formed Catholic religious faculty, a faculty already targeted by the state that desperately wanted to corrupt them. With the 1884 decree, the American Catholic school system already contained nearly all the elements necessary for total breakdown. It lacked but a single piece.

The Heresy of Americanism

Given the decrees of the Second Plenary Council, the eventual appearance of someone like Father Hecker was almost a given. Isaac Thomas Hecker was originally a student of the very Transcendentalism the Second Plenary Council warned against. Befriended by Orestes Brownson when both lived at the Transcendentalist settlement in New Harmony, Indiana, Brownson soon turned away from the fad and towards the Catholic Faith. He was so impressed by Catholicism that he encouraged his friend Hecker to join him in study.[6]

Oddly enough, though Hecker began study months after Brownson, he was baptized into the Faith before Brownson – a friendly bishop had given him a single month's instruction and deemed it sufficient.[7] Once in the Faith, Hecker almost immediately began to study for the priesthood. Unfortunately, by his own admission, he rarely attended class during his four years in seminary.[8]

Consecrated a Redemptorist priest in 1849, he had already been thrown out of the order for disobedience by 1855. He petitioned Pius IX for permission to establish a new order, the Paulists, and this permission was granted in 1858. As Hecker became a publicly

---

6   New Harmony's school was run by Joseph Neef, a former schoolmaster under Heinrich Pestalozzi in Prussia. The semi-illiterate Pestalozzi had invented a non-literary, experience-based industrial arts teaching method that the Prussians very much liked. New Harmony and its school, however, fell apart in three years. That's what happens when you don't have Prussians to run things.

7   Joseph F. Gower and Richard M. Leliaert, ed., *The Brownson-Hecker Correspondence* (Notre Dame, University of Notre Dame Press, 1979), pp. 18-19.

8   Charles Maignen, *Father Hecker, Is He A Saint?* (London, Burns and Oates, 1898), p.27.

recognized figure, Brownson became increasingly dissatisfied with Hecker's theology. Brownson would eventually come to consider Hecker a semi-Pelagian heretic, a man who rejected the concept of original sin and supported the heresy of the total separation of church and state. In fact, Father Hecker even asked Brownson, a famous essayist, to write in support of Church-state separation. Brownson did produce an essay, but in it he pointed out that the separation of Church and state was anti-Catholic.[9]

After Father Hecker's death, the Paulists produced a biography of Hecker's life. This biography was translated for French publication in 1897, where it touched off a storm of controversy. The Catholic Faith in France had been under direct assault by the French government since the 1870 Franco-Prussian war. French republicans considered monarchism and anything that smacked of it treasonous, if only because a monarch had lost to the Prussians. Given the dogmatic definition of papal infallibility made in 1870 by the first Vatican Council, however, Catholic priests understandably saw human government as good only insofar as it conformed to the divine government of the monarchical Church. Thus, many French priests tended to reject French republicanism and instead clung to the monarchical model of government. The resulting political furor caused enormous divisions among French Catholics.

The preface to Hecker's biography just added fuel to the fire. After a commission of bishops studied the matter, Pope Leo XIII wrote a January 22, 1899 brief to American James Cardinal Gibbons in which he pointed out several trends in American thought that were inimical to Catholic Faith. These trends included the following erroneous ideas:

(1) The Church should shape her teachings in accord with popular custom, relax her disciplines or omit or de-emphasize doctrines that non-Catholics find scandalous, that is, a tendency towards silence that omits or neglects Catholic doctrine;

(2) The Church should grant to the faithful the same kind of freedom in spiritual matters that the state grants in civil matters;

(3) Catholics need only adhere to infallible teachings of the Roman pontiff;

(4) License is coterminous with liberty;

(5) External spiritual guidance is not necessary;

(6) Active virtues are superior to "angelical virtues, erroneously

---

9   ibis., Gower and Leliaert, *Correspondence*, Introduction, pp. 38-42.

styled passive" virtues;

(7) Religious life and vows are harmful to human perfection and/or society.

Leo termed these absurdities "Americanism" – the first heresy in centuries to be named after a specific geographical region. Unfortunately, as can be seen from a quick perusal of the list above, the decrees of the Second and Third Plenary Councils already embodied several of the points.

Catholic Faith has always been part of the public sphere, indeed, it formed the public sphere for most of its history. The American episcopal silence on slavery and the explicit command that Catholic priests remove Catholic Faith and commentary from the public sphere conformed perfectly to the first principle. Resulting flights of uncontrolled political fancy would quickly allow principles two through six to follow. Indeed, the Second Plenary Council's decree essentially embodied the fifth principle in regards to the place of religious commentary in political life. After all, if priests were explicitly told not to provide guidance on political matters, it could only be due to the fact that the bishops did not feel such external spiritual guidance was necessary either for Protestant politicians or the Catholic men and women who followed them.

One could argue that the American bishops saw the necessity but questioned the prudence of political commentary in a situation where Catholics were a hated and impoverished minority with virtually no political clout. While prudence is always a concern, of course, false prudence is an equally significant concern. The anti-Catholic political situation would not go away unless someone made it go away. By withdrawing from the arena, the crux of the problem was not confronted.

Worse, consistently and deliberately refusing to proclaim the truth engenders within the individual a distaste for the truth. Thus, by 1897, it is not surprising to discover that the orthodox preaching of Father Pio Maria, formerly Edgardo Mortara, was met with opposition from the archbishop of New York City. He told the Vatican that he opposed Mortara's efforts to evangelize the Jews on the grounds that Father Pio's preaching embarrassed the Church.

But the distaste for Father Pio was not the only example of Americanism put into practice. Consider, for instance, the insistence on the education of children over that of adults, a subtle bow to the

Protestant understanding of how education is to be run. Luther had insisted precisely on emphasizing the formation of children through compulsory education. His Small Catechism is eminently suited for it, and it was the first catechetical tool he published.

Consider also Luther's theological principle, so eloquently stated in his work *Table Talk,* that "reason is the whore of the devil." He held this position because his theology, in debate after debate with adult Catholics, was constantly shown to be irrational and absurd. Rather than blame his theology, he blamed the rational arguments that highlighted his absurdities. Thus, the Protestant denominations that have their roots in Lutheranism have always been more or less anti-intellectual; they have always stood in various degrees of opposition to the education of adults.

Recall also that Luther was the man who destroyed the sacramental understanding of marriage. Because of his own lusts, he concluded that marriage was not truly a sacrament, but just an accommodation God gave man in order to legally absolve him for indulging his sexual lusts. This culturally pervasive Protestant understanding of matrimony's low status did not overtake the Catholic episcopal mindset, rather, it undermined it. In council after council, the American bishops warned about the problems of a mixed marriage: a marriage between a Catholic and a non-Catholic. None of the bishops, however, seemed to recognize that their own attitude towards compulsory schooling might itself be a threat to the stability of Catholic sacramental marriage.

In short, strains within the American Protestant culture, strains of anti-intellectualism and degradation of the sacramental status of marriage, were unavoidably part of the formation of nineteenth century American bishops. When combined with events abroad and fast-moving events at home, it unconsciously distorted their understanding of Catholic Faith to a substantial degree. As a result, they instituted a fatally flawed educational system, a system inadvertently compromised in curricula, staffing and outlook. All that was necessary for the complete collapse of the Catholic school system was a suitably acceptable heresy, a heresy that could sweep through religious orders unchecked. Americanism provided the last piece of the puzzle. As we entered the twentieth century, the American Catholic school system was already locked into the path that would guarantee its failure.

Chapter 8: Contraception *IS* the Curriculum

In Loco Parentis

> In places where there is a Catholic school parents are
> obliged under the pain of mortal sin to send their children
> to it... And even if there is no school attached to the
> congregation of which parents are members, they would
> still be obliged to send their children to a parochial school,
> college or academy, if they can do so without great
> hardships either to themselves or to their children.[1]

The quote above from Archbishop Elder illustrates a mistake
quite common to his era. He forgot the sacrament of marriage ordains
the married couple. That is, it creates of them an ecclesial *ordo*, a
governing body of the Church.[2] In this description, the *Catechism
of the Catholic Church* broke no new ground. A millennium earlier,
Aquinas implied that parents are not only equal to, but in a certain
sense, greater than priests when it comes to their service to their
own children: priests nurture only the spiritual life while parents are
responsible for both the physical and spiritual. That is, parents are
responsible for the body-soul unity of the child's person in a way
priests are not.

In fact, this is the basis for calling the family "the domestic
Church." Parents are the priests, their congregation is their own
children. The very fact of sacramental marriage creates in the spouses
rights and duties towards their children. The Catechism tells us why
in quite remarkable terms:

> The fecundity of conjugal love cannot be reduced solely
> to the procreation of children, but must extend to their
> moral education and their spiritual formation. *"The role of
> parents in education* is of such importance that it is almost
> impossible to provide an adequate substitute." "The right

---

1   William Henry Elder, Archbishop of Cincinnati, *The Catholic Telegraph*, 18 August
1904, p. 4. This was common in America. Indeed, from 1958 to 1970, Archbishop
Zuroweste of Belleville Diocese put Catholic parents in Clinton County under interdict
if they did not send their teens to Mater Dei, the new Catholic high school established in
Breese, IL. This cut the parents off from the sacraments. cf. *Belleville News Democrat*,
January 1, 2006, http://www.belleville.com/mld/belleville/13528107.htm

2   *Catechism of the Catholic Church* #1537.

and the duty of parents to educate their children are primordial and inalienable (emphasis in the original).[3]

If Christian marriage had been the subject of a dogmatic constitution in Vatican I, as was originally intended, the entire history of the twentieth century would have been radically different. The statement above demonstrates how. Consider the phrase "conjugal love." It is conjugal love -- specifically, its physical expression in conjugal relations -- which creates not only the child, but also the parents and their duties. This is a point worth dwelling on.

> The problem of catechists in our schools is not the only one that we face. The catechists in the parish are at least equally problematic. My husband's assistant is a catechist in his parish but he is also pro-choice, pro-contraception and pro-gay marriage. As a matter of fact he and my Protestant husband have had go-rounds on some of those topics since my husband is not pro-abortion or gay marriage (the no contraception thing he isn't convinced on, but was willing to go along with when I became Catholic). What sort of catechesis do you suppose the young teens he teaches get? - *email from the Midwest*

Conception Creates Parents

We tend to define conception primarily as an act which creates a child, but that isn't very accurate. Of course, conception does create children. But, conception creates parents first, if only because the act that conceives is an act whose consequences the spouses must first in some sense embrace. Conception creates parental duties. It creates parental rights. It creates the rights and duties of the child. All of these are created at once, in the single act that conceives. But there is more. All of these creations - child, parent, rights and duties - are oriented towards a specific purpose. Conjugal love is not fully life-giving until the parents show their children how to love and serve God. Only when the child learns this do the parents become fully parents.

---

3   *Catechism of the Catholic Church*, #2221, cf. *Gravissimum Educationis*, #3.

Human beings do not reproduce. Dogs, cats, horses, and fungi reproduce. Human beings procreate. We participate in the creative power of God Himself. We participate in the creation of an immortal person, a person who will still exist when even time itself has ceased to exist.

Thus, according to the Catechism, the life-giving quality of married love, that is, the life-giving quality of sexual relations, cannot be reduced to just this biological act of participation in divine power. The act of sex is an act that becomes really life-giving only when the children we conceive learn to love and serve the God who brought them into existence through our human act. Procreation doesn't stop at a tangle of bedsheets. It includes the diaper-changing, the teaching of prayers, the introduction of little ones to Scripture and the sacraments, the help given to a little ones to recognize God's call, realize his full personhood. That is the full procreative act. It takes years, not minutes or hours.

Pope John Paul II famously said, "Conjugal life becomes, in a certain sense, liturgical."[4] Once we see the full extent of the conjugal act, we can now also see that moral education and spiritual formation are indissolubly embedded within the procreative sexual act. Conception, the existence of a child, is a natural consequence of conjugal love. The parental duty to morally educate and spiritually form the child is a natural consequence of the child's existence. Conjugal love results in sex; sex results in children; children result in both the parental duty and the child's right to education. According to the *Catechism of the Catholic Church*, each is a natural consequence so tightly intertwined with what precedes it that they can together be considered one, single entity: fecundity.

Contraception and Education

But this raises a terrible problem. After all, Pope Paul VI, in *Humanae Vitae* #14, described contraception in this way:

> Similarly excluded is any action which either before, at the moment of, *or after* sexual intercourse, is specifically intended to prevent procreation—whether as an end or as a means (emphasis added).[5]

---

4   John Paul II, general audience, July 4, 1984.

5   Paul VI, *On Human Life, (Humanae Vitae),* #14.

The moral education and spiritual formation of children are embedded in the sexual act; they are natural consequences of sexual intercourse; they are part of what makes the act *procreative*. Pope Paul VI, in reiterating the constant teaching of the Church, succinctly describes the problem America's bishops created for themselves. Put simply, by interposing themselves between the parents and the children, first the nation and then the bishops began to engage in an activity remarkably similar to contraception. The reader may think this quite a serious charge and the evidence brought forward so far certainly inadequate to the task of proving it. So, let us consider the problem in more depth.

Parents are the primary catechists of their own children. The fact is witnessed to constantly in the life and documents of the Church. Indeed, twenty centuries of Christian history attest to it. Now, as is also pointed out:

> The family is the primary but not the only and exclusive educating community... the State and the Church have the obligation to give families all possible aid to enable them to perform their educational role properly.[6]

Notice how Pope John Paul II phrases this sentiment. The state and the Church are to support the parents, not replace them. In this phrasing, he echoes every document on catechetics, on the teaching of the Faith, the Church has ever produced. It is worthwhile noting that the documents on Christian education of the youth that come out of the early part of the century are all tirades against the hegemony of the state. Even as nation after nation passed compulsory schooling laws, the Church insisted over and over again that the state stop telling parents how to raise their children. In short, the bishop of Rome was beginning to realize that the compulsory mass school system was very problematic, but he was having trouble articulating exactly why. This is not surprising. It had been a long time since the Albigensian heresy had walked the earth, and its contraceptive mentality had been dressed up in a brand new form.

The Albigensians taught that the world was created by an evil god, that matter was evil, that only the spiritual was good. Men and women were really spiritual souls trapped in the prison of their material bodies. When Marlowe's Faust asked Mephistopheles how

---

6   John Paul II, *Family in the Modern World (Familiaris Consortio)*, #40.

he could be here on earth tempting men when he should be in hell, the devil replied mockingly, "This is hell, nor am I out of it." An Albigensian would agree with that sentiment most heartily. Earth was hell. Physical existence was hell. Marriage was evil because it permitted sex. Sex was evil because it resulted in procreation. Procreation was evil because it trapped immortal souls in physical bodies, trapped the human spirit in the hell of the material world.

Ask any student in a compulsory school today and he would readily agree with Mephistopheles. With the advent of the compulsory mass school system, a system that was intended to destroy all ties of religion and family, a system built on Darwinian eugenics and intended to reduce the fecundity of the lower classes, we see the state engaging in a contraceptive act that rivaled the best attack on procreation the Albigensians ever dreamt up. Even as Congress passed the 1873 Comstock law that made contraception illegal, state legislatures were creating the moral equivalent of contraceptive schools.

By forcibly interposing itself between parents and children, the state actively attempted to take over spiritual education and moral formation. It *intended* to rupture the parental procreative act, the teaching act by which parents fulfilled their duty to teach their children about the God who made them. It *wanted* parents to have a distorted understanding of themselves. It *wanted* to keep the parents from becoming whole. It *wanted* the lower classes to stop being so fecund. It is no coincidence that the American contraceptive movement leaped forward into the public eye in the 1920's, just as compulsory schooling began to hit its stride. It is no coincidence that 1930 saw the first Christian denomination accept contraception as moral, or that this denomination happened to be Anglican.

By 1930, the English had a fifty-year history of compulsory schooling and a century of mass schooling behind them. England introduced the mass school to the West. England created Darwin, Huxley, Galton, all of the great eugenicists of Europe. England trained the eugenicists of America. By 1930, both the Anglican bishops and their advisors meeting in conference at Lambeth were, to mix metaphors, products of the contraceptive mentality. The English intellectual class, such as it was, brought us the seeds of the disease in the 1800's. It was only appropriate that their faith be the carrier of the full-blown illness in the 1900's.

Contraception and Compulsory Schools

When the American bishops signed on to create their own system of compulsory schools, they unknowingly bought into its contraceptive mentality. They were sold a bill of goods.

Now, some might argue that this is absurd. The bishops have every right to regulate education. Just as the Church had a right to withhold the distribution of the Eucharist under both species or forbid the consumption of meat on Fridays, so She had the right to forbid and/or require certain kinds of schooling.

Unfortunately, while some bring forward this argument, any analogy of this type fails to consider the sacrament of marriage as a sacrament. When we consider the regulation of Eucharistic species for instance, or Friday abstinence, we are considering aspects of liturgy and discipline, subjects which are proper to Holy Orders and Church administration. Furthermore, there is no impediment of grace through these regulations. Anyone who receives either the Body or the Blood receives Jesus *in toto*. The regulation of the Eucharistic species does not change our ability to receive grace. Likewise, fasting and abstinence are both means to gain more grace, so requiring them is laudable. But with the education of children it is different.

As we saw in the passage discussing subsidiarity, the married couple receives grace, receives the fullness of their sacrament, precisely by truly being the primary catechists of their own children. Like a bishop, like the Pope himself, the grace of the sacrament that ordains and consecrates the spouses as primary educators of their children streams directly from Christ. Marriage is unique in that no priest or bishop, no matter how holy, confers the grace of that sacrament.

In fact, the grace is peculiar in this way: anyone who interposes himself between the parent and the child without the parents' permission and without acting precisely on the parents' behalf violates the grace of the sacrament. Indeed, certain aspects of parenthood are so intrinsic to being a parent that they cannot be given away at all.[7] This third party interference in education is a violation very much akin to contraception precisely because such a post-coital interference in the power that parents receive to teach

---

7   Thus, in vitro fertilization (IVF), Gamete Intra-Fallopian Transfer (GIFT) and every similar means of artificial procreation which introduces a third party between the parents during the course of the sexual act are all immoral and deadly sin.

their children actually prevents the parents from becoming fully parents. The parents are prevented from procreating the spiritual life of their child. Compulsory schooling is, by its very nature, a kind of educational *coitus interruptus* in reference to sacramental grace precisely because it strips away the parental power to determine how best to bring their children to knowledge of God.

Now, it is equally true that every parent involved in sacramental marriage has a duty to make sure the divine teaching given to the child is true and accurate. The child has a right to the truth. The parents have the duty to deliver it whole and uncontaminated. Catholic parents have no right to teach the child other than what the Church teaches. But saying this in no way says that the Church has the right to take away the graces of marriage that are due the parents. If the Church or the State takes over or drains away the task of religious education, the parents are supplanted, they are denied the graces of the sacrament of marriage, they are contracepted in their ability to become fully parents, and the bond between parent and child is crippled if not irretrievably broken.

A bishop has the right to deny faculties to a priest precisely because that priest's ordination is a share in his episcopal power. But, it is not at all clear that the bishop has the same right to supplant a parent ordained by the sacrament of matrimony, because that ordination is not a share in the bishop's power. Rather, it comes directly from Christ Himself, conferred by each spouse upon the other. But we still have not touched on the heart of the matter, and it is time to do so.

The Christian Mysteries

> Through the grace of the sacrament of marriage, parents receive the responsibility and privilege of evangelizing their children. *Parents should initiate their children at an early age into the mysteries of the faith of which they are the "first heralds" for their children.* They should associate them from their tenderest years with the life of the Church. A wholesome family life can foster interior dispositions that are a genuine preparation for a living faith and remain a support for it throughout one's life (emphasis added).[8]

---

8   *Catechism of the Catholic Church, #2225, also see Rite of Confirmation #3, footnote p. 201.*

We often read through Church documents without fully appreciating just what those documents say. Take the phrase above: "mysteries of faith." One might be forgiven for reading through this phrase without a second thought. However, to read it this way would be a serious error. The phrase "mysteries of faith" is a technical phrase, one fraught with meaning in Catholic theology. If you would know what it means, you have only to look at the Catechism's table of contents. A quick browse will reveal that the Catechism is broken into four major sections: creed, liturgy and sacrament, moral life, and prayer. The entire second section, the section on liturgy and sacrament, is entitled, "The Christian Mystery." Think on that.

The phrase "mysteries of faith" means "sacraments." The Catechism says parents are to prepare their own children for the sacraments.

Parents. Not bishops. Not priests. Not grade school teachers. Not Directors of Religious Education. Not CCD instructors. Parents. Parents are to prepare their children to meet Christ in the sacraments. Of course, many readers would reply, "But how can parents do that? We are not prepared!" Of course you are not prepared. We already know why. But that does not remove the obligation.

The bishops in America were supposed to follow the dictates of the Council of Trent, dictates reiterated by Pope Pius X in *Acerbo Nimis*. They were supposed to teach adults. As the parents became confident in the Faith, the parents would teach their own children, and thereby become fully parents:

> The Bishops ensure that the authentic Catholic faith is transmitted to parents so that they, in turn, can pass it on to their children. Teachers and educators at all levels also assist in this process. The laity bear witness to that purity of faith which Bishops take pains to maintain.[9]

What some bishops are beginning to understand now was not widely understood a century ago. The bishops of nineteenth-century America did not do their work, thus the Pope chastised them in *Acerbo Nimis*. The several Councils of Baltimore, through the remarkably difficult circumstances they found themselves in and their own subsequent failure to follow the decrees of Trent, had created a situation in which the parents were no longer capable of

---

9   *World Synod Document on Bishops and The Ministry of the Word, 2001*, #105.

doing what the sacrament of marriage consecrated them to do. By the late 1800's, due to forces beyond their control, episcopal attention was more and more concentrated on the education of children. Thus, instead of obeying the principle of subsidiarity and beginning to concentrate on adults in order to remedy their error, the bishops chose a different route.

Egged on by the depersonalizing culture, the culture of use that industrialization was already creating, they ignored the parents and instead followed a mistaken understanding of what Pope Pius IX had done: they directly targeted the children. In that moment, they cut off every Catholic parent in their care from significant portions of the sacramental graces of marriage. It was a mistake they simply would not have made had the Vatican Council been able to complete its work, but the Vatican Council hadn't completed its work. In the space of a single year, the Council was suspended due to military action, Darwin illustrated that everyone needed to think eugenically, the Prussian army proved eugenics worked, and American industrialists decided to implement it via mass schools.

Clericalism is the idea that priests are the only real authorities on matters spiritual and that the laity has little to say and less to do. Clericalism is the heretical idea that parents assist priests in the religious instruction of their own children, when it is actually the priests who assist parents. Now that we understand what happens when parents are stripped of their power, one thing becomes clear: clericalism is a spiritual form of eugenic contraception. The compulsory Catholic school was clericalism *par excellence*.

The Fecundity of Truth

Education and conjugal fecundity are intertwined. Bishops dictated the form of education to parents by allowing parents, either through statement or silence, to think it was a mortal sin to send their child to a public school. By dictating to parents how to raise their children, bishops attacked the parents' right to form their children morally and spiritually as the parents judged best.[10]

Parents may, for instance, have had good spiritual reason to send their child to a public school or to avoid the local Catholic school,

---

10 For anyone who needs a demonstration that contraception is morally wrong, they need look no further than the effects of the compulsory mass school system, both public and private, upon the nation.

but were coerced into doing so anyway in order to avoid putting their own salvation at risk. Priests of this era typically treated children who did not attend Catholic schools as second-class citizens. Parents had no way of knowing the bishops had overstepped their bounds, that the bishops had violated their parental rights as Catholics pursuing sacramental grace. They didn't know this precisely because the bishops had not been teaching them as they deserved to be taught. By violating the rights of the parents, both the state and the bishops were committing an offense remarkably similar to unchastity:

> Chastity presupposes respect for the rights of the person, in particular the right to receive information and an education that respect the moral and spiritual dimensions of human life.[11]

The bishops were not respecting the moral and spiritual dimensions of the sacrament through which human life is begotten. It is often remarked that Catholic parents showed no compunction about using hormonal contraception from the moment it became available. We know the pre-Vatican II Church exhibited a widespread expectation the Church would accept the birth control pill. The advisory council Pope John XXIII formed even suggested that this would be perfectly acceptable. Why would they think this? Because those council members had been raised in compulsory Catholic schools. The members of the council innately knew a large number of the world's bishops had already been contracepting parents through compulsory attendance at Catholic schools.

The shock to the world came when the Pope categorically denied that contraception was moral. With *Humanae Vitae*, America's priests and bishops – many of whom had been in the forefront of the push to accept artificial contraception – began to get a glimmer of what they had done wrong. It is no coincidence that compulsory Catholic schooling ended in dioceses around the world precisely as Vatican II and *Humanae Vitae* brought powerful light to bear on the practices of many shepherds. But, to this day, most bishops do not fully understand the connection, nor do the great majority of the Catholic flock they are supposed to teach. The bishops and their flocks are only now beginning to arise from their sleep as from a dream - or a

---

11 *Catechism of the Catholic Church*, #2344.

nightmare. If you would like to know why American Catholics so quickly accepted contraception, the answer is simple.

Our country and our bishops, by their example, taught us how to be unchaste, taught us how to contracept. Catholic parents embraced the physical act of contraception in the sixties because the bishops had forcefully taught them how to be spiritual contraceptors in the decades prior. We are sacramental people. We just lived out in our marriages what we had been taught from the pulpits regarding our children.

> Our Catholic school board voted to provide health care benefits for *all* domestic partners, because "Catholics don't do enough for their teachers." - *email from Arizona*

Creating Adolescent Parents

> ...[I]n exceptional circumstances the State can also exercise a substitute function, when social sectors or business systems are too weak or are just getting under way, and are not equal to the task at hand. Such supplementary interventions... must be as brief as possible, so as to avoid removing permanently from society and business systems the functions which are properly theirs... to the detriment of... freedom. In recent years the range of such intervention has vastly expanded, to the point of creating a new type of State, the so-called "Welfare State."[12]

Pope John Paul II took the welfare state to task in his 1991 encyclical *Centesimus Annus*. The welfare state contradicts the principle of subsidiarity. It directly intervenes and deprives society of its responsibility. This "leads to a loss of human energies and an inordinate increase of public agencies which are dominated more by bureaucratic ways of thinking than by concern for serving their clients and which are accompanied by an enormous increase in spending." It creates an adolescent culture, a culture artificially stripped of its responsibility.

---

12   John Paul II, *The Hundredth Year (Centesimus Annus)*, #48.

> Malfunctions and defects in the Social Assistance State
> are the result of an inadequate understanding of the tasks
> proper to the State. Here again the principle of subsidiarity
> must be respected: a community of a higher order should
> not interfere in the internal life of a community of a lower
> order, depriving the latter of its functions, but rather
> should support it in case of need and help to coordinate
> its activity with the activities of the rest of society, always
> with a view to the common good.[13]

Just as the American bishops ignored *Acerbo Nimis*, so the American Bishops ignore *Centesimus Annus*. They do not appear to realize that what is said about the welfare state also applies to the Catholic school system. Remember how the secular schools struck at apprenticeship in order to create the adolescent mindset? The adolescent is simply an artificially emasculated adult, an adult who has no purpose in life because his life's work has been taken from him. The combination of parochial school and clericalism has created the adolescent parent, the parent who is mature enough in body to undertake adult tasks, but who has been marginalized spiritually by a system that takes over parental function. Today's parish is a welfare state designed to create adolescent parents.

If proof of this needs to be brought forward, simply converse with consecrated men concerning the points raised in this book. Whenever a priest or bishop rejects the idea that parents are to do sacramental formation, one of the first counters brought forward is inevitably, "But the parents aren't formed in the Faith. They can't do the work. If we don't teach these children, who will?"

Maybe nobody will. But that is hardly relevant. There are times when it is better to leave a task undone then to attempt it without sufficient grace. Consider, for instance, the layman who, upon entering the church for Sunday Mass, is informed the priest was struck by a car minutes before and is en route to the hospital. There is no priest available for Mass. Does this lack of a properly ordained priest give the layman the right to say, "Well, if I don't celebrate Mass, no one will! Help me into that chasuble!" Of course not. Even though there is no priest present, the layman has not the grace to take over the functions of a priest. He is not consecrated to that *ordo*. He must suffer, wait for a priest, and if none appears, find another Mass.

---

13   ibid.

If he cannot find another Mass, there is nothing more to be done. Though he has a right to the Eucharist when he is in a state of grace, that right won't be fulfilled today. Perhaps it won't be fulfilled for quite some time.

> The family's catechetical activity has a special character, which is in a sense irreplaceable... [14]

It is the same with children. Baptized children not only have a right to know God, they have a right to be introduced to God by their parents. The parents are consecrated to this *ordo,* this governing body, by marriage. Parents, in turn, have a right to be formed by the Church so they can do this. Sacramentally married Catholics have a right to be fully parents. It is hardly reasonable for the bishop to fail in his duty to instruct the parents and then insist on instructing the children because the parents are incompetent.[15]

"But the parents aren't formed in the Faith! They can't do the work!" Indeed? So form them. If parents can't do their work, it is because the priest and bishop have not done theirs. Parents are ordained with the grace to teach their own children. If they are not competent to use that grace, it is the pastor's task to form them and make them competent. He has neither the grace nor the right to supplant living sacramentally married parents. The parents are irreplaceable. That means neither the priest nor the bishop can replace them.

If the parents refuse to be formed, then the priest must fast and pray for them, organize others to fast and pray for them, plead with them until they choose to begin to exercise the graces of their ordination. There are many instances of Catholics who must wait for months or years between Masses. Similarly, the pastor may have to wait months or years for the parents to do what they are uniquely ordained to do. But he cannot trample on the child's right to be formed by her parents simply because he is himself incompetent in forming those same parents. Indeed, if he is incompetent to form adults in a Faith specifically designed for adults, what makes him competent to perform the much more difficult task of adapting this adult Faith to a child's understanding?

---

14   John Paul II, *Catechesis in our Time (Catechesi Tradendae),* #68.

15   The response of the consecrated man in this situation embodies the definition of *chutzpah. Chutzpah* is that quality by which a child kills his parents and then throws himself on the mercy of the court because he is an orphan.

The bishop is the primary catechist of the diocese. He has a duty to teach in union with the Pope. The parents are the primary catechists of their family. They have a duty to teach in union with the bishops and the Pope. But just as bishops can fail in their function, and yet not be replaced, so parents can fail in their function, yet this does not give anyone the right to attempt to replace them. The Pope has the power to replace a bishop in his see only for very grave reason. Similarly, bishops require very grave reason to attempt to replace a parent. As the example of Pope Pius IX shows us, they must be willing to bear every single consequence if they do.

If the pastor attempts to interpose himself into the parent-child relationship without first forming the parents to do their work, if he steps in as a crutch instead of a supplement, he is depriving those parents of the opportunity to become truly parents. He has made the Church into the Welfare State, taken away the parents' apprenticeship, the work that trains them for heaven. He cripples the parents, he treats them as asexual children... no, it is worse than that.

He treats them as if they are already dead. A priest or bishop who would fight passionately to keep one man off death row often thinks nothing about taking over the sacramental preparation of another man's child. He dictates to the parents all manner of irrelevant conditions as if he was the primary catechist while the child's biological father was but his lowly aide.

Instead of accomplishing the much more difficult task of pastoring those parents into doing this sacramental preparation themselves, the pastor too often ignores their need to wield the sacramental graces of their marriage; he impedes their salvation. A parent who never takes the time to slow down and show a child how to do something is abusing that child. He is ignoring her, treating the child like an object instead of a person who needs to learn how to grow in grace and wisdom before God and man. Priests and bishops who dare to do these things to parents act in exactly the same manner as the uncaring parent. They are in grievous error and they must reform themselves. It would be pleasant if there were a kinder way to phrase it, but there is not.

As it is, pastors cripple parents, make them co-dependents, using the parish bureaucracy to drive them to spiritual and emotional exhaustion, crushed by the system. Any pastor can see the evidence himself. How many parents are deeply, passionately involved in the second grade formation of their first child? Nearly all of them. How many are still deeply, passionately involved in the Confirmation preparation of that same child in eighth grade or in high school? Almost none of them. What happened in those six years? Simple. The parochial school system destroyed the parents.[16]

> A second-grade teacher preparing the children for First Communion habitually told her students that anyone who attempted to receive the Eucharist on the tongue would be severely punished. The pastor, aware of this abuse, did nothing. - *email from Nebraska*

The Effects of Sterility

After their appalling second grade experience, where the pastor, the parochial school teacher, the PSR/CCD teacher, the Director of Religious Education (DRE) made them know their place, told them what to do, where to sit, what they would and would not be allowed to say, they were battered. After years spent fighting the system through seventh, eighth, ninth grade or higher, they become cynical and depressed. These are the parents who deliberately turn Confirmation into a charade, an excuse for a party. Why? Because they have complete contempt for the system that treats them with complete contempt.

How often have we heard the sweet story of the second grade child who converted his parents back to practice of the Faith! When we hear such a tale, we make soft mewling noises of awe and wonder. Oddly enough, however, we almost always find that these parents have returned to their pagan ways by the time the child reaches eighth grade, assuming their child is still in the system at all. "But certainly *they* at least had a good school experience!" we cry, "Why the change?"

They reverted to their old ways because a second-grader cannot typically evangelize anyone at more than a second-grade level. Adults need an adult understanding of the Faith; a second-grade understanding isn't good enough. It is a sad commentary on

---

16 "Any attempt to diminish human beings by depriving them of spiritual paternity and maternity... is incompatible with the natural development of man." Karol Wojtyla, *Love and Responsibility*, Ignatius Press, San Francisco, 1993, p. 261

adult formation when an adult is so under-taught that second grade evangelization is a step up for him. Certainly the parents suddenly catch fire, but there is no fuel. There is no adult catechesis. The parochial school system not only has no place for parents who would wield their sacramental graces, it actively crushes parents who dare to step outside the factory system of administering the sacraments. That's why the fire is dead in a year, perhaps two.

But the fire is not just dead. It is worse than this. This time, when they fall back into apathy, they take their child with them. After the fire within burns into cold ashes, they fall back into their old ways with a vengeance. They spend the next few years implicitly or explicitly teaching their child that the Faith is for second-graders and not to be taken seriously by adults. As one wag says, the whole family is now inoculated against the Faith – they got just enough of it to catch the fever, but now the immune response has kicked in and they will never suffer that fever again. Like every welfare state, the parochial school system as it was originally constituted, as it is run today, creates quiet hopelessness, silent rage, and despair. It creates the adolescent mindset. We must get past this problem. If we do not, the Catholic Church in America is subject to judgement. It is doomed.

> Hence it is evident that both by right and in fact the mission to educate belongs preeminently to the Church, and that no one free from prejudice can have a reasonable motive for opposing or impeding the Church in this her work, of which the world today enjoys the precious advantages.[17]

Pius XI is sadly misinterpreted today. What too many Catholic bishops and priests forget is that every baptized person is part of the Church. The mission to educate belongs preeminently to the Church precisely because baptized, sacramentally married parents *are* part of the Church, and *do* exercise their ministry towards their own children on behalf of Christ, whom they represent to their own children. The Church is not just the bishops, priests, deacons and religious. It is also those who are members of the *ordo* of marriage.[18]

---

17 Piux XI, *On Christian Education (Rappresentanti in Terra)*, *#27*.

18 Some argue that *Provido Sane Consilio* #25-30 forbids parents doing sacramental prep. In fact, *PSC* stresses the importance of catechism classes. Catechism instruction provides an intellectual understanding of the Faith. Sacramental preparation prepares the catechumen for a direct encounter with Christ. While these two things are related, they not identical. Note also #31 re-emphasizes the central importance of adult instruction.

Creating Adolescent Americans

On January 14, 2005, Nicholas Cafardi, dean of the Duquesne University Law School and chairman of the National Review Board, commented on the priest sexual abuse scandal by saying, "The numbers support the idea that this was an epidemic... This epidemic started in the 50's and 60's and peaked in the late 70's and 80's."[19] For those who still do not believe bishops taught us to contracept, watch the timeline.

In 1950, Margaret Sanger, an ex-Catholic, underwrote the research necessary to eventually create Enovid, the first hormonal contraceptive. Another Catholic, John Rock, had Enovid in trials by 1956. During the summer of 1957, it was on sale in America for menstrual problems. Three years later, Enovid was approved for contraceptive use. In that same year, John F. Kennedy publicly repudiated his Catholic Faith, saying it could have no effect on his governance.[20]

With that pronouncement, American politics proclaimed Catholic Faith irrelevant. Despite his substantially heretical statements concerning the separation of Church and state, Kennedy was voted into office. Pre-Vatican II Catholics across the nation once again breathed life into the Frankenstein heresy of Americanism. Meanwhile, the problem of homosexuality in the seminaries had become so serious that Pope John XXIII directed the Sacred Congregation of Religious to issue "Instruction on the Choice and Formation of Candidates To The State of Perfection and To Holy Orders."[21] The document expressly forbade the ordination of homosexual men. Rome does not produce a document except to address an obvious, serious problem. In America, the document was virtually ignored.

Even as seven decades of spiritual contraception gave way to an equivalent physical product, both America's political life and her seminaries had already begun to self-destruct. On January 25, 1959,

---

19   Wayne Laugesen, *National Catholic Register,* "New Study Calls Abuse an Epidemic", Jan 30-Feb 5, 2005, http://www.ncregister.com/current/0130lead3.htm.

20   Pope John XXIII set up a review board in 1963 to study the problems created by John Rock's birth control pill. Upon his death, the new Pope Paul VI expanded the review board to sixty members. The final board contained sixteen bishops, with the sixty laity now acting as advisers. In their June 1966 report, nine of the sixteen bishops and all but two of the sixty advisers agreed that there was no problem with artificial contraception. All were products of the celebrated pre-Vatican II Church.

21   Issued January 23, 1961.

Pope John XXIII announced that a second Vatican council would soon be convened. But it was already too late.[22] In America, the temporary floodwall created by using Catholic teaching orders as faculty had already begun to collapse. By 1960, as American politics ran amok, as the seminaries imploded, and as Enovid became the first hormonal contraceptive on the world market, the opening of Vatican II was still two years away.

> The Catholic school... would no longer deserve this title if, no matter how much it shone for its high level of teaching in non-religious matters, there were justification for reproaching it for negligence or deviation in strictly religious education... The special character of the Catholic school, the underlying reason for it, the reason why Catholic parents should prefer it, is precisely the quality of the religious instruction integrated into the education of the pupils. [23]

Creating Adolescent Bishops

When did many bishops clearly stop teaching sexual morality? We in the United States can point to June 22, 1965 and the amazing statement from Boston's John Cardinal Cushing regarding legislation that would legalize contraception, "I could not in conscience approve the legislation [supporting legalization of contraception, but] I will make no effort to impose my opinion upon others... I do not see where I have an obligation to impose my religious beliefs on people who just do not accept the same faith as I do."[24]

Now, every bishop and every priest is responsible for the salvation of every person living within his diocese and/or parish. He is not just responsible for teaching and sanctifying the Catholics in

---

22 There are reports that on May 23, 1923, Pope Pius XI and several cardinals discussed the possibility of calling a council, while Pope Pius XII apparently even made preparations in 1948 to call such a council. Both were said to have been talked out of the idea.

23 John Paul II, *Catechesis in our Time (Catechesi Tradendae)*, #69.

24 Note that Cushing's publicly erroneous remarks were made in regards to contraception. Ironically, a prince of the Church is the source for one of Planned Parenthood's most absurd and important arguments. cf. Diogenes, "Personally Opposed, But..." *Catholic World News*, 2003, http://www.cwnews.com/news/viewstory. cfm?recnum=26364.

his diocese; he is responsible for teaching and sanctifying *everyone* in his diocese. This is Catholic doctrine.

What would we say of a math professor who opined, "I do not see where I have an obligation to impose my belief that $2 + 2 = 4$ on students who just do not accept the same mathematics I do"? The Catholic Faith is more true than math, more certain than the sunrise, indeed Catholic truth is the source from which the sun draws its ability to rise. But Cardinal Cushing reduced the eternal and divine Truth to the level of human opinion. He repudiated his responsibility to teach Truth to the people of the world. This was the ultimate expression of spiritual contraception, the refusal to be a parent, the refusal to teach the adults under his care about the God who made us.

When Lyndon Baines Johnson wanted to promote birth control world-wide in an attempt to prevent foreign countries from competing with U.S. interests, he brought Joseph Califano Jr. in to speak to the bishops of the United States. LBJ was concerned that American bishops might tag his plan as an attempt to spread error and sin throughout the world. He need not have worried.

As Califano told the story, America's bishops agreed to let LBJ undertake his plan as long as he used a different phrase.[25] Birth control is intrinsically evil, after all. The bishops agreed to the phrase, "the population problem," tacitly pretending that it referred to the problem of feeding the poor when they knew full well it actually referred to the US policy of eliminating the poor through eugenic contraception.

The bishops lied to themselves. Worse, they permitted phrasing that is essentially heretical. After all, what is a population problem but too many people? And what are people but images of God? So America's bishops said, "It is permissible to talk about the problem of having too many images of God in the world. It is permissible to work on reducing that problem." Compare it to Mother Teresa's opinion on overpopulation.[26] "Children are like flowers. How can

---

25   Joseph Califano, "How I Squared Church and State," *Washington Post*, Sunday, June 24, 2001, B-1, http://www.washingtonpost.com/wp-dyn/articles/A7325-2004Jun26.html.

26   It is in this comparison that we recall an interesting fact. These were the same bishops who allowed their liturgy directors to stop "the proliferation of sacred images." They got rid of statues, of icons, of the images of saints. The proliferation of sacred images is confusing to the people, said the liturgists. For the same reason, they moved the tabernacle from the center of church. The dual location of Christ in the Blessed

you say we have too many flowers?" This is the difference between many American bishops in the 1960's and a saint.

The American bishops had become as lax towards the mortal sin of contraception as they had been a century before towards the mortal sin of holding another human being in slavery. Their first sin led to the Civil War, the largest war-time slaughter of Americans the world has ever seen. Now, their custom of spiritual contraception led to an even greater slaughter of Americans, and of people throughout the world: the slaughterhouse of abortion.

As Califano says, "Those were the days when you could sit down with the bishops; they were sensitive to the separation of church and state in the wake of the cliffhanger election of the first Catholic president, John F. Kennedy. The bishops and the laity accepted the assertion of the Jesuit theologian Gustave Weigel, in his widely reported 1960 lecture at Catholic University, that 'the Roman Catholic Church would not attempt to interfere in the political activities of a Catholic president, nor would a Catholic president be bound by Catholic morality in deciding public issues.' "[27]

Now, the idea that the Church and the state are distinct is Catholic doctrine. But the idea that they are separate or separable is Catholic heresy. The Church has power over the state, the state has the duty to uphold Catholic truth, both are duty-bound to support the family.

Thus, Gustave Weigel was himself proclaiming a substantially heretical position. The American bishops sat still for it because the American bishops were... what? The charitable explanation is that the bishops were, like their brother bishops in the generations before them, not particularly well-formed in the Faith. That is the best one can say.

The Bloodbath

To any who would like to disagree, we now turn our attention to the American bishops' Pastoral Plan for Pro-Life Activities. Though they began working on it within twenty-four hours of the Roe v. Wade decision, the 1975 document that was eventually issued

---

Sacrament during Mass (tabernacle and altar) is confusing to people, said the liturgists. They merely parroted Califano: the proliferation of images of God is problematic to U.S. foreign policy. The bishops meekly agreed to both abuses because they themselves were deeply confused.

27   ibid.

treated only abortion, euthanasia and sterilization. It did not mention contraception at all. To this day, the United States Conference of Catholic Bishops (USCCB) has maintained almost complete silence in regards to the subject. Now that we have seen the connections, we might perhaps understand the peculiar blindness our bishops have towards this particular sin. Most of them never really understood the connection between contraception and abortion. Many still don't. This is not so odd as one might think. None of us tend to understand the sin that force of habit compels us to repeat over and over again. The mind does not want to dwell on what is being done. It offends our self-image.

> A Catholic school teacher told her fourth grade students that Jesus had brothers and sisters. When a Catholic parent called the instructor to confirm this was taught, the instructor readily admitted to it. When the parent pointed out that this was actually a heretical teaching, the instructor began insisting she had actually never taught such a thing. The children had merely misunderstood her.
>
> Concerned by this experience and other reports, the parents investigated further. They discovered, among other things, (a) the music teacher publicly refused to make the sign of the Cross, (b) the grade school library stocked anti-Catholic books, including the notorious *Left Behind* series, which teaches the Pope as anti-Christ and the heresy of the Rapture, and (c) the Catholic school religion teacher was not Catholic. - *email from Kansas*

Unfortunately, this unwillingness to examine our sins has lead to a much higher death toll than ever the Civil War created. *The Physician's Desk Reference* points out that every hormonal contraceptive acts as an abortifacient. Every single one. But the USCCB has never made a single statement concerning this fact. Instead, they campaigned against the abortifacient aspects of the morning-after pill (MAP), even though the MAP is merely a high-dose contraceptive, that is, it is *exactly* as abortifacient as every other hormonal contraceptive. What irony! Like the boy who cried wolf, the one time Planned Parenthood tells the truth about a contraceptive its adversaries refuse to accept it.[28]

Even though the MAP is simply one more hormonal contraceptive, America's bishops seem intent on drawing an artificial line between it and every other hormonal contraceptive. In fact, the only difference between MAP and everything else is dosage and timing: the regular birth control pill is taken before the act of sex while the MAP is taken after. In this respect, the MAP reflects compulsory schooling – both act upon the parents after fertilization, both keep the parents from becoming fully parents.[29]

Contraception schizophrenia is also mirrored in the current American Catholic schism, for it can be called nothing but schism when a politician is given the Eucharist in one diocese, but refused if he walks ten feet into the neighboring diocese.[30] Again, the spectral silence we saw on the slavery issue hovers ominously over us as Americanists among today's bishops refuse to exert their authority. Again, if anyone disagrees, we have only to turn to Rome to confirm the facts.

In a now famous February 11, 2005 EWTN interview, Cardinal Arinze, the Prefect of the Congregation for Divine Worship and the

---

28   In a December 12th, 2003 *New York Times* article, Cathy Cleaver Ruse, the USCCB's Director of Planning and Information for the Secretariat for Pro-Life Activities, said, "When it comes to contraception as a policy issue - access, availability - the Catholic bishops do not get involved in that debate." In March, 2004, I asked her to clarify this remark. She replied, "Legal bans on contraception were ruled unconstitutional by the U.S. Supreme Court in 1965 for married couples and then for everyone in 1972, so without a constitutional amendment there is little that can be done to ban contraception by law." When I pointed out that the USCCB lobbies to ban abortion despite the Court, she replied "No, there is no 'lobbying to ban abortions for everyone' as that too has been precluded by the Supreme Court." It seems the Supreme Court trumps the Vatican.

29   Similarly, despite Senator Edward Kennedy's constant, vociferous public support for contraception, abortion and other mortal sins, the USCCB has criticized him by name only once: when he opposed tuition vouchers for Catholic school children following Hurricane Katrina. "Denying educational aid to victims of Katrina because they attended Catholic schools... makes no sense... Senator Kennedy said he is "extremely disappointed" that in President Bush's plan for hurricane relief aid would go to students no matter where they attend school. He's not half as disappointed as his fellow citizens [are in him]" said the USCCB's secretary for education, Sister Glenn Anne McPhee, OP, (Sept 21, 2005). http://www.usccb.org/comm/archives/2005/05-213.shtml

30   Canon #751 "Schism is the refusal of submission to the Roman Pontiff or of communion with the members of the Church subject to him." Since the communion of Faith rejects abortion, endorsing it equals separation.

Discipline of the Sacraments, was asked if pro-abortion politicians should be denied communion. The Cardinal responded, "The answer is clear. If a person says 'I am in favour of killing unborn babies whether they be four thousand or five thousand, I have been in favour of killing them. I will be in favour of killing them tomorrow and next week and next year, so, unborn babies, too bad for you. I am in favour that you should be killed,' then the person turn around and says 'I want to receive Holy Communion.' Do you need any Cardinal from the Vatican to answer that? ... Simple, ask the children for First Communion, they'll give you the answer."

After surviving three centuries without adult formation, we are no longer faced with the problem of evangelizing parents at a second-grade level. Rome tells us we now need to evangelize many American bishops and cardinals as if they had not yet reached a second-grade level of understanding Catholic Faith. But even though these same bishops appear to be incompetent to carry out their duties, the bishops have authority. No one can act without regard for their authority. They are members of an *ordo*. The principle of subsidiarity must be respected.

When the parent fails to guard the table, the dogs eat the children's food. That isn't good for the parents, the children or the dogs. It is a principle many American bishops do not yet grasp. But all hope is not lost.

Hope Springs Anew

It is said that when seeking ways of regulating births, only five percent of you consult God. In the face of this unfortunate fact, we your pastors have been remiss: how few are there among you whom we have reached. There have been some couples eager to share their expertise and values on birth regulation with others. They did not receive adequate support from their priests. We did not give them due attention, believing then this ministry consisted merely of imparting a technique best left to married couples.

Only recently have we discovered how deep your yearning is for God to be present in your married lives. But we did not know then how to help you discover God's presence and activity in your mission of Christian parenting.

Afflicted with doubts about alternatives to contraceptive technology, we abandoned you to your confused and lonely consciences with a lame excuse: "follow what your conscience tells you." How little we realized that it was our consciences that needed to be formed first. A greater concern would have led us to discover that religious hunger in you.[31]

In 1990, the bishops of the Philippines discovered their voices. The people of that country are truly blessed to have such consecrated men. A few bishops on this continent have also begun to rejoin the eternal college of bishops and are now speaking out against contraception; a few American bishops have forbidden pro-abortion politicians from approaching the Christian mysteries they guard. But, as will shortly become clear, much remains to be done, for there is more than one way for a bishop to contracept the parent-child relationship.

---

31 Janet Smith, "A Mistaken Church?" *Catholic Dossier*, Volume 6, No 3, May-June 2000, http://www.catholic.net/rcc/Periodicals/Dossier/2000-5-6/column.html.

Chapter 9: Systematic Infiltration

Pre-Vatican II: The Wasteland

The Catholic schools failed because secularism had laid waste to the Catholic Faith prior to Vatican II. Older readers will snort in disgust, "That's simply untrue! We all knew the Faith then, attendance at Mass was strong, confession lines were long, religious vows were high. How can anyone make such a foolish statement?"

Easy. Consider Church history. If we wish to see how well-taught adult Catholics act, we need only review the Council of Ephesus. This Council met because a bishop named Nestorius had begun to insist that Mary was not the Mother of God, but only the mother of Christ. The assertion provoked a storm of controversy, and a meeting of bishops in the town of Ephesus was called to settle the issue.

Unfortunately, while Nestorius and his main opponent, Cyril of Jerusalem, both arrived in Ephesus in a timely fashion, many of the other bishops did not. The start of the council being delayed due to the bishops' slow arrival, the people of Ephesus began holding processions in the town, during which participants chanted "Mary is the Mother of God!" These were adults who had been taught an adult grasp of the Faith. They insisted on orthodoxy and brooked no confusion in matters of faith. They were, perhaps, part of the reason Nestorius ultimately refused to show his face in the streets or at the council. You see, he would not even venture outside his house unless he was accompanied by a large contingent of his supporters, and he could not seem to find a large enough contingent.

Now, contrast this event to the American response towards the latest council. When the heretics came out of the woodwork and started talking about "the spirit of the Vatican II," was there a mass uprising of faithful Catholics, an uprising so uniform in active orthodoxy that it broke the backs of the heretics before they even finished their heretical sermons? In a word, no.

Pre-Vatican II Catholics had already been broken by a half-century on the wheel of compulsory Prussian-style education. They had been taught how to live clericalism, how to bow to authority not because it was based in eternal Truth, but simply because it was authority.[1] They responded to the bishops just as the industrialists had intended them to respond to the foreman.

In the years before the Council of Trent, the ghetto created by Catholic culture had not prepared the faithful to deal with heterodoxy among their own authority figures. When Martin Luther rose up, the people did not know how to respond. The spirit of Martin Luther rose from its moldering grave at the Second Plenary Council. Made visible to the assembly after Vatican II, albeit with grumbling at the stench in some quarters, he again tormented Catholics. Like the serfs who had to endure Luther, post-Vatican II Catholics were again taught Purgatory no longer existed and sin was no impediment to salvation.

Just as in the decades prior to Trent, virtually none of the pre-Vatican II faithful had an adult grasp of the Faith. Certainly few knew the Faith well enough to engage and destroy the arguments of the heretics. Indeed, few had the self-sufficiency even to buy a copy of the Council documents and read what was said for themselves. Their homeschooled, voraciously well-read great-grandparents, the lads and ladies who were 95 to 100% literate, would have read every word of the Council and used the Council documents to skewer the heretics. But the 1860's were gone. It was the 1960's, and the compulsory schools had done their work.

Consider again Christopher Spiller's analysis of John F. Kennedy's 1960 run for President of the United States:

> To posit a conflict between [the Church's] teachings and one's private conscience as JFK did is to fundamentally misunderstand the nature of conscience in the first place. Conscience means, quite literally, "with knowledge" (*con scientia*). To separate it so radically from one's faith formation moves [conscience] from the realm of the intellect to that of the will. It moves from being a means of discerning the truth to positing the truth by *fiat*. JFK's comments in 1960 clearly demonstrate that such a position, now rather wide spread in some circles of Catholic moral theology, was already a problem. This

---

1   This is, by the way, an example of the condemned heresy of fideism, the idea that we believe doctrines not because they are true, but simply because they are taught with authority. Priest and theologian Raymond Brown displayed his fideism when he opined that the Virgin Birth was not historical fact. He insisted he still believed it, but only because the Church taught it. That is fideism in spades.

faulty understanding of conscience not only helped to get JFK elected, but also weakened the acceptance of the classical view expressed by Aquinas that Church and State, while distinct, are not in conflict.[2]

Remember, JFK proposed his essentially heretical position three years prior to Vatican II, when the Catholic Faith was supposedly like unto the Rock of Gibraltar. His heresy was so little-noticed that no bishop spoke out against his remarks, while the majority of adult Catholics showed no hesitation at all in voting for him, yet his heresy was no less serious than Senator John Kerry's scandalous promotion of abortion. The Baltimore Catechism was an excellent teaching tool for children, but its marvelous and succinctly distilled answers were meant for children, not adults. As post-conciliar events demonstrated, such a catechism was no match for adult situations.

When the heretics who claimed to represent the Council taught error, Catholic adults armed only with eighth-grade answers found themselves laughed out of the room by adult heretics and their razor-sharp theological patter. Meanwhile, the men and women who could only repeat stock answers to completely inadequate questions stood shaking with frustration, unable to marshal their thoughts, wondering how the principles of Catholic Faith they knew so well could be so quickly shattered.

The point was quickly driven home: Catholic Faith was inadequate to the issues of the day. After a few such public humiliations, very few were even able to muster the backbone to publicly denounce the heretics. Certainly there was never a question that riots would break out or that priests or bishops would be physically removed from their rectories, as American Catholics had done for much less reason a century before. The great mass of Catholics had been taught docility, acceptance of authority, and how to contracept, how to be sterile in everything. The sterility conceived in the Third Plenary Council's decisions gave birth to the stillborn heresies fully revealed in the light of Vatican II, heresies whose corpses still infuse the rank odor of decay into American culture as the stench settles over it like a shroud. Prior to Vatican II, Catholic Faith in America was a mile

---

2   Christopher Spiller, *Church and State: The Sacred, the Profane, and the First Amendment,* presentation at Duquesne University's 11th Annual *GSO Conference: The Academy and the Polis,* (2005).

wide and an inch deep. Vatican II simply ripped old bandages off the leprous wound.

The Cult of the Expert

As we have seen, despite the exhortations of *Acerbo Nimis* in 1905, nothing much changed in America. For almost a century, the majority of America's bishops had been in the habit of supplanting the teaching authority of parents and abdicating their own teaching authority to religious orders. Most bishops did not teach adults. Instead, they insisted on educating Catholic children themselves, but even then, they actually handed the task over to religious orders outside of their own control. They had gotten into the habit of spiritual contraception. As a result, seminary oversight slowly fell away as bishops, who had themselves now been formed by the mass schools, found other things to do with their time. When this tendency was combined with a second, disaster loomed.

As the industrialists had hoped, as the Prussian system intended, the cult of the expert had emerged in the United States. The Ph.D., ironic short-hand for "doctor of philosophy," was invented in Germany around 1870. The irony of the Ph.D. lies in the fact that it generally signifies a complete absence of philosophy. After all, the whole point of the degree is to take the departmentalization of subject matter to the nth degree. Whereas the highly literate but unschooled man is a jack of all trades, equally capable with a pick or a pen, equally at home at the desk or the dance, the "Doctor of Philosophy" is a tiresome technician, someone who devotes his life to a specific branch of knowledge, putting the single part in the place of the whole. His expertise is in a single subject, not in all subjects.

This is, of course, precisely the opposite of the philosopher. The philosopher is one who loves wisdom and pursues it. While we all know the word "philosophy" is composed of two Greek words, *philo*, which means love, and *sophia*, which means wisdom, most of us are unaware that *wisdom* is likewise a compound word, created from two words with Germanic roots. *Wis* means "to know the right path" and *dom* means "judgement." The word *dom* is the source of the word "doom." A "kingdom" is the area subject to a king's judgement, for instance, while "Dooms-day" is Judgment Day. So, "wisdom," strictly speaking, means "proper judgment concerning the right path."

A philosopher loves and pursues proper judgment concerning the right path. In order to do this well, a philosopher must know as much about the world as possible, he must know how all the different parts of the world fit together into a harmonious whole. But a Ph.D.? The one who is awarded this contradiction in terms has declared himself a monomaniac, caught up in the study of one discipline, seeing the whole world through its lens. The only Ph.D. which is, perhaps, not self-contradictory is that of theology – it alone attempts to study the world through the prism of God's eyes. Every other Ph.D. produces a philosophical Cyclops.

But the Prussian system taught deference to Ph.D.s as "experts." American bishops, like everyone else in American culture, did not consider what this implied. As was previously noted, the seminaries began to experience problems in the 1950's, well before Vatican II. The 1948 release of Dr. Alfred Kinsey's substantially faked report, *Sexual Behavior in the Human Male*, followed by the fraudulent 1953 sequel, *Sexual Behavior in the Human Female*, put talk of sex into the public forum. Though Kinsey's doctorate was in entomology, the study of insects, though Kinsey himself was arguably mentally unstable and though his research was clearly flawed, the Ph.D. behind his name was enough. The reports rocked America.

As seminarians began to emulate the behaviour described in the reports, the bishops did the only logical thing, the thing every mass-schooled American had been trained to do – they turned to the experts. Many of the bishops apparently failed to realize that when it comes to sin and how to keep men from its near occasion, *they* were the experts. In any case, the experts on human sexuality told the bishops the conditions being exhibited among some seminarians and priests were treatable. The bishops believed the experts.

As the problems in the seminaries worsened, Vatican II convened, drawing attention towards Rome and away from home. The realization of impending change quickly swirled through the culture. The problems in the priesthood worsened. Many bishops redoubled their consultations with the experts. Actively homosexual priests were treated primarily as if they suffered from a psychological problem instead of a sin problem. The psychological experts at the time, desperate to gain respect in the larger scientific community, convinced themselves that they could successfully treat any condition, including homosexual pedophilia. When the experts completed their treatments and told the bishops the priests were cured, the bishops believed the experts. The priests re-entered ministry.

As priestly vocations underwent a sharp drop following the Council, the pressure to return priests to ministry grew. By the 1970's, the situation was essentially uncontrolled as the bishops attempted to juggle a dozen post-conciliar balls at once. Bishops are not experts in psychology, nor has anyone ever thought they were or should be. By this time, most bishops were relying on secular experts for advice. They had to rely on psychologists about sex because the majority of them had stopped teaching Church doctrine about sex. They had stopped teaching Church doctrine on sex because the mass schools had, by their very existence, already distorted their understanding of Christian sexuality. By and large, the bishops of America didn't know what to do. That's why they were stuck with the answers of lay Ph.D.s. As things got steadily worse, the American bishops largely retreated into silence.

The History of Silence

> We anathematize [both] the inventors of the new error... [and the pope] who did not attempt to sanctify this Apostolic Church with the teaching of Apostolic tradition, but by profane treachery permitted its purity to be polluted.[3]

With this statement, Pope Leo II affirmed the conclusion of a general council: Pope Honorius was condemned as a heretic. In the early 600's, Pope Honorius faced a heresy within the Church. When he was asked how to handle the heresy, he replied by forbidding discussion of the topic at all. Because he failed to teach the Faith, and because he forbade the use of both orthodox and heretical phrasing, the council found him derelict in his duties and condemned him as a heretic. His condemnation was confirmed by two ecumenical councils and the very liturgy of the Church, which for two centuries repeated Honorius' condemnation in the papal oath. The condemnation still stands.

Note well: he was not a heretic for having mistaught. No Pope has ever mis-taught Church doctrine. Rather, his heresy lay in his silence.

---

3   Leo II, confirming the Third Council of Constantinople, as quoted in the *Catholic Encyclopedia*, http://www.newadvent.org/cathen/07452b.htm

Now, he was a good bishop in all other respects. He did much good for the people of Rome and for the Church as a whole. He died well-respected in most circles. But, his silence on one point of doctrine eventually condemned him.

From all the evidence, he was silent because he didn't know what to do. That's the problem with being infallible: infallibility means you won't teach the wrong answer. Sadly, infallibility does not mean you know the right answer or that you are able to competently teach the right answer even if you do know it. Competent teaching is a skill like any other skill: use it or lose it. Pope Honorius was condemned simply because he retreated into silence.

In the Mass, and through the Confiteor, every Catholic is reminded that sin lies both "in what I have done, and in what I have failed to do." Silence is a failure to teach. Silence can be a sin. Silence, as the history of the Church shows, can even be a heresy.

When Cardinal Cushing denied that a doctrine of Catholic faith would have any relevance for non-Catholics, he expressed a materially heretical misunderstanding. He spoke of "his" Faith. The doctrines held by a Catholic bishop are not his anymore than the Mass he celebrates is his or the baptisms he confers are his. These are all Christ's, that is, they are all God's. He does not hold beliefs, he holds Truths. We believe these things because they are true, and they remain true whether or not we believe them.

Professors Aren't

It is important that we fully understand this point. The Creed I repeat every Sunday is ultimately not a statement of what I believe, it is a statement that I recognize reality. The secular world has a somewhat similar practice: psychologists will sometimes ask a mental patient to name the year or the president of the United States. If the patient answers correctly, it is likely he has at least some grip on reality. So it is with the Creed. I repeat the Creed at Sunday Mass to demonstrate that I am not yet theologically insane. I hold to the teachings of the Church because I am made for Truth, and this is it.

I profess the Creed. Thus, I am a professor. Indeed, this is where the title used by all university faculty finds its source. Nearly every European university in existence was founded by the Catholic Church. For a thousand years, every person who taught at such an institution had to first publicly profess that he held onto reality. That is, he had to be a professor of Catholic Faith. This point is completely lost on most of the universities and colleges in America.

It is, perhaps, understandable why secular institutions no longer grasp this. But why would Catholic institutions fail to see the connection? Or given the ground covered so far, perhaps the better question is, when did Catholic institutions begin to lose their grip on reality?

That answer has been researched and explained in books far thicker than this one, so a synopsis will have to suffice. In July 1967 twenty-six Catholic men flew from Chicago's O'Hare airport to a conference center in Land O'Lakes, Wisconsin, a center owned and operated by Notre Dame University. Even though there were many Catholic women's colleges, no women were invited, since the conference would ostensibly focus on research institutions, and none were run by women's orders. In fact, virtually none of the men who showed up ran research institutions either. Like so much that emerged from this conference, it was built on a lie.[4]

Another absence was notable: William Joseph McDonald, rector of the Catholic University of America, the only American university under direct Church control, declined to attend. He sent a dean, Roy Deferrari, in his stead. The meeting was a serious one. These Catholic institutions were intent on increasing their market share.

The reason was simple: federal dollars for higher education were flowing like beer at a frat party, and the leaders of these institutions wanted a bigger stein. By 1967, the GI Bill had swelled the attendance at colleges and universities across the United States. In a country where four in five Americans were not Catholic, attendance at a truly Catholic institution would appeal only to a market niche, not the whole market. If Catholic leaders like Notre Dame's Fr. Theodore Hesburgh or St. Louis University's Fr. Paul Reinert wanted federal aid, and lots of it, they had to get rid of the Catholic culture. This unspoken fact undoubtedly lay on every administrator's mind. So did another fact. As even proponents point out, if Catholic schools began accepting government money, the administration would have to change. Government loans force into the public sphere accountability

---

4   It is a little-known fact that orthodoxy tends to correlate to a population's male-female ratio. When the sex ratio in a population is equal, or nearly so, odd religious cults and heresies are much less likely to occur than when the population is substantially skewed.

issues that would otherwise be handled by provincials and bishops in a much less public fashion. Government money would change the way institutions run.[5]

Instructors Don't

> Since however the younger generations must be trained in the arts and sciences for the advantage and prosperity of civil society, and since the family of itself is unequal to this task, it was necessary to create that social institution, the school. But let it be borne in mind that this institution owes its existence to the initiative of the family and of the Church, long before it was undertaken by the State. Hence considered in its historical origin, the school is by its very nature an institution subsidiary and complementary to the family and to the Church. It follows logically and necessarily that it must not be in opposition to, but in positive accord with those other two elements, and form with them a perfect moral union, constituting one sanctuary of education, as it were, with the family and the Church. Otherwise it is doomed to fail of its purpose, and to become instead an agent of destruction.[6]

What the Catholics assembled in Wisconsin did was simply a repetition of what Protestant universities had already done sixty years earlier. By 1910, the Protestants had agreed to strip personal faith and religion out of their curricula, replacing these things with scientific inquiry.

Now, everyone agrees that science operates very poorly as a religion. It can never claim full knowledge of the material world or material truth, rather, it can claim only knowledge concerning

5   In *The Underground History of American Education*, John Taylor Gatto relates an interesting story concerning William Wirt. After the New York City school riots, Wirt returned to Indiana. While on a business trip in Washington D.C., he attended a private dinner party at the home of a high government official.

In later Congressional testimony, Wirt swore he heard dinner guests discuss how the government would control commerce by becoming the major source of long-term capital loans. The dinner guests claimed to have made propaganda a science. They claimed they could make newspapers and magazines jump through hoops simply by taking away advertising. Labor leaders would be bought off with government contracts, colleges and schools bought off through federal aid and large farmers purchased through government subsidies. Wirt's testimony was ridiculed as absurd by the prominent journalists of the period and his testimony was ignored. Whether true or false, it was certainly prescient.

6   Pius XI, *On Christian Education (Rappresentanti in Terra)*, #76-77.

what it can see. What it does not see, it does not know. Worse, even what science does see can become the fuel for erroneous logic, and therefore falsehood, concerning material reality. But for Protestant schools, this was not much of a concern.

> On April 1, 2005, the Queer Alliance at the University of San Francisco hosted a "Gender Bender Ball... attire is very encouraged [but] not essential for admission." The party organizers intended to host "all the bay area schools." According to the university website, "The University of San Francisco is a Jesuit Catholic university with regional campuses throughout California that offer quality graduate and undergraduate programs." - *email from California*

The Catholics at the conference failed to realize a significant difference between Catholic and Protestant institutions. Protestant institutions, by definition, never had the fullness of Divine Truth to begin with. Thus, when Protestants traded their religious convictions for scientific convictions, they suffered no significant loss. Indeed, one might argue that the gained quite a bit, since they at least traded error-ridden theologies for relatively certain knowledge of some material truths. But, when Catholicism approaches the table of science and considers making the same trade the Protestants made, She is at a distinct disadvantage. Catholics have full knowledge of the truths of Divine Faith. It would be absurd to trade this for the partial knowledge yielded by material truths.

Unfortunately, the men at the table were, to put it mildly, not thinking very clearly. They had seen the lessening influence of Protestant theology on American public life and noticed that this seemed to be a relatively good thing for Catholic Faith. Indeed, between compulsory schooling and waning Protestant influence, Catholic Faith had grown rapidly in the previous decades. After all, the major teaching tool of Catholic Faith, the child-centered Baltimore Catechism, was a perfect match for the kind of adult the public schools now routinely produced.

The Catholics seated around the table decided that following the Protestant lead and reducing the influence of Catholic theology would improve the situation even more. The religion of science seemed more robust, more appealing. Besides, everyone else was doing it. Catholic institutes of higher learning had to conform to the times. The men who ran these institutions, all raised in the mass school system, had learned the importance of conformity in kindergarten. Like sheep, they followed their Protestant shepherds.

Catholics had spilled blood to prevent the takeover of the great Catholic universities during the Protestant Reformation and the French Revolution. Not here. The Catholic universities of America would nearly all simply hand their institutions over to lay boards. University corporations took over.[7]

St. Louis University and Notre Dame had already essentially done this in the years leading up to the meeting. They formally incorporated the changes later that year. By 1972, nearly all Catholic colleges and universities in America had followed their lead. If bishops had found dealing with the head of a religious order cumbersome, they soon discovered that dealing with a lay board is like herding cats. One more buffer against episcopal authority had been placed between the bishop and the Catholic university. With this change, bishops were now more than ever administrators, not teachers.

If there is any question that the bishops knowingly permitted the surrender of the Catholic colleges and universities, consider a single fact. Following the 1968 publication of *Humanae Vitae*, theologians throughout the country who had been trained in the pre-Vatican II Catholic colleges and seminaries of the nation, men who had staked their reputations on the idea that John Rock had created a morally acceptable contraceptive alternative, became open heretics. They dissented from Pope Paul VI and the eternal teaching of the Church loudly and vigorously. The American bishops responded with perhaps the most curious document the Catholic Church in America has ever produced: the November 1968 Pastoral Letter *Human Life in Our Day*. Though it was superior to many national documents in that it strongly agreed with Pope Paul VI, it also made the most amazing statement anyone had ever seen. It invented out of thin air the concept of "licit dissent."

> ...There exist in the Church a lawful freedom of inquiry
> and of thought and also general norms of licit dissent. This
> is particularly true in the area of legitimate theological
> speculation and research. When conclusions reached by

---

7   And why not? Corporations are persons too, aren't they?

such professional theological work prompt a scholar to dissent from noninfallible received teaching the norms of licit dissent come into play.[8]

The statement was simply absurd. No one had ever heard of licit dissent before, primarily because the concept doesn't exist. Worse, since the ordinary Magisterium is infallible, no one knew what the bishops meant when they referred to a "non-infallible received teaching." In short, this portion of the document made no sense, except... except in the context of the Land O' Lakes insistence on every university's "institutional autonomy and academic freedom."

It would appear that just over a year after the Land O' Lakes conference, the NCCB publicly signaled their surrender here, in a paragraph phrased so that it would make sense only to university administrators and faculty. The faculty took the hint. Heresy in seminaries and universities across the nation exploded, as heretics publicly taught that contraception was moral. As expected, the bishops made no move to discipline them.

The Reign of Incompetence

With this decision, most American Catholic universities became functionally indistinguishable from their secular counterparts. In 2003, The Cardinal Newman Society published the Higher Education Research Institute Study through Catholic World Report.[9] In the 38 major "Catholic" universities surveyed, students actually increased their opposition to Catholic teaching as their attendance at the Catholic institution lengthened. As Catholic freshmen, 45 percent believed abortion should be legal. Four years later, 57 percent of seniors thought so. Premarital sex was acceptable to 30 percent of freshman, but in four years, 49 percent accepted the idea. As freshman, 55 percent of students approved of legal marriage for homosexuals, but by graduation, 71 percent believed it was just.

Clearly, the scandal is not just at the university level. If one-half of incoming Catholic freshmen think abortion is legal, if one-half think homosexual marriage should be legal, it is hard to say the Catholic parochial school system is working well either. If even

---

8   NCCB, *Human Life in Our Day*, #49, November 16, 1968.

9   Patrick J. Reilly, "Are Catholic Colleges Leading Students Astray?" *Catholic World Report*, March 2003, pp 38-46, available at http://www.cardinalnewmansociety. org/Publications/News/catholic_world_report.htm.

larger numbers graduate with these beliefs, the colleges are just as incompetent as the grade schools. When Catholic universities have predominantly non-Catholic faculty, when they remove crucifixes, permit pro-abortion speakers and groups and/or promote homosexual lifestyles, we can say with perfect confidence that most Catholic schools have one too many words in their titles.

Rome became aware of the absurdity that is the Land O'Lakes Conference and considered her response. In 1990,[10] after the most significant consultation ever conducted prior to the release of an apostolic constitution, Pope John Paul II published *Ex Corde Ecclesiae*, the Apostolic Constitution on Catholic Higher Education. Among its recommendations and requirements is the requirement that the theology staff of Catholic universities and colleges take the mandatum. The mandatum is the oath by which Catholic professors swear they will faithfully teach Catholic theology. Most university leaders have consistently rejected the concept. Most bishops refuse to publicize who has taken it.

Thus, while the requirement to attend Catholic elementary school fell away after Vatican II, the episcopal insistence on contracepting the parents has not. Now, instead of interposing themselves between parents and children, most bishops have taken the opposite tack. They refuse to assist parents at all. If psychological terminology were appropriately applied to an entire group, one might term this behaviour passive-aggressive.

Some might argue that this is a false conclusion. After all, the early commentary in this book took great pains to point out that adolescents and young adults are not properly children at all. It hardly seems reasonable to change the standards now and attack the bishops for failing to assist parents in reference to their children's college education. Besides, college attendance is not mandatory. How is this contraception?

These are all valid points. Throughout history, the Church has insisted that adolescents are functionally adults. But remember the context. For most of Church history, the culture was agrarian. That is, for most of Church history, the culture did not artificially extend childhood. For most of human history, the purpose of being a child

---

10   Notice the time lag. The conference was in 1967, the apostolic constitution only released in 1990. Compare this to Pope John XXIII's decree forbidding the ordination of homosexuals in 1961. How much time had passed since the seminary problem began?

was to grow into an adult. The sooner this growth was completed, the better off everyone would be.

Today, the situation is strikingly different. We have invented the concept of childhood, even invented the concept of adolescence, a term that only came into the American vocabulary in 1904. We study childhood, encourage childhood, extend childhood. As business has discovered, it is easier to separate children from their money. So, we have taken away useful apprenticeship and replaced it with useless schooling, schooling so useless that today's college graduates know less of the world than a barely pubescent boy knew in 1850. Because we have crippled the children, they now need parental guidance at an age and with an urgency that was simply unknown to earlier generations. Likewise, while college attendance may not be mandated by the bishops, it has become very difficult to avoid because of the way the mass school has forced society to restructure itself.

Thus, when parents attempt to help their children identify a Catholic college in order to receive the employment certificate that is today's college degree, they need the support and assistance of bishops. The family is the heart of the nation. The family is the heart of the Church. Every aspect of society is meant to nurture and assist the family. Bishops who refuse to publicize the mandatum are doing neither. The whole purpose of the mandatum is to assist families as they attempt to identify solid Catholic educational opportunities for their children. When bishops refuse to make the mandatum public, they are contracepting the parents by preventing the parents from learning what they need to know in order to assure their child's continued growth in the Faith.

It is a matter of supreme irony that the 1873 Comstock law, the American law which made the sale or use of contraceptives in the United States illegal, was almost entirely the work of Protestant churches and politicians. This Protestant law was overthrown by secular courts in 1965, just two years before the Land O'Lakes conference, precisely because the Catholic bishops were silent at the moment their voices were most needed. Most bishops are still silent. It is not for nothing that St. John Chrysostom, a father and doctor of the Church, said, "The floor of hell is paved with the skulls of bishops."

*   *   *

The story of Catholic education in America is riddled with ironies, and one of these leaps forward from this short history of Catholic higher education. Recall that the Land O'Lakes conference was ostensibly held to advance research in Catholic institutions. In the aftermath of that conference, only one institute of Catholic higher education refused to endorse the conference conclusions: the Vatican-operated Catholic University of America. Today, when one studies the entire roster of the Association of American Universities, a group of the most prestigious research institutions in the country, only one Catholic institution can be found upon its roll: the Catholic University of America.

Part IV: Studying the Wreckage

The Current Situation

As Leo XIII declares in another memorable encyclical, where He thus sums up the rights and duties of parents: "By nature parents have a right to the training of their children, but with this added duty that the education and instruction of the child be in accord with the end for which by God's blessing it was begotten. Therefore it is the duty of parents to make every effort to prevent any invasion of their rights in this matter, and to make absolutely sure that the education of their children remain under their own control in keeping with their Christian duty, and above all to refuse to send them to those schools in which there is danger of imbibing the deadly poison of impiety." - *message from Pope Pius XI to Catholic parents and consecrated men in* On Christian Education *(Rappresentanti in Terra), #35.*

Chapter 10: The Parish

[T]he parish community must continue to be the prime mover and preeminent place for catechesis... [for] it is supremely important that all these catechetical channels should really converge on the same confession of faith, on the same membership of the Church, and on commitments in society lived in the same Gospel spirit: "one Lord, one faith, one baptism, one God and Father."... Without monopolizing or enforcing uniformity, the parish remains, as I have said, the pre-eminent place for catechesis.[1]

The parish *is* the curriculum (emphasis in original).[2]

Historically, the Catholic Church has run two kinds of schools: mission schools, in which the unbaptized were taught, and Catholic schools, whose attendance was restricted to Catholic students. Today, these sharp distinctions are gone.

America's bishops originally established compulsory Catholic education in order to teach children to keep the Faith. That is, the schools exist so as to make sure both parents and children recognize the centrality of the parish life, which finds its highpoint in the liturgy. The schools exist to support the parish. Unfortunately, most Catholic adults involved in parochial schools emphatically deny this.[3]

The USCCB, as quoted in the sentence that opens this chapter, is completely correct. The parish *is* the curriculum. The parish

---

1   John Paul II, *Catechesis in Our Time (Catechesi Tradenda)*, #67.

2   USCCB, *Our Hearts Were Burning Within Us*, #118.

3   "The parish can survive just fine without a parochial school, but the parochial school cannot survive without the parish." I have personally witnessed pastors speak this truth to parish councils and then watched in amazement as every member of these parish councils strenuously argued with their respective pastors. Experience teaches that parish council members are often notorious for (1) their refusal to attend parish adult formation events and (2) their striking ignorance of Magisterial documents, particularly those on education. But this attitude is not limited to parish council members.

When I wrote an opinion column in which I observed that parish schools typically absorb between 50% and 80% of a parish budget, one parish administrator disagreed. He argued that the parish school budget was separate from the general parish budget. In other words, in the administrator's eyes, the school was not only an entity distinct from the parish, it was an entity completely separate from the parish. When I pointed out that the school was a line item in the parish budget, that the school's job was to bring parishioners into the liturgical life of the parish, he stopped responding.

forms parents and all parish adults. Parish relationships define for its members what is important and what is not important when it comes to the Faith. As the USCCB itself notes, this is precisely the problem:

> [T]he Church wisely and repeatedly insists that adult faith formation is "essential to who we are and what we do as Church" and is "situated not at the periphery of the Church's educational mission but at its center." *Despite the consistency and clarity of this message, the Catholic community has not yet fully heard and embraced it.* While most Catholic parishes place a high priority on the faith formation of children and youths, far fewer treat adult faith formation as a priority. This choice is borne out in parish staffing decisions, job descriptions, budgets, and parishioner expectations (emphasis added).[4]

The Catholic community has not fully heard and embraced this teaching concerning the importance of adult formation precisely because the American bishops have not done so. In two hundred years, the bishops have never been able to concentrate on forming Catholic adults. True, great emphasis has always been placed on instructing the non-Catholic adult in the Faith, but apart from an occasional booklet published by the bishops' conference, Catholic adults, especially Catholic parents, have been roundly ignored. By and large, this is not the fault of individual parish pastors. They have been given marching orders that cannot be carried out.

Blood-Sucking Parasites

Consider the first fact of parochial school existence: they cost more than everything else in the parish combined. Schools no longer have essentially free staffing supplied by religious orders. Parish staffs require a just wage, health benefits for their family and a decent retirement plan. The parish does not have the funds to do justice to any of these legitimate needs, much less all of them. The parish is the curriculum. So parish businessmen, seeing how well the parish treats its own employees, learn an important lesson: "The Church does not provide a just wage or any form of economic justice to its own employees. Neither shall I for mine."

---

4   USCCB, *Our Hearts Were Burning Within Us*, #43.

But that is just the beginning. The parochial school, like a parasite on the parish, sucks away every dime parish activities generate and snuffles eagerly through the parish bank account, still hungry for more. The school is such a notorious black hole for parish resources that some dioceses have actually been forced to implement rules forbidding schools from taking more than a certain percentage of the Sunday collections or a certain percentage of the parish budget.[5]

> Make a commitment of financial resources. It is not enough to talk about the need for adult faith formation; actions are also essential. Budgets and personnel decisions will need to be reconsidered in light of this plan. *The challenge will be to provide resources to build adult faith without undermining other educational activities already engaged* (emphasis added).[6]

"Other educational activities already engaged" is, of course, simply a code phrase for the parish school. Now, combine the statement above with the USCCB command to "Give adult faith formation the best of our pastoral resources and energies,"[7] and the whole situation is revealed as the farce it is. Consider: the parish must maintain the physical plants of church, parish offices and rectory, pay parish staff salary and benefits, pay the diocesan tax levied on each parish (this tax keeps the chancery offices running) and operate all non-school parish activities out of, at best, less than 50% of the parish budget. Many parishes do all of this out of 30% or even 20% of the budget – the rest is being poured into the school.

So, adult faith formation receives "the best of our pastoral resources and energies." In daily parish operation, this means "whatever is left once all the other bills are paid." It is not unusual for this amount to be precisely zero. The Rite of Christian Initiation for Adults (RCIA), adult formation, Bible studies, adult speakers, all of it is zeroed out in the budget, or virtually so. It is not at all difficult to find parishes in which the parochial school's annual budget approaches one-half million dollars while the entire adult formation budget, including RCIA, has to be self-funded by the volunteers who

---

5   The financial situation generally precludes any real efforts to accommodate special needs children in the schools. There simply isn't enough money available to do the job.

6   USCCB, *Our Hearts Were Burning Within Us*, #178.

7   USCCB, *Our Hearts Were Burning Within Us*, #78.

work the ministry. Adults get nothing of perceived value from the parish. Catholic adults are fair-minded people. They give as much as they see they are getting. That is, they give nothing.

Catholics give less to the upkeep of their church than nearly any other denomination precisely because the Church, in this country at least, has never taught them at an adult level. In this sense, our separated brethren are far ahead of us. Protestant churches may not understand the duties and responsibilities owed to the baptized, but they do understand that adults have larger bank accounts than children. When working in concert with grace, even pragmatism can be baptized.

It should be said in their defense, however, that the bishops understand this. They know the conflicting commands in their otherwise superb document on adult education are impossible to implement. But they are trapped. Any bishop who attempts to close down a parish school faces a scourging in the press and from the public that is impossible to overstate. Hard feelings will linger for years, decades, over every school closing. The reason is simple: the parish *is* the curriculum.

The *Real* Life of the Parish

Since 1884, every diocese, every parish has taught generations of adult Catholics that children's education is the most important kind of education the Church can do. It has taught adults that the education of parents and other adults is, to put it in the most generous light, secondary. Most Catholics see adult education as a *non sequitur*. They have never seen it and they really don't know what the pastor is talking about when he refers to it. Often, the pastor isn't quite sure either, since he's never seen it outside of a seminary classroom or one-on-one instruction.

As a result, it has become impossible for pastors to teach adults. All we needed to know we learned in kindergarten. Catholic adults tend to view adult formation events as a magnet for the overzealously religious, the ignorant and those who like warm, soft fuzzies from Scripture. In the experience of most adults, the parish has no intellectual content that would seriously challenge a teenager, much less an adult.

Thus, in a parish of 2000 families, the pastor is pleased if 20 people – one-quarter of one percent of his parish population – shows up for an adult event. After all, he can only get 30% of the parish to Sunday Mass. Parish events in large cities may reliably draw hundreds, but only because the population it draws from numbers in the millions. Adult populations reliably turn out for only two things: sports and the annual parish festival. The parish is the curriculum.

The parish exists to keep the school running. If this were not the case, why is the parish bleeding red just to keep the school running? Businesses only keep a department running at a loss if that department is critical to overall business function. The parish doesn't bleed that kind of money for adult formation, but only for children's formation. When given the choice between the importance of liturgy and the importance of a parish school, or the importance of adult versus child formation, that's quite a commentary.

Precisely because the school absorbs so much of the parish's resources, the entire life of the parish does not telescope down into the liturgical year or the Mass. Instead, most parish activities are built around the school. They have to be. It's the only way to raise the funds necessary to keep the school running. The school must be kept running because the bishop doesn't want to deal with the pain that comes from closing a school. It is painful to close a school because the school is the life of the parish. The Mass is not.

Oddly enough, ordained men already *know* this. Cut Masses out of the schedule all you want. Run confession down to a half hour each week or even "by appointment only." The bishop can even remove the resident pastor and hold communion services three Sundays out of four. None of this will raise the squawk that closing the parish school does. Parish school activities take up nearly a decade of each Catholic child's life. Catholic parents build their life around their children. If their children attend the school, then the school *is* the parish. They cannot imagine parish life without a school. So, when Catholics are told, "We will have to close your parish school," what those Catholics *hear* is, "We will have to close your parish."

But we haven't hit the bottom yet, because parish life gets telescoped down even further. When we look at the life of the school, what is the single most important aspect from everyone's perspective? Academics are important, certainly, but we don't over-emphasize academics. These schools were built to fail, remember? The point of the Prussian system is not to build academics but to build unthinking cooperation, "Teamwork" with a capital "T". And where do we see teamwork most thoroughly exemplified? Why, on the sports field, of course!

The most important sport in the school is never a solitary one like track and field, golf or tennis. The long distance runner is too lonely. No, the games that most thoroughly exemplify teamwork are football and basketball, sports whose season runs during the school year, so students get maximum exposure to teamwork. If teamwork is the most important thing we can learn in school (and Prussian military experts say it is), then the school exists to support the sports team.

The bishops say the parish is the source and summit of liturgical life. In fact, the parish is the source and summit of athletic life.

> In Nebraska, an assistant football coach, married with two children, was put on trial for the statutory rape of one of the female high school students. He was acquitted solely because the date of the sexual encounter was at issue – the jury couldn't establish if the two had sex just prior to or just after the girl's seventeenth birthday. Several parishioners were disappointed that such a fine football coach had to be fired, and was thereby lost to the school. - *email from Nebraska*

If this seems an unduly harsh assessment, we have the recent example of a bishop who was applauded for what was certainly an excellent homily in nearly every respect save one. When one considers the art of rhetoric, of homiletics, of giving a rousing speech, one rule holds constant as the northern star: start with your weakest point and end with your strongest.

The bishop in question is a wonderfully personable Catholic man. His homily at a Mass kicking off a large Catholic festival reviewed a series of affronts to Catholic Faith. The attacks he listed were, in order, attacks on humanity, hope, morality, community, on the doctrines of the Faith, the integrity and holiness of the Pope, even attacks on the great and glorious Blessed Virgin. Clearly he is building up to a rousing close. Clearly the only attack more vicious than an attack on the Mother of God would be… the state's threat to decertify the Catholic schools.

> How can any politician without any fear of consequence, decertify our Catholic schools… that do so much enormous good for the whole state and save taxpayers an absolute fortune? And why do we as Catholics not stand up and fight, and defend our faith? What will it take to finally get us mad?

He didn't say, nor did he need to say, what was on every mind. State de-certification would render Catholic athletes unable to compete on the field. The homily was a rousing success. The Catholic base was activated. The state de-certification project was shelved.[8]

Helpless

Given these facts, the pastor literally has no way to present adult doctrine to the adults in the parish. Despite the fact that we live in a culture soaked in sex and death, most pastors are loathe to speak the doctrines which heal the misunderstandings this deadly culture inflicts upon adult lives. Why?

Well, the pastor has ten minutes to deliver his sermon. If he goes longer on a consistent basis, he will be mildly chastised by the bishop. Ten minutes is barely enough time to mention that masturbation is evil, contraception is evil, abortion is evil, homosexual activity is evil, certainly not enough time to explain the rationale behind the teachings. It would take weeks of homilies to lay out the foundations, and such a homily series would eventually reach the ears of the bishop. "Father, aren't you supposed to be speaking on the readings?" The bishop is right. The pastor *is* supposed to be speaking on the readings. As *Acerbo Nimis* points out, the homily is for discussing the Scriptures, not for doing adult catechesis.

But even if a pastor is brave enough to speak these truths when it is possible to do so in conjunction with the readings, he will quickly discover a remarkable phenomenon: parents use their children as human shields to avoid hearing doctrine. That is, the moment one of the afore-mentioned topics is raised, parents besiege the pastor. He is chastised for daring to use the word contraception, masturbation or fornication during the sermon. There are *children* present!

These parents have never heard of the Curé d'Ars. Thus, they have never heard of the sermon he gave, in which he rebuked his

---

8   Shortly afterward, this same bishop publicly stated that he could not, in good conscience, refuse the Eucharist to a pro-abortion politician.

townspeople for their foul language. During his rebuke, he read aloud during Mass from the ambo a list that contained each offensive word. The Curé wanted to be sure his adult flock clearly understood what he meant by the phrase "foul language." The Curé would be run out of town today.[9]

The pre-teens may watch MTV, the teens may watch worse, the young ladies may read *Cosmopolitan* at recess, the young men may peruse the sports magazine swimsuit issue, but God forbid the pastor mention what the children study more assiduously than their homework.

Similarly, the parish website cannot reference any doctrine that might prevent parents or children from living the culture of death. As with the sermon, the website may not contain words like "masturbation," "fornication," "contraception," "sex," "sodomy," "condoms," or "abortion." The parents solemnly inform the pastor that their *children* surf the web. It matters not that these same parents throw used condoms or empty contraceptive pill packages in the family trashcan. The parish website may not address the issue.

Similar woe is heaped on those who place the wrong links on a parish site. "There is a separation of church and state in this country, Father," comments the adult parishioner, blissfully unaware that he has just repeated a Protestant heresy. How could he know? Most bishops, and therefore most priests, would rather remain silent concerning the Gospel than comment on the interaction between the Good News and current politics. Bishops don't want to pay the taxes their parishioners pay.

---

9 Conversely, pastors frequently complain about adults who sit in the last pew during Mass. They shouldn't. After all, the pastors trained them to do it. Look at any parochial school Mass. The older the child, the closer he sits to the back. Thus, every schoolchild knows that liturgy is for children. Adults stay far away from it. The parish *is* the curriculum.

Chapter 11: The Parents

The post-Vatican II heresies were legion, but nearly all had at least one virtue: they were right. They were not entirely right, of course – that's why they are heresies – but they were right about one thing consistently. They were right to point to the Church doctrine that Vatican II emphasized, the doctrine Vatican I might have emphasized if it had completed its work: lay involvement is vital for the life of the Church.

One of the most long-lived heresies that arose out of Vatican II involves ordination: the perceived need for a female priesthood. Combine this with the push to remove the celibacy discipline by allowing married priests, and a common theme emerges. Like every heresy, female ordination was built around a core truth, but a truth so deeply hidden that the heretics themselves did not recognize it:

> The family's catechetical activity has a special character, which is in a sense irreplaceable... family catechesis therefore precedes, accompanies, and enriches all other forms of catechesis. Furthermore, in places where... invasive secularism makes real religious growth practically impossible, 'the church of the home' remains the one place where children and young people can receive an authentic catechesis. Thus there cannot be too great an effort on the part of Christian parents to prepare for this ministry of being their own children's catechists and to carry it out with tireless zeal.[1]

The family is an irreplaceable teacher. We know this precisely because its role has been usurped. Both the world and the Church are suffering because of it. Parents are, by and large, no longer competent to pass on the Faith to their own children. They themselves have but an eighth-grade understanding of the Faith, if that. They know this. So, we may say Catholic parents recognize two things: (1) they are supposed to pass the Catholic Faith on to their own children, (2) they are incapable of passing that Faith on to their children.

This is a problem. Rather, this is *the* problem. It's been the problem for over a century. These two facts, taken together, create enormous subliminal frustration, frustration that eventually mutates

---

1   John Paul II, *Catechesis in our Time (Catechesi Tradendae)*, #68.

into a simmering rage against the Church that failed in its duty to teach.[2]

The post-Vatican II heresies are almost all rooted in the Third Plenary Council's decision to contracept Catholic parents by taking over their rights and duties. The family is the domestic Church, it is the sanctuary of life.

Recall Catechism articles #2221 and #2225. The parent is the first educator, the educator who cannot be replaced, the educator who initiates his children into the sacraments. We must consider these two articles again because they lie at the heart of nearly every heresy and scandal that has swirled through the Church in the last century.

Parents do sacramental preparation. The bishop, or his delegate, the priest, or his delegate, the DRE, or her delegate the CCD teacher, or the parochial school teacher; these people are required to *assess* the child to determine readiness, but they may not take over the child's formation. Parents are the primary catechists. That means *the parents* determine the appropriate curriculum for their own children: not the bishop, the priest, the DRE, or the schoolteacher. It is *the parents* who choose when to present the child for the reception of a sacrament. If the child is not prepared, the bishop or his delegates are required to point this out in order to guard the sanctity of the sacraments, but it is *the parents* who determine how to remedy the identified lack, not the bishop or his delegates.

The parents must give the child the fullness of the Faith. The child has a right to the Truth in all its glory and without any falsehood mixed in. But that child also has the right to receive the divine Truth from his parents first, so that they might be fully parents, and he might be completely the child of his parents. When someone acts to assist the parent, whether bishop, pastor, DRE, parochial school teacher or CCD teacher, the fact that this is merely assistance must be clear as crystal. The bishop and his delegates may dictate content. The child must know what the sacrament does, must desire that for himself, and must know enough about the liturgy to be able to move through it and receive the sacrament.[3] That is the extent of what can be dictated. Anything else belongs to the competence of the parents, and no one else.

2   We could dance around the issue with many words, but bluntness has its virtues.

3   Canon 889.2 "Outside the danger of death, to be licitly confirmed it is required, if the person has the use of reason, that one be suitably instructed, properly disposed and able to renew one's baptismal promises."

Primary catechist means just that. When teaching in a classroom, the primary catechist is the one who judges the appropriateness of every method used. The teacher's aide stands and waits. It is the Bridegroom and the Bride who has the child, not the teacher's aide. The bishop is the primary catechist in the diocese, he teaches the adults and any children who might through unhappy circumstance have no parent or guardian to care for them, but when it comes to children of a sacramental marriage still extant, the situation is quite different. He is a catechist, he is the catechist the parents train their children to respect and obey as the child prepares to assume the mantle of maturity, but he is not the child's primary catechist. Until the child reaches maturity, the parent is the primary catechist. The parent forms and prepares the child. Anything the assistants do, whether those assistants are bishops, priests, DREs, or school teachers, is done with the express consent of the parent. The parents prepare the child for the sacraments.

But what does it mean to say the child is prepared? For every sacrament except baptism, reconciliation, and anointing of the sick, the child should first be in a state of grace, so for Confirmation and first Eucharist, the child should have confessed prior to and fairly close to the event. Other than that, there are only three conditions, assuming the child is old enough to have the use of reason.[4] He must (1) know what the sacrament will do to him (2) want that sacramental transformation and (3) know enough about the associated liturgy to be able to move through it. The third condition can be dispensed with if need be.

That's it. That describes the complete sacramental process for Confession, Confirmation and reception of the Eucharist. The child doesn't have to understand *everything* concerning the Eucharist. If that were true, none of us could receive. He needs only know that this is Jesus, Body, Blood, Soul and Divinity, fully present in His glorified body and that Jesus enters him to make him holy. The child doesn't have to know everything concerning Confirmation either – he need only know that this sacrament matures and completes the graces of baptism so he can fully proclaim the Gospel to all peoples everywhere. Once he knows what the sacrament does, he has to express a desire for it. Once he does that, he needs to be taught the

---

4   Age seven or thereabouts, according to the judgment of the parents and the agreement of the bishop.

liturgy so he can move through it to obtain what his heart desires. That's it.

The enormous realm of "experts" and "programs" built up around this learning process is absolutely absurd. Sacramental preparation stopped being about the sacraments a long time ago. Today's sacramental preparation, especially the preparation for Confirmation, is consciously seen and used as a last chance to "fully catechize" the child before he becomes an adult and sloughs off his Catholicism for good, as today's adults do.

For all those who believe it is proper to withhold the sacrament until "full catechesis" is accomplished, there is but one thing to say. Stop. First, only adults can be fully catechized, so the attempt to fully catechize a child is doomed to failure. Second, even if it *were* possible to do such a thing, the only teachers who have the grace to accomplish it are the parents.

Today, most catechists simply teach the child and the parent to hate both them and the Catholic Faith. The grace, the power, to catechize a child in the sacraments comes from his parents' marriage, or in extraordinary circumstances, from the sacrament of Holy Orders. If the parents' marriage graces are not allowed to work, the whole effort is useless.

That is the meaning of *Catechism of the Catholic Church* #2221 and #2225, it is the meaning of the dozens of documents on the family that the Church has produced in the two millenia of her existence, from the Scriptures right up to the latest encyclical. This is the key teaching that Pope John Paul II elaborated in painstaking detail for over a quarter century. He did it in every encyclical, every apostolic exhortation, every Wednesday audience that ever leapt from his lips or his pen. The parents are the primary catechists of their own children because the sacrament of marriage requires them to be so. You see, Vatican I never got that dogmatic constitution on Christian marriage written and Vatican II forgot to include it. John Paul II noticed the omission. So, he consciously became a one-man ecumenical council. Christian Marriage finally got its dogmatic definition through his pontificate. Better late than never.

> I don't know what the overall answer is. My own kids are convinced that it will require either parents homeschooling their kids or parent-run (as opposed to diocesan) Catholic schools. I suspect that reflects their sense that the diocesan schools are beyond repair.
>
> They make that judgment after meeting a lot of kids who've gone to diocesan schools in various parts of the country. Interestingly, the kids they've found to be the most faithful Catholics are either converts or cradle Catholics who've had a profound conversion experience late in high school or early in college and most of them went to public schools. The kids who were "good Catholics" all along are for the most part "pick and choose" type Catholics.
>
> The Catholic center tries to encourage them to be more faithful, and I think is perhaps succeeding baby step by baby step. The cradle Catholic students certainly don't arrive on the scene as fully committed to the teachings of the Church as the converts for the most part, but that's because of what they've been taught. Their hearts are a whole lot more wanting to believe the Church than their heads would sometimes indicate. - *email from Midwest*

Living the Meaning

Every person is consecrated priest, prophet and king by baptism. We normally live these roles out through our assistance at Mass every Sunday and through our acts of charity in the world. But for parents who are ordained by the sacrament of marriage to be the first heralds of the Gospel, priest, prophet and king take on a very specific form. The family is the domestic church. The parents are the priests, their children are the congregation. The parents are the prophets, the children are the people. The parents are the kings, the children the subjects they rule over and care for every moment of their lives.

Grace is *power*. It is the power to do what God does, it is a power that burns within the one consecrated by it, a power that cannot be contained. When it is frustrated, the human person who was meant to exercise the power of grace, to wield that power as a skilled swordsman wields a blade, that person is trapped into uselessness.

When the Third Plenary Council erroneously insisted it had a right to teach children that was superior to that of the children's own parents, when the Code of Canon Law seemed to reiterate this erroneous idea, the priestly faculties of every Catholic parent in America were stripped away like flesh from the bone. In that instant, the parents were transformed from the priests, prophets and kings of their own children into teacher's aides. They were changed from men and women who trained to use and wield the power of sacramental grace into ignorant cheerleaders standing on the sidelines.

This stripping away of responsibility might have worked in any situation but that of a sacrament. Though the responsibility was stripped away, the sacramental grace still burned within each parent and every person instinctively knew it. The parents *had* to exercise the power, the people around them *had* to help them exercise it. Their bones burned with it. What to do?

If the parents could not be true parents, perhaps they could simply avoid being parents at all. Perhaps that would relieve the burning of grace. So they contracepted. But contraception helped not at all. The *ordo* of sacramental marriage still burned within them, it would not let them rest. What to do?

Through the long decades of Catholic compulsory school, the laity had learned. They could never hope to be teachers unless they lived consecrated life, like the nuns and priests. Only the religious had a right to teach the children. "Your child will not receive the Eucharist unless the following conditions are fulfilled!" "How can you expect us to confirm that child unless he finishes his worksheets?!" "I'm sorry, your child has not learned the twenty-seven required prayers."

Laity were ignorant. Laity weren't allowed. But the ordination of marriage burned in them. They *needed* to teach their own children, parents *needed* to become fully parents, they *needed* their children to see them as the primary catechists. But they also knew they were called to be married, they were not called to be celibate. Father might permit them to assist, but they could not make any substantive decisions. They burned with grace. They burned with resentment.

Then the heretics opened what seemed for all the world to be a door. The Council said lay people were to get involved. "But," thinks the laity to themselves, "we cannot be primary educators unless we are celibate religious. Instead, we are married. What could the Council mean? Perhaps it means we must take the cloth. It *must* mean married priests. It *must* mean women should be ordained. That is how we parents gain the ability to teach our own children!"

The laity knew that marriage is a stumbling block, an impediment to the full life of grace. The secular culture has always said it. The pre-Vatican II Church certainly seemed to say so and the teachings of the Church never change so the Council must have confirmed it. The nuns, the priests would never have been so imperious towards our parents unless they had the right!

Women petitioned for priesthood because their own priestly role as teaching mother had been taken over by the school. Men supported them because justice demanded the grace be allowed to work. Both lobbied for married priesthood. Entering Holy Orders was the only chance anyone had to teach their own children the sacraments and thus allow the sacramental power of marriage to be finally exercised. Supporters spoke of the universal need for sexual release, but what they meant was the universal need for life-giving release. The system did not allow the parents to create their family as a sanctuary of life, so they clamored to enter the only sanctuary they could find. Giving physical life is easy. But giving spiritual life – only priests and religious can *really* teach children about God. We are not permitted to do *that* unless we are ordained, so we must all be ordained. We must all be ordained. We must all be ordained…

The Return of 1884: Orwell's Nightmare

Almost forty years after the end of the council, at a conference renowned for its orthodoxy, a bishop, likewise renowned for his orthodoxy, gave a talk on children's catechesis. During the course of the talk, he said, "You know, bishops cannot know every child in the diocese," and he paused to let that thought sink in.

Too true, but no one expects them to. What was he driving at?

"Even priests will not necessarily know every child in the parish," he added, and paused again. The audience waited in silent expectation. The air crackled with anticipation.

"That's why *the assistance of parents* is of such importance to us in catechizing children."

In the audience, heads nodded in agreement.

'Since parents have conferred life on their children, they have a most solemn obligation to educate their offspring. Hence, parents must be acknowledged as the first and foremost educators of their children. Their role as educators is so decisive that scarcely anything can compensate for their failure in it...'

The right and duty of parents to give education is essential, since it is connected with the transmission of human life; it is original and primary with regard to the educational role of others on account of the uniqueness of the loving relationship between parents and children; and it is irreplaceable and inalienable and therefore incapable of being entirely delegated to others or usurped by others.[5]

> I believe that there is hope for our youth, but I think that hopeful things are unconnected to diocesan schools for the most part. I place a whole lot more trust in Youth 2000 and the Franciscan University summer conferences to challenge our young people than I do in parochial schools as they currently stand. So I think that people should listen to what [the author] is saying and try to figure out just how we can begin to make some changes.
>
> I know of at least one priest in our diocese who would agree. His comment on our parochial school was that "it raises cafeteria Catholics because it's a cafeteria Catholic school." ...Of course he's not particularly popular for his ideas in some circles, but he's one of the best priests around here. To criticize diocesan schools is to essentially gore the sacred cow. Parishes pour so much of their budget into the schools that they are reluctant to hear the truth about them. Putting blindfolds on and refusing to see the truth, however, won't fix the problem. At the moment there are a lot of people who prefer to keep their blindfolds on and really resent people... who are asking them to really see what's happening. - *email from the Midwest*

---

5   John Paul II, Family in the Modern World *(Familiaris Consortio), #36.*

The Students

For a book on Catholic education, it might be observed that remarkably little is said about the students. There is a reason for that. Schools reflect the culture onto the student, and culture is formed by adults. When we talk about the problems with schools, we must necessarily first discuss the adults who have packaged their problems into the specific form we call "the school."

But it would be remiss not to discuss some of the problems adults introduce into the school in the form of their own children. In that spirit, we shall examine the problem of school from the perspective of the student.

> The Catholic school... would no longer deserve this title if, no matter how much it shone for its high level of teaching in non-religious matters, there were justification for reproaching it for negligence or deviation in strictly religious education... The special character of the Catholic school, the underlying reason for it, the reason why Catholic parents should prefer it, is precisely the quality of the religious instruction integrated into the education of the pupils.[6]

The earliest Catholic schools were mission schools that admitted only non-Catholics. When schools for Catholic children were created, not only did they admit only Catholics, many were sex-specific: one academy for boys, another for girls, in accordance with the principles of Catholic education. Unfortunately, with the collapse of the religious orders, this separation could not remain. In city after city, the individual boys' and girls' academies coalesced into a single coeducational facility. Even so, it was not enough. As school staffs disappeared and Catholic parents turned to contraception at roughly the same rate as the general populace,[7] the number of Catholic children inexorably dropped. Even the coeducational facilities began to shrink and close.

This should have been the death-knell for Catholic schools. But, though Catholic parents attempted to contracept Catholic schools out of existence, they found their quarry was not so easily caught and killed. The schools that were not forced to close as a result of the loss of religious and the birth-dearth soon found that they could stay

---

6   John Paul II, *Catechesis in Our Time (Catechesi Tradendae)*, #69.

7   Roughly 80% of Catholic married couples contracept.

afloat by opening their doors to non-Catholics. The irony is rather extreme – historically, Catholic schools were built almost exclusively to evangelize pagan children and to form priests. In 1884, Catholic schools switched to teaching Catholics exclusively. But, when the religious orders collapsed, the schools found they had to return to teaching pagan children just to exist, only this time without the religious orders to fund and instruct in the endeavor.[8] This, of course, changed the rules of the game.

You see, once non-Catholic students are admitted through the doors in such a way that the school depends on the money of non-Catholic parents, these same non-Catholic parents have to be encouraged to keep those children there. Whereas Catholic mission schools had always been free, and could therefore teach the Catholic Faith without adulteration, Catholic contraception means Catholic parochial schools have lost this luxury. So, Catholic schools, originally built exclusively for Catholic children, are forced into an adulteration of the Catholic curriculum just to survive.

> We renew and confirm [previous papal] declarations, as well as the Sacred Canons in which the frequenting of non-Catholic schools, whether neutral or mixed, those namely which are open to Catholics and non-Catholics alike, is forbidden for Catholic children, and can be at most tolerated, on the approval of the Ordinary alone, under determined circumstances of place and time, and with special precautions. Neither can Catholics admit that other type of mixed school, (least of all the so-called "ecole unique," obligatory on all), in which the students are provided with separate religious instruction, but receive other lessons in common with non-Catholic pupils from non-Catholic teachers.[9]

It is the unusual Catholic school today that would not fall under Pope Pius XI's prohibition, either because baptized and unbaptized are in the same instructional classes or because the instructors

---

8   The USCCB document *Renewing Our Commitment to Catholic Elementary and Secondary Schools in the Third Millennium (June 2005)* even acknowledges this: "Catholic schools should be available to students who are not Catholic and who wish to attend them. This has been a proud part of the history of Catholic schools *in the nineteenth and twentieth centuries.*" *(emphasis added).*

9   Pius XI, *On Christian Education (Rappresentanti in Terra), #79.*

themselves are often not Catholic or both.[10] For reasons that will be discussed shortly, it is nearly impossible today to infuse a Catholic worldview into the classroom even under the best of conditions.

Once we add in the need to placate non-Catholics, we instantly realize that Catholic schools actually face a determined effort from their own customers to keep the Catholic worldview out of the classroom entirely. What Assembly of God Christian will permit their little Johnny to hear that his lack of baptism puts his salvation in danger? Johnny is too young to understand these things – he comes home crying when he hears it, his classmates tease him, this teaching is unconscionable! Johnny and his three thousand dollars in tuition will leave immediately unless something is done.

So, something is done.

Once the Assembly of God is placated, the Catholic who is divorced and remarried without benefit of annulment must be placated, then the one who contracepts, then the parents living in open fornication, the parents of the child conceived through IVF, the lesbian Rainbow Sash parents, etc. Every parent has to be equally welcomed, lest we lose the chance to evangelize Johnny and his parents (with what?) or, worse, we lose the tuition that keeps the school afloat.

As the school's hallmark Catholic teaching is inevitably watered down in a wild attempt to keep the doors open for Catholic children, its mission changes. It becomes an essentially non-sectarian private school that happens to be run by the local Catholic parish for reasons that are no longer entirely clear.[11]

---

10 Compare the papal statement to the USCCB statement in *Renewing Our Commitment:* "We gratefully acknowledge the contributions of school personnel who are not Catholic, but who support and cooperate in accomplishing the mission of the Catholic school."

11 Canon law recognizes that name and nature do not always correspond. Consider canon 803.3 "Even if it really be Catholic, no school may bear the name *Catholic school* without the consent of the competent ecclesiastical authority." This implies the reverse is also true, i.e., a school may inadvertently bear the title without actually being Catholic. Church law recognizes that the two are separable.

Chapter 12: The Rest of Us

[F]or catechesis to be effective, it must be permanent, and *it would be quite useless if it stopped short at the threshold of maturity*, since catechesis, admittedly under another form, proves no less necessary for adults (emphasis added).[1]

When we consider the role, or lack thereof, adult catechesis has played in the United States over the course of the last two centuries, the passage above is earth-shattering. Essentially, Pope John Paul II tells us that it is no surprise to find the American Catholic school system essentially incapable of carrying out the role the Third Plenary Council implicitly assigned it. The parochial school cannot be the focus of parish educational efforts. Without adequate adult formation, the work of the parochial school is *quite useless.*

The importance of adult catechesis as the ground and support for the catechesis of children cannot be overstated. In the passage immediately preceding this, the Pope points out:

> I cannot fail to emphasize now one of the most constant concerns of the synod fathers, a concern imposed with vigor and urgency by present experiences throughout the world: I am referring to the central problem of the catechesis of adults. *This is the principal form of catechesis*, because it is addressed to persons who have the greatest responsibilities and the capacity to live the Christian message in its fully developed form. *The Christian community cannot carry out a permanent catechesis without the direct and skilled participation of adults*, whether as receivers or as promoters of catechetical activity. The world, in which the young are called to live and to give witness to the faith which catechesis seeks to deepen and strengthen, is governed by adults. The faith of these adults too should continually be enlightened, stimulated and renewed, so that it may pervade the temporal realities in their charge (emphasis added).[2]

Lay Teachers

This problem cannot be ignored for very much longer. The public schools are at least as unacceptable today as they were in

---

1   John Paul II, *Catechesis in Our Time (Catechesi Tradendae)*, #43.

2   John Paul II, *Catechesis in Our Time (Catechesi Tradendae)*, #43.

1884, but there are no religious teaching orders to man the bulwarks. The number of elementary school students served in 1919 is roughly comparable to the population served today (1.8 million versus 2 million), but class size has dropped from 43 to 18. This means the number of classroom teachers has more than doubled. Worse, today's secular teachers cost much more to maintain even though they tend to know much less about the Faith. Thus, today's bishops find themselves in a dramatically worse situation than the one they faced in 1884.

Religious orders are self-sustaining communities. They not only take care of the physical needs of their members, they also take care of the theological formation of those same members. Religious must meet minimum internal standards of piety and Catholic knowledge in order to be accepted into the order. When a bishop brought in a teaching order, he brought in inexpensive, highly skilled labor.

Unfortunately, lay staff have none of these advantages. Consider the costs first. Laity have neither the financial support of an entire community nor the vows of poverty which religious typically take. They require payments into social security, unemployment, and retirement funds.[3] Because lay people tend to have families, their health care costs are higher, and their base salaries must be much more robust. And precisely because lay people do not take vows of stability, that is, they do not promise to live in a specific place for an extended period, they tend to move away. They must therefore be more frequently replaced, with the cost for the search borne by the parish, not a religious order. Finally not only does each teacher cost much more, the bishop must hire two for every one previously required. But the monetary costs are trivial compared to the real problem.[4]

Ignorance is Not Bliss

> Any pastoral activity for the carrying out of which there are not at hand persons with the right formation and preparation will necessarily come to nothing. The

---

3   Unfortunately, some parishes do not pay into unemployment, which causes no end of misery when a fired employee suddenly discovers this.

4   Due to shrinking vocations, most teaching orders now need "lay equivalency", thus, they are now compensated exactly as lay people are.

working tools themselves cannot be effective unless used
by catechists who have been rightly formed.[5]

Religious receive a pre-ordained amount of theological formation,
formation that the bishop can assess fairly easily, even if only in a
general way. This is not true of today's lay people. Because bishops
have not spent time teaching adults, today's adults tend not to be
well-taught in the Faith. Hiring any specific lay person is essentially
a shot in the dark. Even if a principal or bishop requires the oath of
fidelity to the Magisterium from lay teachers prior to allowing them
into the classroom, it means little. They might want to be orthodox,
but there is no guarantee they actually know what the Magisterium
teaches. This is true even of regular Mass participants.

> Diocesan pastoral programs must give absolute priority
> to the *formation of lay catechists* (emphasis in the
> original).[6]

In fact, adult Catholics tend to know no more about their Faith
than they did when they received Confirmation.[7] The reason is clear.
Confirmation is functionally no longer considered a sacrament, it
has become a rite of passage into adulthood. After Confirmation,
the individual puts away the things of the child, that is, religious
instruction, and gets on with adult life, that is, he ignores the Faith
entirely. After all, there is no such thing as adult knowledge of the
Faith. If there were, someone would surely have devoted serious
resources to it. American culture and American bishops, whether
they like it or not, have a system that reinforces this attitude. Neither
the lay Catholic nor his parents nor his grandparents have ever seen
adult formation for Catholics and thus they ignore statements that
hint adult faith formation might be a matter of any consequence.

---

5   Sacred Congregation for the Clergy, *General Catechetical Directory*, #108.

6   Sacred Congregation for the Clergy, *General Directory for Catechesis*, #234.

7   Compare Rome's "absolute priority" language to the USCCB's "build adult faith
without undermining other educational activities already engaged" directive, cf. Pius
XI, *On Christian Education (Rappresentanti in Terra)*, #79.

> Last fall I was hired to teach religion in our Catholic middle school... I taught in the school for the first six weeks of the school year ... I was still in everyone's good graces [when I left], but I'm not sure how much longer that would have been the case. I found the catechesis level of the majority of the students to be appalling. What was worse was the theological training/ viewpoints of my colleagues. When I took the "radical" position that Adam was a single individual, one of my colleagues told the student who asked her about this that I was wrong. This teacher had been hired to teach French and felt that she was not duty bound to even know what the Catechism taught, far less to actually accept it. I had to show the principal what the Catechism said on the subject in order to put the matter to rest and even then the French teacher still disagreed. - *email from Midwest*

So, the parochial school faculty suffer from a number of defects. First, it is not possible for the Church to pay a just wage. Catholic teaching positions are for single people and secondary wage earners. No primary wage earner can afford to feed his family while in the employ of a parish. As a result, the pastor and/or principal actually violates Catholic social teaching on just wages by employing the teacher at all.

The low pay creates the second situation. The pay drives out all who are not totally dedicated to Catholic teaching, while incompetent teachers tend to be driven in. Thus, after a few years, three kinds of teachers are generally left: (1) the extremely proficient, highly dedicated Catholic teacher (2) the teacher, generally single, who just puts in time while waiting for a better-paying job in a public school, and (3) the teacher so incompetent he could not even get a job at a public school.

Groups (1) and (3) tend to have long careers at the school. Group (2) experiences a rather high turnover rate. None of this helps morale. Teachers who have worked both the private and the public school system frequently comment on this.

But it doesn't end there. Of the three kinds of teachers listed, groups (2) and (3) tend not to be Catholic. Indeed, it is now unusual for a school to even have a completely Catholic staff, much less a completely orthodox Catholic staff. It is not difficult to find allegedly Catholic grade schools with a non-Catholic "teaching" religion courses, or a Catholic high school with a Protestant principal, generally hired because he is an excellent football or basketball coach.

A non-Catholic teacher can be just as good, often much better, at teaching certain technical aspects of a subject than an allegedly Catholic teacher, but, by definition, a non-Catholic teacher cannot be the best.[8] He cannot infuse a subject or a school with a Catholic worldview. If the subject is not embedded within a Catholic worldview, the student's understanding of the world is inevitably incomplete. Thus, no matter what it might say over the door or upon the sign out front, any school with this kind of staffing does not have Christ as the center nor is He the reason for everything it does. This is why Pope Pius XI expressly forbade the kind of schools America tends to run.

> Neither can Catholics admit that other type of mixed school (least of all the so-called "ecole unique," obligatory on all), in which the students are provided with separate religious instruction, but receive other lessons in common with non-Catholic pupils from non-Catholic teachers.[9]

Unfortunately, even if the entire staff is Catholic, life is not necessarily any better. Thirty- and forty-year-old adults who have no more than the equivalent of an eighth-grade grasp of Catholic Faith attempt to live and imbue in their students a Catholic life and Catholic viewpoint they do not have. Now, ask yourself, who makes a better accountant: a man who has studied math through eighth grade, or a man who has studied the principles of accounting at an adult level for several years? Most would choose the second. Some might even remark that eighth-grade math skills alone will not lead to a successful adult life as an accountant. Similarly, no adult can live a successful adult life as a Catholic with only an eighth-grader's understanding of Catholic Faith.

---

8   Non-Catholic teachers were not exactly what Vatican II had in mind when it said "Teachers... should therefore be prepared for their work with special care, having the appropriate qualifications and adequate learning both religious and secular." *Christian Education (Gravissimum Educationis)*, #8.

9   Pius XI, *On Christian Education (Rappresentanti in Terra)*, #79.

.

Parochial elementary schools and diocesan high schools are often outstanding private preparatory schools, doing excellent work in secular education. But for the vast majority of schools, that is all they are. Apart from a monthly Mass, there is nothing particularly Catholic about them.

Ship of Fools

Now, there are some who, ignoring the Magisterial teaching on this subject, argue that an adult grasp of Catholic Faith is not required to be a teacher in a Catholic school. All that is necessary is participation in an active Faith community. Let us ignore the difficulties in finding such an active adult Faith community. Let us instead focus on the heart of the question. Would those making such an argument accept a grade school teacher who had only an eighth-grade understanding of math, reading, writing or literature as an instructor in a parochial school? Would the pastor, the principal or the parents be edified to know that such a well-qualified instructor was hired to teach? Put another way, if adult grasp of a discipline is unnecessary to qualify as a teacher, why have teachers at all? Couldn't we just get eighth-grade dropouts to teach second grade? In terms of Faith formation, isn't that what we have in many ostensibly Catholic teachers today? For make no mistake: the Catholic grasp of a subject is the only truly adult grasp of that subject.

People who insist an adult grasp of Catholic Faith can be acquired as easily as a six-pack at the community liquor store haven't got an adult grasp of the Catholic Faith. If this were easy, none of us would need to live as long as we do. Put bluntly, it is embarrassing for everyone involved when an eighth-grade English teacher, asked to do Confirmation preparation for her eighth-grade class, has to decline. Although she had attended Catholic grade school and high school, and had even spent a year in the novitiate of a religious order (was this not an active Faith community?), she did not feel confident enough in her knowledge of the Faith to teach children about the sacrament. This situation is as sad as it is typical.

Think about this. This woman is trying to teach English literature, trying to introduce children to mature themes, yet she is so unfamiliar with the sacrament that imparts spiritual maturity she doesn't trust herself to teach it. To what extent do you think she is competent to teach literature, that is, a mature outlook on life as discussed by mature adults, if she doesn't understand the source from which maturity springs? At best, such an English teacher will produce excellent language technicians. She will never produce young adults with a Catholic, that is, a solid, understanding of maturity.

Or take the case of the married Catholic adult who had been preparing second grade CCD children for the reception of the Eucharist for the last ten years. After a new DRE was appointed in the parish office, he not only resigned the volunteer position as CCD teacher; *he left the Catholic Faith entirely* and joined a Protestant community. Why? Well, he wasn't being fed. It boggles the mind: the man who taught children about Jesus' presence in the Eucharist wasn't being fed. How well do you suppose that decade's worth of CCD children were served?

In the defense of parochial school teachers, it is not as if their life were easy. They not only receive an unjust wage, they are commanded to teach children they did not beget a Catholic worldview they do not possess or understand. Even if they did possess that understanding, the classroom textbooks neither possess nor understand it. Apart from a single textbook series that issued its first volume in 2004, there are no parochial school textbooks in any departmental subject that embody a Catholic worldview.

Catholic schoolteachers are accredited through secular education schools. Even if fully orthodox Catholic textbooks in the appropriate subject matters were presented to these teachers, the contents would be so radically at odds with their own training the teachers would be loathe to use them.

Catholics trained in a secular mindset don't just fail to teach the Faith. They actively spew secular humanism into the classroom. It is not their fault. We each teach what we know. Furthermore, we only teach what we are allowed to teach. As many a Catholic teacher has discovered, even if Catholic principles, teachings or textbooks are brought into the Catholic school, many Catholic parents deeply resent their introduction. The parents were trained in secular humanism as well, you see.

Subjects cannot overlap. Thus, a parochial school teacher may not mention God in math class. He may not point out that the triangle is an ancient symbol for the Trinity, nor mention the circle signifies the eternity of God. Numbers associated with the presence of triangles and circles -- numbers like pi, sine, cosine, tangent, cotangent, secant, and cosecant -- permeate mathematics in much the same way God's presence permeates the universe. Mentioning this in math class brings down the wrath of parents. Such discussion is dangerously off-topic and decidedly odd.[10] Both parents and students are Prussians who insist that knowledge stay separated into little compartments. No overlap can be permitted lest the children transition to adulthood.

> For the mere fact that a school gives some religious instruction (often extremely stinted), does not bring it into accord with the rights of the Church and of the Christian family, or make it a fit place for Catholic students. To be this, it is necessary that all the teaching and the whole organization of the school, and its teachers, syllabus and textbooks in every branch, be regulated by the Christian spirit, under the direction and maternal supervision of the Church; so that Religion may be in very truth the foundation and crown of the youth's entire training; and this in every grade of school, not only the elementary, but the intermediate and the higher institutions of learning as well. To use the words of Leo XIII: "It is necessary not only that religious instruction be given to the young at certain fixed times, but also that every other subject taught, be permeated with Christian piety. If this is wanting, if this sacred atmosphere does not pervade and warm the hearts of masters and scholars alike, little good can be expected from any kind of learning, and considerable harm will often be the consequence."[11]

How many Catholic schools can actually accomplish what the Pope here commands? Very few. The most obvious reason is simple: even orthodox Catholics tend not to have an adult grasp of the Faith. What the teacher does not know, the teacher cannot infuse into even one lesson, much less into every aspect of learning.

---

10 In 1931, the Austrian mathematician Kurt Gödel proved that any logical system as complex as addition and subtraction contains assertions that are either (1) logically contradictory or (2) cannot be demonstrated to be true or false – they have to be taken on faith. This is considered the most important mathematical discovery of the twentieth century. What few realize is that Gödel thereby demonstrated that science and math are just as faith-based as religion. It is not surprising to discover this brilliant mathematician was also deeply theological. He also converted St. Anselm's proof of God's existence into modal logic, demonstrating its coherence.

11   Pius XI, *On Christian Education (Rappresentanti in Terra)*, #80.

2000 Years of Catholic Education

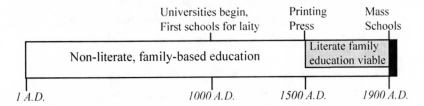

Universities begin, First schools for laity | Printing Press | Mass Schools

Non-literate, family-based education | Literate family education viable

1 A.D.   *1000 A.D.*   *1500 A.D.*   *1900 A.D.*

Schools are Fundamental

Some say Catholic parochial schools are the key to passing on the Faith. They have evidence: studies indicate that most adults who practice the Faith were taught in a Catholic parochial school or had contact with a Newman Center. This demonstrates, they say, how necessary the school system is for Faith transmission.

As the history presented in this book has already shown, as the graph above indicates and as a moment's thought illustrates, the conclusion is absurd. As we have seen, the Catholic Faith in the last century has not been presented anywhere but in the Catholic schools. There has been virtually no adult evangelization. If information concerning the Faith is offered in only one place because all other venues have been shut down or left untried, can we be surprised that virtually all Catholics learned about the Faith from that one remaining venue?

As the above graphic demonstrates, for ten of twenty centuries, schools for baptized children didn't exist. For fifteen of twenty centuries, inexpensive printed books didn't exist. For nineteen of twenty centuries, mass schools didn't exist. So, if we were to survey all the Catholics in the world through all the ages and ask each whether or not they (a) were a practicing Catholic, and (b) had attended a Catholic school as a child, the survey results would be quite different. In at least nineteen of twenty centuries, practicing Catholics have had no parochial school experience at all. The idea of the school, specifically the idea of the parochial school in the modern American sense, is just over a century old. Now, how can something that short-lived be essential for Faith transmission?

To make sense of today's survey numbers, the argument has to be turned around. Consider that fifty percent of Catholic children attended school in the early 1900's (which means fifty percent did not). Only twenty percent attend today. If schools are critical to passing on the Faith, and we once had a fifty percent attendence rate at schools, why has the percentage of practicing Catholics and of school attendees dropped? Doesn't this drop show that the schools did not work very well in the past and they work even less well today?

When we consider the studies in this light, they are actually quite an indictment. Those who wave about studies showing most practicing Catholics learned the Faith in parochial school or at a Newman Center advertise the fact that bishops have failed in their task. Catholics are supposed to change the culture, convert the world. An evangelizing Church would have a large percentage of practicing Catholics who had no contact with Catholic culture or teaching in their youth, but came into the Faith as adults because the example of Catholic laity and the teaching of Catholic bishops had changed their hearts.

Catholic bishops are meant to lead Catholic laity so that we together transform the pagan culture. Catholic Faith is revolutionary, it is subversive, it razes the idols as it renews society. Instead, as it is currently constituted, the Catholic parochial school system razed the family without renewing the culture. *It failed because it was designed to fail.* There is no particular reason to think it can or should be salvaged.

> While it is true that parents are the first and foremost educators of their children and that the rights and duties that they have in this regard are "original and primary with respect to the educational role of others", it is also true that among the means which will assist and complement the exercise of the educational rights and duties of the family, the school has a value and an importance that are fundamental.[12]

Now, make no mistake: Catholic schools are fundamental but only if they are Catholic. If they are not fully Catholic, they are not fundamental. When the Sacred Congregation says the school is "fundamental," it does not necessarily mean this particular school in this particular town is fundamental. Rather, it must first be demonstrated that a school which claims to be Catholic is, in fact, really Catholic – in teachers, textbooks, curricular design, and leadership, in parents, students and culture. Having the name

12   Sacred Congregation for Catholic Education, *Lay Catholics in Schools, #12.*

is insufficient, the name proves nothing. The fact that Catholic colleges are indistinguishable from secular colleges when it comes to transmitting doctrine proves this much.

But even if all these things obtained, is a school fundamental in the way a parent is fundamental? In a word, No. The Sacred Congregation cannot be using the word "fundamental" in the way that some would assume. Parents are persons. Despite what corporate law says, universities are not persons. The meaning of the word "fundamental" changes according to whether it is ascribed to a real person (like a parent or the Church or Christ) or a non-person (like a school or college or university corporation).

The reason is simple. Individual persons are subject to grace, they are transformed by their baptism. Sacraments permanently change persons into something they were not before: Catholics. Even if persons do not recognize the presence of grace, even if they choose never to use the grace, baptized persons are indelibly and irretrievably marked as members of Christ's body, their status as persons has been infinitely elevated. They have always the ability to be Catholics, if only they choose to rely on the power infused in them by baptism. Baptism is fundamental. Persons are fundamental.

With colleges and universities, it is different. They are not persons in any real sense. We cannot baptize a college or confirm a university. There is no sacrament which transforms their character permanently, no outpouring of grace which guarantees they will always have the ability to live up to their name. As objects, they don't even have real names. They are fungible, interchangeable. Thus, when we speak of how a school is "fundamental" we must always be speaking in the abstract, not in the concrete. "School" is fundamental in the sense that children must grow up and learn to live holy and honorable lives in the society of men. However this transformation is accomplished in the child, that is the school. Whoever teaches them how to live this transformed life, he is the catechist. So, yes, school is fundamental. But the statement is so obviously true when considered in this light, that it needs no elaboration.

Many bishops suffer from the mistaken idea that the particular schools they administer are fundamental. They believe that if we simply supply enough funding to those schools, the erosion in the Catholic culture can be ended.

It can't.

We don't need money. We need doctrine. We need parents and secondary catechists who can deliver doctrine. Just as Vatican II merely highlighted a pre-existing problem, so the current money woes merely highlight a pre-existing problem. Neither the Council nor the bank account lies at the root of the problem. Neither of these things will ultimately solve the problem. We know the solution. We always have. We just have to implement it.

> A professor at a Catholic university tells his graduate theology students that a group of nuns on a desert island would be able to confect the Eucharist. - *email from Pennsylvania*

Bonzo Teaches College

An apostolic constitution is the strongest possible exercise of the ordinary Magisterium. It is generally reserved for the most important definitions the Church makes: the promulgation of liturgy to the universal Church. *The Catechism of the Catholic Church,* the first universal catechism in five hundred years and only the second in the entire two millenia history of the Church, was promulgated through an apostolic constitution. So, when you see the phrase "apostolic constitution" on a document of the Catholic Church, you are looking at an extremely weighty and important document. The only way to pronounce on an issue with more authority is to gather an ecumenical council to discuss and rule on the matter.

Ex Corde Ecclesiae, the document Pope John Paul II issued on the Catholic university, is an apostolic constitution. The carefully-chosen title, taken from the first two words of the document, translates roughly as *Out of the Heart of the Church.* Remember, catechesis which stops short on the threshold of maturity is quite useless.[13] In a post-industrial society, the age at which Christians are able to attend university is the threshold of maturity. Today, this age is the heart of the Church.

Now, an adult does not need a university degree to be a Catholic, but it is certainly the case that Catholics who intend to teach other Catholics about the Faith need to be well-educated in the Faith. Before compulsory schooling was instituted, Catholic institutes of higher

---

13   The 1884 parochial school system was therefore quite useless.

learning had little direct impact on the vast majority of Catholics in America. Today, schooling holds a much more central place on life's stage. With the religious orders largely gone, the parents emasculated and the general adult population ignored by the bishops, the quality of the Catholic university now dictates the quality of the parochial schools and thereby dictates the quality of parish life. If Catholic higher education fails to form good teachers, the parochial schools are dead in the water. If Catholic higher education skews the formation of Catholic adults, those adult graduates will be unable to live adult Catholic lives. As parents, they will fail to pass on the Faith.

Today's universities produce the teachers and the textbooks that will be used in the only place anyone learns anything about the Faith: Catholic parochial schools.[14] The university has become a lay version of Trent's seminary. Now we can see why the apostolic constitution was titled as it was. The Church has put all her eggs into one basket.

So, how is the basket doing? We saw some measure of the man (assuming corporations are persons) in Chapter Nine's discussion of the Newman Center Survey, but many consider that survey to be flawed. In deference to their fine sensibilities, we will bring forward the bishops themselves to comment on the effectiveness of the Catholic university in America.

> It would help if the texts chosen were faithful. I spent much of my time "editing" the areas of the textbooks which were either less than helpful or downright misleading. The texts were not only not as faithful as they could have been, they were also deadly boring and some of the time over the kids' heads. - *email from the Midwest*

---

14 Today, the university has taken the place of the labor union. The university degree is the union card that allows you to work in most of the closed shops in the nation. It doesn't signify the acquisition of real knowledge any more than the union card of old necessarily signified real skill. All it means today is you owe somebody somewhere some money. In that sense, the university is the ultimate union-busting tool, a fact that could not have escaped the notice of the industrialists who first fought against the unions and for the universities.

Bonzo Writes a Textbook

In 1997, Archbishop Daniel Buechlein and the Ad Hoc Committee to Oversee the Use of the Catechism released a list of the elementary catechetical materials series approved for use by the committee. The list was short, only four series were approved. Of the dozens of submissions made, all the rest suffered from major deficiencies, deficiencies which one member of the committee described as "appalling." The top ten deficiencies were:

1) Insufficient attention to the Trinity and the Trinitarian structure of Catholic beliefs and teachings;
2) Obscured presentation of Christ as the center of salvation history, insufficient emphasis on Christ's divinity;
3) Indistinct treatment of the ecclesial context of Catholic beliefs and magisterial teachings;
4) Lack of a distinctively Christian anthropology;
5) Insufficient emphasis on God's initiative in the world with a corresponding overemphasis on human action;
6) Insufficient recognition of the transforming effects of grace;
7) Inadequate presentation of the Sacraments;
8) Deficient teaching on original sin and sin in general;
9) Meager exposition of Christian moral life;
10) Inadequate presentation of eschatology.[15]

The Catholic textbook companies were shocked, shocked to find their texts were deficient. They worked hard for the next two years, and after close consultation with the bishops' committee, finally managed to start producing something acceptable at the parochial school level.[16] Five years later, in December 2003, the same committee, though now under different leadership, reported on its progress in identifying good high school catechetical materials. Keep in mind that the same publishers produce both grade school and high school material. This is what the committee found.

Of the twenty-five series examined, none were adequate. Two-thirds were judged so bad the bishops recommended the entire book

---

15   The USCCB report on grade school textbook deficiencies may be found at http://www.wf-f.org/NCCBSpring97.html.

16   Grade schools would have to re-purchase the now-corrected textbooks. "What a pity!" said the textbook publishers.

be thrown out and a new one re-written from the ground up.[17] So how did the high school text mistakes compare to the grade school text mistakes?

- Overemphasis on the humanity of Jesus, no emphasis on the Holy Spirit (see #1,2 in the grade school list);
- Overemphasis on the role of community, under-emphasis on hierarchy (see #3);
- Relativism and religious indifferentism (see #4, 5);
- Social teaching grounded in personal initiative rather than divine initiative (see #4,5);
- Bad or entirely missing sacramental theology (see #6,7);
- Reluctance to call fornication or adultery a sin (see #8);
- Language that implies morality and belief are matters of personal opinion (see #8,9);
- De-emphasis on the importance of the priest, to the point of disappearance (see #7);
- Inadequate explanation of the Real Presence (see #7);
- Ambiguous and misleading discussion of women's ordination (see #7);
- Marriage theology that refers to "partners" instead of "husband and wife" (see #7);
- Avoids masculine pronouns in reference to God (see #1);
- Exclusive use of the historico-critical method of reading Scripture, including denial of miracles (see #2-6).[18]

In his report, Archbishop Alfred Hughes of New Orleans, the head of the commission, described the cause of the problem. "The committee recognizes that the causes are manifold. A particular area of concern is the way in which catechetical leaders, catechists and potential textbook writers are being taught and formed in our institutions of higher learning."[19]

The people who write these textbooks were trained in Catholic universities. One would assume that the authors of Catholic textbooks had more thorough training in the Catholic Faith than the regular college student. The bishops call the result of the work of these

---

17 High schools would have to re-purchase the now-corrected textbooks. "What a pity!" said the publishers again, as they drove to the bank.

18 The USCCB report on high school text deficiencies can be found at http://www.catholicculture.org/docs/doc_view.cfm?recnum=5879.

19 "When Catholic Catechetical Works Don't Teach the Faith," *Zenit*, December 4, 2003, available at www.zenit.org, Code: ZE03122421.

specially trained men and women "inadequate" and "appalling." The bishops, through the evidence they present and the words falling from their own mouths, explicitly tell us that Catholic universities are not forming Catholics.

No educational college or degree in the United States trains teachers in anything except Prussian departmentalism and secular humanism. No college or university shows prospective teachers how to integrate the Catholic Faith and/or the Catholic worldview into any of the particular disciplines. Essentially no one is being trained to teach the trivium and quadrivium. From the standpoint of formation, there appears to be no difference between hiring a Protestant teacher and hiring a Catholic teacher, with one possible exception: the Protestant teacher may be more serious about using Scripture in the course of his work than the Catholic teacher is.

And, remember, these textbooks were produced by those who presumably made an in-depth study of Catholic theology at the university level. Results for the rest can only be imagined.

Now, let us be perfectly clear on this. Catholic adults who attend most of the nation's Catholic "institutes of higher learning" are being defrauded, their money is being taken under false pretenses. They are neither getting what they paid for nor what they have a right to expect from the college or the Church. The defrauded adults these universities graduate are fed into the parochial schools and form many of our families, either as parents or as schoolteachers. Worse, these "appalling" adults become professors and administrators at our colleges and universities. It is a horrifying thing to contemplate.

The Pope issued a requirement to Catholic colleges and universities that all theology and philosophy professors take the mandatum. He used the most powerful expression of the ordinary infallible Magisterium to order it done. Catholic universities and colleges largely ignore it. Bishops collude in this disobedience and refuse to publicize who has taken it. Similarly, bishops are directly told by the head of the Congregation for Divine Worship to refuse the Eucharist to active homosexuals and public supporters of abortion. Many of these bishops either publicly dither or actively refuse to comply. The Church in America is in schism. The Catholic school system put it there.

On that subject, there is nothing else to say.

Part V: Picking up the Pieces

The Solution

If ideologies opposed to the Christian Faith are taught in the schools, the family must join with other families, if possible through family associations, and with all its strength and with wisdom help the young not to depart from the faith. In this case the family needs special assistance from pastors of souls, who must never forget that parents have the inviolable right to entrust their children to the ecclesial community.
- *message from Pope John Paul II to all parents. It can be found in Family in the Modern World (Familiaris Consortio), #40*

Chapter 13: Recommendations to Priests and Bishops

So, the adults are untaught, the schools are no good, the teachers are ignorant, the texts are useless, the pastor can't get people to listen, and the colleges are incompetent.

Thanks be to God the situation isn't too serious. Through the sacraments of Matrimony and Holy Orders, God provides the graces necessary to heal these defects, the graces necessary to transform not just a nation or a people, but the world.

That's good enough. Let's start there.

The key to solving the Catholic education problem is to empower the parents to exercise the graces of the sacrament of marriage. In most cases, their ability to wield this power is atrophied. They've never seen it used, they don't understand how to do it themselves. Indeed, many parents will fight the whole idea of accepting the responsibilities the sacrament already requires of them.

As every bishop knows, it is his task to pastor parents into dropping their crutches. Today, when it comes to teaching their own children, the bishop is their crutch. They intend that bishops and priests do their work for them, form their child spiritually and morally, initiate their child into the sacraments.

Consecrated men must refuse to do the parents' work. Instead, parents must be pastored into doing the work they were meant to do. This will not only relieve bishops and priests of an enormous burden, it will make parents stronger. It is a win-win situation. All that is required of bishops is a bone-deep willingness to be crucified. But that is not a problem. After all, it *is* why a man becomes a priest.

Everyone must pray for the bishops. Pray long.

Fast. Fast hard.

Fear not.

Bishops are asking parents to turn and embrace their sacrament. The sacramental principle *ex opere operato* applies. What is lacking in either the one who confers the sacrament or the one upon whom it is conferred is not particularly relevant. God supplies the lack. Pastors know this is true. The grace of Matrimony, like the grace of Holy Orders, springs new every day. Even though the parents might not be fully competent in a natural sense, even though they may actively fight what needs to be done, God will supply what they lack. All involved must trust the graces of marriage. Let those graces work.

The First Principle: Family catechesis

> There may be no place more significant for catechesis than the family.[1]

The bishops of America have said it, now they must believe it. The parochial schools are not set up for family catechesis in any sense of the word. They may make fine private schools, they may be marvelous at preparing children to enter into the mindset of a secular university, but they are not equipped to do spiritual or moral formation. The teachers aren't married, and even if they are, they didn't birth all the children standing in front of them. They don't have the grace to do the work the parents do: spiritual and moral formation.

> The family's catechetical activity has a special character, which is in a sense irreplaceable... family catechesis therefore precedes, accompanies, and enriches all other forms of catechesis. Furthermore, in places where... invasive secularism makes real religious growth practically impossible, "the church of the home" remains the one place where children and young people can receive an authentic catechesis. Thus there cannot be too great an effort on the part of Christian parents to prepare for this ministry of being their own children's catechists and to carry it out with tireless zeal.[2]

Can anyone honestly look out at American culture and say, "Well, this passage doesn't apply to us"? Of course not. Sadly, Christian parents do not know they need to be prepared to become their own children's catechists. Bishops must teach them to teach their children.

> The family is the primary but not the only and exclusive educating community... the State and the Church have

---

1   USCCB, *Our Hearts Were Burning Within Us, #102.*

2   John Paul II, *Catechesis in our Time (Catechesi Tradendae), #68.*

the obligation to give families all possible aid to enable them to perform their educational role properly.[3]

"Give families all possible aid" means exactly that. Help the parents do what only parents can do: provide spiritual and moral formation. Now, in order for parents to do their work, the bishops must form them first. Parents cannot give what they don't have. They cannot use the graces of the sacrament of marriage if they are sinning against their own marriage.

Parents need to hear frequent sermons from the ambo and in encyclicals on sins that have heretofore been covered over in silence. The Onan passage is a marvelous discussion of contraception. Paul's insistence that we must not to mutilate our bodies leads to discussion of surgical sterilization. Jesus asking about the green tree and the dry, speaks of in vitro fertilization. When the readings for a wedding Mass come up, so should the teaching on contraception. When the disciples point out this saying is hard, and ask who can hold to it, speak on contraception. Bishops must frequently preach on the mortal sin of hormonal birth control, the mortal sin of condoms, the mortal sin of surgical sterilization, the mortal sin of IVF, the mortal sin of abortion, the mortal sin of masturbation. Eighty percent of adult Catholics have done at least one of these things within the past month or so. The Scriptures give myriad opportunities to discuss the problem. Use those opportunities.[4]

The liturgy gives life. The homily is meant to help people apply the grace of Mass to their daily lives, to help people take the Mass out into the world because the Mass gives life to the world. If homilies don't frequently show how the Mass readings address the life issues – all the life issues – the graces of priestly ordination are being wasted. If priests are not preaching frequently on all the life

---

3   John Paul II, *Family in the Modern World (Familiaris Consortio), #40*.

4   In 1956, Senator Lyndon Baines Johnson, facing political opposition from pastors in his re-election bid, silenced them. He slipped into law the now infamous tax code change which strips pastors of their civil rights. The USCCB must get this absurd law off the books. It violates the divine rights of the person and the integrity of the Faith. The Church is required by God to guide the state, both in private discussion with state leaders and in public remonstration and invitation to follow the teachings of the Gospel. Separation of Church and state can mean only one thing: the state may not interfere in Church matters. The Church always has the right to guide the state. The mistake of Baltimore's Second Plenary Council should not be enshrined in law.

issues, bishops are allowing the men consecrated to assist them to be placed in danger of hell.

So, what does "frequent" mean? The Church tells us to attend reconciliation "frequently," and we are told that this means about once a month. It is with reason that St. John Chrysostom, the father and doctor of the Church, said, "The floor of hell is paved with the skulls of bishops." He knew the responsibility he bore. If bishops don't preach it, parents won't hear it. If parents don't hear it, bishops are at least partly responsible for their mortal sins. Who needs that?

We are permitted to be selfish when it comes to our salvation. Even the imperfect love of pure self-interest should drive the urge to break open the Mass readings and apply them to daily life. Parents discipline their children precisely because parents have enough trouble with their own sins. We have no desire to be partly responsible for the poor choices our children may make. Parents want their children to have the whole Catholic Truth not only because it is beautiful, but also because we do not wish to be held an accomplice to their sins. If that is true for us, who have but a few children, how much more true is it for Father, who has so many?

The Organizing Principle: Adult Catechesis

Every bishop knows children don't read encyclicals. If the bishops really believe elementary school education is of primary importance, they should consider this one fact.[5] Encyclicals are not written for grade school children, so they are never introduced to grade school children. It's not part of their formation. If the bishop only trains children, then he is training every generation to ignore him. If he throws the bulk of parish resources into training children, then the bulk of parish resources is devoted to training every generation to ignore him. This seems unwise.

The bishops have told us adult faith formation is to be the center of parish catechesis. They must make it so. As long as the bulk of parish resources go to the parish schools, the parish schools are the center of

---

5   The most recent USCCB statement, *Renewing Our Commitment to Catholic Elementary and Secondary Schools in the Third Millennium (June 2005)* includes the curious statement, "We are convinced that Catholic schools continue to be 'the most effective means available to the Church for the education of children and young people' who are the future of the Church." The internal quote in the previous sentence comes from the NCCB document, *To Teach as Jesus Did*, #118, published November, 1972.

parish life. Every consecrated man knows this. Those schools cannot exist on less than they already have. Thus, adult formation cannot be the center of the Church's educational mission as long as the parish school exists. Bishops and priests know that, too.

So, priests cannot be asked to do the impossible. If family catechesis is to be the first and foremost means, if adult formation is to be the center, then the parish school will have to be at the periphery. That means in most cases it has to be eliminated.

If the school cannot be eliminated, then the rules have to change. Parents cannot be permitted to enroll their children in Catholic schools unless they themselves promise to attend adult formation during the school year. That must be part of the parents' service requirement. This must apply to both Catholics and non-Catholics. If the parents aren't willing to receive adult instruction in the Faith, then why enroll the children?

The life of the family revolves around the raising of the child. If the parish won't help the parents get that work done, then the parents will rightly ignore the parish. In most cases, the school doesn't help the parent, it actively interferes with, it replaces the parent. If bishops aren't willing to close down elementary schools in order to funnel resources into helping adults do their tasks, then in what sense are bishops treating "adult faith formation as a priority"?

"This choice is borne out in parish staffing decisions, job descriptions, budgets, and parishioner expectations." Bishops staff the parishes with pastors. Job descriptions, budgets, parishioner expectations: the bishop is the leader here. Pastors know what they can safely ignore and what they cannot based on the priorities the bishops provide. Articles #42 and #43 of *Our Hearts Were Burning Within Us* are not just directed at priests or laity – they are directed squarely at the United States bishops. The episcopacy wrote it. They must live it.

Until the bishops do this, there will never be enough money to fully subsidize all the parish schools in a diocese. In rural dioceses, even one elementary school per town is often one school too many. Trying to raise money at the diocesan level for all the elementary schools just re-arranges the deck chairs, it doesn't keep the ship afloat. We all know why. Adults earn the money, not children. As long as diocesan adults aren't well-formed, they won't provide the money needed to run the schools. It's that simple.

> The *organizing principle*, which gives coherence to the various catechetical programs offered by a particular Church, is attention to adult catechesis.[6]

According to the *General Directory of Catechesis*, most diocesan parochial schools are incoherent. If this word seems harsh, it cannot be helped. It is in the documents. Find a parish that has a school but no serious adult formation process, a process that at least half the parish adults attend on a regular basis, and you will have found an incoherent parish school - in fact, a useless parish school.

> I cannot fail to emphasize one of the most constant concerns of the synod fathers, a concern imposed with vigor and urgency... the central problem of the catechesis of adults. This is the principal form of catechesis... The world... is governed by adults... For catechesis to be effective, it must be permanent, and it would be quite useless if it stopped short at the threshold of maturity...[7]

This is the Holy Father's teaching. This book is but a messenger. If there is no adult formation going on, then it doesn't matter how good the grade school is. According to the Holy Father, the parochial school is, under such conditions, a waste of time, of money and ultimately of grace. Bishops are the stewards of diocesan resources. Why throw resources away by funding elementary schools at the expense of adult education?

The lives of parents revolve around their children. The lives of single adults, whether young or old, revolve around forming relationships with other adults. Adult formation has to play on those themes. The diocese has to make adult formation the centerpiece of its presence in the nation.

> Every apostolic activity "which is not supported by properly trained persons is condemned to failure."[8]

Recall again what the *Catechism of the Catholic Church* says of parents: they are "the first heralds of the Gospel." In undertaking the spiritual formation and moral education of their children, they are engaged in an apostolic activity. They will fail unless they are properly trained by the bishops and the priests. Since family catechesis is, "in

---

6   Sacred Congregation for the Clergy, *General Directory of Catechesis* #275.

7   John Paul II, *Catechesis in Our Time (Catechesi Tradendae)*, #43.

8   Congregation for the Evangelization of Peoples, *Guide for Catechists*, #19.

a certain sense irreplaceable," that means catechesis as a whole will fail unless the parents understand and live out their responsibilities.

> The training [of catechists] should not be improvised or left to the initiative of the candidates themselves.[9]

The Church specifically says the parents – the primary catechists – cannot be left without support. They are supposed to be given a systematic instruction in the adult principles of Faith. That means they need to know and understand the Theology of the Body, they need to know and understand that marriage is the form of our salvation. Parents live out in their bodies and in their families the sign of Christ's salvation for the whole Church. They don't know how it works unless bishops help them understand. In short, the most crying need for sex education is not with the children, it is with the parents.

If the parents have a proper understanding of sexuality, they will form their own children properly. If the parents do not have a proper understanding, no one will be able to heal the children's worldview. Period. These principles cannot be taught in grade school, but they cannot fail to be taught by adulthood, for if they are not taught, the transmission of the Faith will fail.

> The qualities of persons, in particular those involved in direct apostolate, takes precedence over structures, and so funds earmarked for catechists should not be diverted to other purposes.[10]

> Diocesan pastoral programs must give absolute priority to the *formation of lay catechists* (emphasis in the original).[11]

Notice the phrase "absolute priority." Apart from the pastor himself, parents are the foremost catechists in the parish. That means forming parents outranks operating the parochial school. If it is a choice between forming parents and forming children, there is no contest. Parents come first. For America's bishops, if if it is a choice between funding the parochial school and funding an adult formation process for parents, the infallible Magisterium of the Church requires

---

9   ibid, #28.

10   ibid., #32.

11   Sacred Congregation for the Clergy, *General Directory for Catechesis*, #234.

the schools to close. That's what the Sacred Congregation is telling all Catholics when it asserts that forming the parents is an "absolute priority."

> I had an interesting talk with the science teacher while I was teaching religion at a Catholic school. She went over a test I had given and said that she could not have passed it and that she had been a catechist in her local parish. The test was not difficult and many of the kids actually did quite well on it. The problem was that the science teacher had been given no particular theological training at all, even to be a catechist. She wanted to transmit the Catholic faith (at least as much of it as she knew), but no one had given her any training, not even a Frank Sheed book or even a book list of helpful resources. - *email from Midwest*

Establish Monasteries

Throughout the history of the Church, the monastery has been the source and summit of adult catechetical activity. Much of the laity formed themselves through close contact with monastic communities. The monastic communities preserved Catholic records, Catholic culture and literacy itself. Indeed, the very concept of the parish actually grew out of circumstances created by the country monastery. Cities became organized into parishes only around the eleventh century, long after the countryside had already adopted the concept because of monastic work. When we see the Church emphasize the importance of the parish today, we must remember the monastic roots from which the parish grew. In emphasizing the parish, the Church emphasizes the monastery.

The monastic life bears great resemblance to the life of a large family. Both the monastery and the families involved with them will enrich each other from mutual contact. Part of the reason adult faith formation never got started in the United States lies precisely in the fact that monastic communities were virtually unknown here. The nineteenth century attempt to substitute parochial schools and parochial teaching orders for monastic communities essentially failed.

While monasteries are certainly subject to the same possibility of heretical teaching that struck down so many of the teaching orders, the level of risk is not the same. Monastic orders do not seek secular formation, they do not require secular accreditation as the teaching orders did. While Catholic children in compulsory Catholic schools were forced to hear and obey the teaching orders, families that associate themselves with monastic work do so on a voluntary basis. Because the monastery has its own work that does not directly intrude into family life, members of the monastic community are neighbors and friends as well as models. The dynamic for monasteries is completely unlike that of the school, for it centers not around a child's view of the world, but an adult's view. The monastic community has always guarded the life of the Church in a pre-eminent way. Its absence in a diocese is always felt.

Fortunately, establishing monasteries is not as difficult as one might think. Every properly ordered Catholic family is a kind of monastery. It lives out a rule of communal religious life led by persons under vows according to a specific spirituality. Bishops might find it intellectually easier to provide families direct support if they view families in this light.

It may be hard to find suitable adult monastic communities, but these communities are necessary to the restoration of Catholic culture. They must be searched out and brought in.

> I don't know about your area but in the South it is horrible. The Adult Ed situation is abominable! I have already lost one child to no faith at all, and find that the other is right on the verge of going to a Protestant church just to get education, fellowship and Christian support for a Christian life for herself and her family. She can find none of that at her Catholic parish in New Orleans. It is truly sad. - *email from Lousiana*

Get Professional Instructors

While the diocese waits for monastic communities to take root and grow, there is an interim approach. Monastic communities are extremely inexpensive centers of adult formation, but other forms of adult formation are generally not very expensive either. Parochial schools are expensive because they are trying to do more than they should. Adult formation costs less than a parochial school and produces better results.

Assume a parish decided to take the expensive route and bring in an outside professional speaker every weekend for a year. Omitting Easter and Christmas to ease calculations, we can assume fifty speakers a year are brought in, one each week. Most professional Catholic speakers can be flown in for a single talk, housed and paid for quite a bit less than $2000. Fifty weeks at $2000 is $100,000. Running a parochial school typically takes anywhere from $500,000 to $5 million per year in immediate costs, depending on the size and location. So, conservatively speaking, for one-fifth the cost of a parochial school, that parish could be running a completely professional adult discussion series using men and women who know the Faith intimately and are practiced in explaining it to others. And for that $100,000, we get dozens, hundreds of adult catechists trained in an adult understanding of the Faith and able to teach in the most effective setting there is: the family.

But that's not all. Outsiders who are brought in to teach on a weekend or even week-long basis don't generate liability problems. They don't get involved in abuse scandals, there is virtually no insurance liability, there are no employment taxes, no health insurance payments, no retirement benefits to deal with. There is a contract cost, and that is it. So, a professional speakers' series is actually much cheaper than even the conservative parochial school comparison above indicates.

Now, such a speaker's series is not all peaches and cream. Outside speakers are generally specialists. A chastity speaker tends to know little about Church history, for instance. If several speakers who are not very familiar with one another's work are used, the catechesis may not be consistent. Gaps in catechesis may easily appear, or information is needlessly repeated. In addition, full catechesis involves a relationship of lived example between catechist and catechumen, whether pre- or post-baptismal. That relationship does not get established with outside speakers who change every week.

On the other hand, a group of adults who are getting together every week to hear a speaker can easily be encouraged to form friendships, groups, local associations of adults who encourage one another in their shared journey. When a speaking event is properly structured to encourage the formation of these groups, the results can be tremendous. When a speaker is brought in on Friday, a parish or family discussion group can be held on the following Saturday, Sunday or Monday to delve further into the speaker's topic, for instance. Similarly, organizers must provide ample time before and after the talk for such discussions to flourish, perhaps including a weekly potluck dinner with free babysitting for the children during the event.

Bringing in outside adult speakers can be an important facet to starting adult catechesis. As native parish adult catechists are identified and formed, the parish catechists-in-training can gather together afterwards, critique the lessons imparted by the outsider, and begin to get an idea of what to deliver and how to deliver it. As each speaker comes in, the parish can test different ways to promote the speaker series, discovering the best way to promote a talk before any of the local speakers take the stage.

This kind of an effort is not only cheaper and more effective than parochial schools, it is also among the most important things that can be done to change parish culture. Such a speaker series demonstrates in a highly visible way that the parish cares about and is capable of dealing with adults and adult issues. It puts the focus on the people who need to be cared for the most: the adults. When adults are well-cared for, the children are well-cared for. When the adults are not cared for, the children won't be, either. It doesn't matter how much money is thrown at the problem if it is thrown at the wrong group.[12]

Create an Adult Space

Of course, if adult formation is the organizing principle of parish catechesis, if it is situated at the center of parish life, then adult formation would have a building devoted to it. An adult formation center is an obviously adult space. Such a center has masterpieces of medieval and Renaissance art on the walls, plush carpet, comfortable and spacious meeting rooms with good temperature control, a good sound system, a fully functional kitchen and a free child care facility

---

12   This really just summarizes the oxygen-mask monologue given by every airplane stewardess. In a flight emergency, oxygen goes to the adult first, not the children. Grace is oxygen. The adults need it first so they can show the children how to use it.

for those evening talks the parents attend.[13] The chairs are comfortable, the tables are good quality, the time before and after a talk is spent gathered around a table laden with good things to eat and drink.

Such a center feels like a lawyer's office, a doctor's office. It is the kind of place where children automatically drop their voices because they feel vaguely out of their depth. This space is for adults. This space respects adults. Imagine what you encounter at a professional conference or a university event. That is what a parish adult formation center looks like. Adults want to be treated with respect. Sending them to the school gym or the eighth grade classroom, to the school cafeteria or the church basement, is a mismatch of message and audience. When parishes respect adults, adults will respect the Faith.

Support Catholic Radio

If all of this sounds too difficult, then consider the examples of the early Church. The apostles did not sit at their desks, writing out what they thought they should say. The apostles did not build community halls and wait inside for someone to show up. The apostles preached in the public square. They went out into the Areopagus and spoke to the pagans there. The cities have gotten a little bigger since this was last done, but it is still possible to go out into the streets and personally speak to people. The most effective medium apart from actual personal contact is called "radio" and it works. It is cheaper than television, more focused than the internet and non-visual, so busy people can listen while they are doing something else – a quality lacking in newspapers, television and the internet.

Bishops can establish diocesan radio stations or encourage and support lay people in this endeavor. Radio is roughly as expensive as a diocesan newspaper and it reaches a lot more people a lot more quickly and a lot more flexibly.

Information distribution is increasingly fragmented. Newspaper readership is plummeting, television is expensive, digital media is too immense. A significant number of people will never go on-line; even if they do, the diocesan web site is but one among millions. Radio is still ubiquitous in a way unrivaled by other media. It can catechize. It can imbue our minds and turn us towards God. It is worth investigating.

---

13   Afternoon talks for second-shift parents.

> I received my B.A. in English from a state university and my M.A. in British and American Literature from a Catholic university. I experienced more mention of God and faith in the state school than at the Catholic university. I took a graduate course in Victorian Literature and neither John Henry Newman nor Gerard Manley Hopkins were mentioned, never mind objects of study.
>
> I teach a confirmation class at my parish (which does not have an elementary school). Most of the confirmandi are woefully ignorant of basic Catholic ideas and ideals. I can only infer that the children's ignorance is a reflection of their parents' ignorance as well.
>
> The pedophile crisis within the American Catholic Church is a direct result of the lack of adherence to and understanding of Catholic doctrine by her priests and bishops. It is incumbent upon the bishops of the United States to use their pastoral powers to re-educate the priesthood and laity both.
>
> Certainly, the prevailing secular culture is antagonistic. Now is the time for Catholics to be emboldened by the Truth and pronounce it with fidelity and fortitude. - *email from the southern United States*

Let Parents Do Their Work

The main aspect of adult formation is parental assistance. The Catechism commands parents to initiate their children at an early age into the sacraments. Parents must be able to do sacramental preparation. Parental competition must be gradually phased out. The sacramental prep done in CCD and parochial school must disappear. Those teachers may act on the pastor's behalf to assess the readiness of the children, but the parents must take on the task of preparing their own children and making the first assessment of their child's readiness for the sacraments.

This may sound horrendously difficult to accomplish, but it is not. Such a process could easily be phased in over the course of five to ten years. It must simply be made clear to parents who attend the infant Baptism preparation sessions this year that they will be required to prepare their own children for first Reconciliation and first Eucharist a few years hence. Between their child's first and fifth birthday's, these parents will be provided with opportunities to learn the Faith at an adult level. As the sacramental years approach, they are shown various ways of scaling that adult information down for their children. Then the task of sacramental formation is removed from the schools as the children of these fully prepared parents approach each sacrament. It is now the full responsibility of the parents.

Understand that not all parents will prepare their children to be ready at the same time. That's fine. In fact, that's the point. The parents bring their own children along as they see fit. Different children mature and prepare at different rates, and the parents are the ones who can assess this the best. You might find that every second or third Sunday, one or more children are making their First Communion, sitting in the first row and coming to the altar before the rest of the congregation. The large-scale Mass in which dozens of children receive the sacraments at once might well become a thing of the past. That is also fine. Just as baptism is accommodated to whatever Sunday parishioners schedule it, so first Reconciliation and first Eucharist will be accommodated to whatever Saturday or Sunday parishioners schedule it.

Confirmation follows the same pattern. The parents prepare their own children. They have the right. They have the grace, the power. If that means some parents prefer their children receive Confirmation years before the diocesan norm, and the child is well-prepared, that is their right. Of course, since the bishop is the one who imparts the sacrament, the parents will have to accommodate themselves to his schedule. Similarly, parents should keep in mind that the bishop will undoubtedly not be able to change his Confirmation liturgy schedule. This is reasonable.

It will simply be the case that the bishop finds he is confirming well-prepared children aged seven or eight rather than seventeen or eighteen. This is good. It means the parents know the Faith. It means the parents are passing the Faith on to their children. It means the parents are fully embracing the graces of the sacrament of marriage. Parents who insist on preparing their seven- or eight-year-old for Confirmation are almost certainly not contracepting. Every good bishop will, of course, welcome the intense parental involvement in the Faith and their child's Faith life that such preparation represents.

Parents must also remember that if they, as parents, find the schedule of the local bishop difficult to manage, the child can always receive the sacrament in a neighboring diocese. Just as any Catholic may receive Reconciliation and Eucharist from any priest, so any Catholic may receive Confirmation from any bishop. Confirmation does not have to happen in the local diocese. Few people realize parents and children have this right. They do. Now, every bishop has the duty to make sure the one to be confirmed is really well prepared, but that consists in making sure the child knows what the sacrament does, the child desires it for himself, and knows how to move through the liturgy in order to receive it. The requirements are not onerous. He can go anywhere in the world to receive it.

Leverage Homeschooling Parents

> If ideologies opposed to the Christian Faith are taught in the schools, the family must join with other families, if possible through family associations, and with all its strength and with wisdom help the young not to depart from the Faith. In this case the family needs special assistance from pastors of souls, who must never forget that parents have the inviolable right to entrust their children to the ecclesial community.[14]

Families have a right to form associations, and these associations should be encouraged. Indeed, one could argue that the pastors have a duty to make sure such associations do form. Thus, it is to everyone's benefit to utilize the talents of homeschooling parents to the utmost.

A word should be said about homeschooling here, though more will be said later. Not all parents have the capacity to educate their child in chemistry, math or other forms of secular knowledge.[15] No one expects they would. The grace of the sacrament of marriage guarantees only that parents have the power to accomplish the moral

---

14   John Paul II, *Family in the Modern World (Familiaris Consortio)*, #40.

15   Grace builds on nature. While marriage infuses parents with the power to teach their own children in spiritual matters, it does not infuse them with the necessary knowledge. Everyone has the power to know God. Not everyone has the power to know, understand or teach calculus or chemistry.

and spiritual formation of their children, the power to initiate them at an early age into the sacraments. Outside of these particular tasks, the parents have no particular charism through the sacrament of marriage to form their children. The teaching of Church history, of apologetics, of Latin, and similar aspects of the Faith are important to a complete Christian education, but many of these might best be accomplished by others.[16] The teaching of math, chemistry, and music may likewise be accomplished by others.

But what parents do have both by right of baptism and marriage is the right of collegiality. They have a right, and a concomitant duty, to associate with one another, to form a body. Much has been written about how television, automobiles and air conditioning have combined to destroy the collegiality of families and neighborhoods. Where families used to sit out on large front porches and watch their children play together in the streets or the fields on a summer's evening, now they sit huddled before an electronic god in the isolated and delicious coolness of their darkened homes. Much of every parent's self-perceived incompetence to transmit the Faith to their own children rests in this modern isolation. Parents living in a world where every couple is made up of two professional employees, where many parents are single and have no one to talk to at all – this has broken parental solidarity. There is no one to talk to.

When this is considered, the advantage of having parents teach parents becomes obvious. Homeschooling parents are among the best of solutions to the problem of unformed parents precisely because they were themselves once unformed parents. They are familiar with the problems of instructing for sacramental initiation and moral/ spiritual formation. They are familiar with all the resources. Because they have a depth of experience in teaching other areas as well, they have a robust knowledge of what needs to be done at various age levels. Ask them to help form the community of parents that is to be established in the parish. Ask them to lead adult formation sessions. Let parents live their marriage grace, their baptismal grace, by assisting one another in leading their children towards holiness.

---

16 Thus, the Rite of Confirmation, #3 says, "The initiation of children into the sacramental life is ordinarily the responsibility and concern of Christian parents. They are to form and gradually increase a spirit of faith in the children and, *at times with the help of catechism classes*, prepare them for the fruitful reception of the sacraments of Confirmation and Eucharist." (emphasis added) Catechism class is not sacramental prep, it is assistance in these ancillary aspects. Parents do sacramental preparation.

Nevertheless, Venerable Brethren and beloved children, We wish to call your attention in a special manner to the present-day lamentable decline in family education. The offices and professions of a transitory and earthly life, which are certainly of far less importance, are prepared for by long and careful study; whereas for the fundamental duty and obligation of educating their children, many parents have little or no preparation, immersed as they are in temporal cares. The declining influence of domestic environment is further weakened by another tendency, prevalent almost everywhere today, which, under one pretext or another, for economic reasons, or for reasons of industry, trade or politics, causes children to be more and more frequently sent away from home even in their tenderest years.[17]

If bishops want to be serious about supporting family catechesis, they would consider subsidizing not Catholic parochial schools, high schools or universities, but homeschooling families. The greatest investment a bishop can make in a child's formation is this: make sure the child can stay at home with his mother or father so as to learn how to live an adult life from the adults who gave him life.

Dioceses give tuition grants to Catholic elementary school students all the time. By giving that money directly to the parents themselves, the parents could more easily form a sanctuary of life for their children in their own home, as they are called to do. This idea may sound radically impossible, and perhaps it is, but has anyone ever investigated the idea to see if it is?

Consider what the latest research says on the subject. Charles Desforges (Order of the British Empire), emeritus professor of education at the University of Exeter, examined research from around the world in order to compare children's academic attainment with the amount of parental support they received. He found that at the age of seven, school has almost nothing to do with academic achievement:

When all other factors bearing on pupil attainment are taken out of the equation, parental involvement has a large and positive effect on the outcomes of schooling... This effect is bigger than that of schooling itself... Let's say we could make all schools equally good. Would all seven-

17   Pius XI, *On Christian Education (Rappresentanti in Terra), #73.*

year-olds be equally good? The answer is no. You would only reduce differences in attainment between them by five per cent. But if you could make all parents equally good at parenting, it would make a difference. It would reduce differences between children by thirty per cent.[18]

What John Paul II said thirty years ago, research today confirms. Even if all grade schools were made equally capable, it would have almost no effect on the child. But, if we made all parents excellent parents, it would have a substantial impact on the child. So, why are we pouring our resources into schools when those resources really need to be invested in parents?

Old habits of thought must be broken.[19] The parochial school cannot remain the focus of concern. Adult education must become the focus. It is what the bishops said they would do in the document they wrote.

Reform the School Curricula

Hence in accepting the new, he will not hastily abandon the old, which the experience of centuries has found expedient and profitable. This is particularly true in the teaching of Latin, which in our days is falling more and more into disuse, because of the unreasonable rejection of methods so successfully used by that sane humanism, whose highest development was reached in the schools of the Church.[20]

Pope Pius XI goes on to point out in the same article that education in godless schools thereby "renews in a real and *more terrible manner* the slaughter of the Innocents" (emphasis added). If one or more Catholic elementary schools or high schools is kept open, the curricula must be reformed. The Pavlovian bell system and the departmental approach must be eliminated. The Catholic high

---

18 "Mums, Dads Key to the Future," *The Sunday Times*, 10 April 2005. The article can be found at http://www.sundaytimes.news.com.au/common/story_page/0,7034,12803677%255E950,00.html.

19 Nine of ten heart bypass patients who are given a stark choice - change your lifestyle or die - die. Lifestyle change only works when it is radical, embraces a simple, joyful life-vision and is intensively coached. See http://www.fastcompany.com/magazine/94/open_change-or-die.html

20 Pius XI, *On Christian Education (Rappresentanti in Terra), #87.*

school graduate should be sufficiently self-assured that he need not raise his hand to participate in an adult conversation.[21]

Catholic education forms good judgment first and foremost. Good judgment is more important then any single subject. The trivium and quadrivium, properly taught, do this job, but the pure classical education is not everywhere compatible with state accreditation. The bishops must decide what they want: an accredited sports team or a Catholic education.

A Catholic education might be harmonized with state goals, but only by a true interdisciplinary approach, an approach to knowledge that is led by adults skilled enough to show the connections between the disciplines despite the inadequate textbooks on their desks. The integration of human understanding into a coherent whole stands at the center of what it means to be Catholic, and this integration is not just an integration of various subjects into a whole, but the integration of divine knowledge and purpose into daily life.[22]

An example of how this might be done can be found in the Pearson's Integrated Humanities Program (IHP) core curriculum, the program that ran at the University of Kansas until 1979. It was a four-semester sequence of humanities courses in which the students read and considered the great books of Western civilization. The first semester studied Homer and other Greek writers, the second, Virgil and the Romans, the third, the Bible and St. Augustine and other writers of the Middle Ages, and finally Shakespeare and other modern writers. But this was not just a Great Books curriculum.

Robert Carlson's book, *Truth On Trial: Liberal Education Be Hanged*, includes a chapter that documents in detail how poetic education in the IHP begins to humanize. In the IHP program, students were not permitted to take notes during the hour and a half twice-weekly lectures. They had to *listen*. The lectures were not lectures. On Tuesdays and Thursdays, three professors, two from English

---

21   Who has not had the disconcerting experience of holding conversation with a group of adults who substitute raised hands for conversational skills? Twenty-something college students often insist on raising their hands and being recognized by one of the other adults in the conversation before they will speak. The habit displays how adults are schooled in adolescence. Adults conversing together should know how to hold conversation without being demeaned in this way.

22   As the Second Vatican Council points out in *Gravissimum Educationis* #1:"True education is directed toward the formation of the human person in view of his final end..." The Trinity is our final end.

and one from the classics department, would simply pick up a book, open to a passage, read it aloud and then talk about it, allowing the discussion to go wherever it would. While the "lecturers" discussed Cicero, Plato or others, the discussions were always meditative, built on commentary, never disputative.

During the Monday-Wednesday-Friday sessions, students memorized poetry. No texts were allowed in these sessions at all. The group leader, who had himself committed the poem to memory, would verbally teach it to the students for memorization.

Students learned calligraphy, took frequent evening sessions for naked-eye star gazing and learned the Greek myths associated with the major constellations. They also learned several traditional songs, which the whole class sang prior to the start of lectures. They learned to waltz. They learned poetry, beauty. Though theology and religion were never formally taught, many IHP students came into the Catholic Church. In fact, several entered consecrated religious life.

Carlson describes the IHP experience this way: "Western tradition has divided the long itinerary of liberal education into three stages each contributing something of its own to the three purposes of liberal education - to humanize, to acculturate, to make happy. These are the stages of poetry, liberal arts, and sciences. According to Plato, the first step in the long itinerary of liberal education is the elementary or poetic stage.... These descriptions of the poetic stage of development mention the powers within the young student -- senses, memory, imagination. Poetic education begins to humanize by developing these powers."[23]

Why did the IHP curriculum work so well? Because the professors who ran it merely exposed their students to what agrarian communities had always exposed their children: the discourse and lives of adults. These students had the opportunity to do what the young Ben Franklin had done: sit quietly at the dinner table and listen to his father's guests converse about the books they had read and the topics of the day. Franklin learned to speak in front of kings by imitating his father's way of speaking to his dinner guests. In an age before light pollution was an issue, the children were taught the

---

23   James Taylor, *Poetic Knowledge*, as quoted on http://www.greatbooksacademy. org/html/pearson_integrated_humanities_.html. See also *Iris Exiled: A Synoptic History of Wonder*, University Press of America (2002).

constellations by their parents in the evening, and what they saw was enriched by what they read from their father's books. For their own entertainment they sang traditional songs, they learned to dance to the music of the pipe and horn. They learned to make beautiful things for the sake of making beautiful things. IHP simply recreated the agrarian experience of maturing from childhood into adulthood.[24]

This is Catholic education. This is the history of how man has always educated himself. It is glorious and it invites others to participate in the glory.

> In fourth grade my daughter announced that her teacher said nothing is wrong with homosexuals, and she was taught artificial birth control and artificial insemination are okay (no, I'm not kidding). She was also being bullied. I was told, "kids will be kids," after I asked why Catholic values weren't being actively taught there. Sad to say, the parish Confirmation class was a joke.
>
> My daughter is now enrolled in a Catholic university, whose president proclaimed that the campus is "unabashedly Catholic" even though it took a while for him to cancel the "Vagina Monologues" after it was scheduled last year. My daughter's in her second theology class - she reports she hasn't learned much in either one, but they ARE basic classes and she and I (and her high school) did cover some of the territory. The first course (comparative religions) was taught by a Protestant. Thank God she's active in liturgy and has joined a Bible study class. I pray fervently that being on a Catholic campus will help my daughter form a life-long love for the Church, and hunger to understand and live the faith.
>
> Can someone please tell me how I can find out whether the Catholic philosophy and theology professors at my daughter's university have taken the mandatum? - *email from California*

Enforce the Mandatum

Pope John Paul II has already told us the basics: "As the family goes, so goes the nation... As the family goes, so goes the Church."

---

24 Even so, the IHP instructors knew they had gotten the students too late. They understood that this formation should have taken place in grade school or at least high school.

Any bishop who does not enforce and make public the mandatum betrays the Catholic family. Papal teaching forbids non-Catholic teachers in Catholic schools, it forbids the mixing of baptized and unbaptized students in the same classroom. Likewise, if a Catholic teacher refuses to publicly embrace the Faith, he betrays the graces of his sacramental Confirmation.

In order to make this perfectly clear, we shall reiterate the principles so far elaborated. As the Pope points out, the bishop is consecrated to support the family. He does so by teaching the parents the Faith and sanctifying all the members of the family through the sacraments. Just as Joseph guarded the Holy Family, the bishop guards and assists the families in his flock against anyone which does not provide unstinting support to the parents as they work to form their children in the Faith.

The word "professor" means "one who professes Catholic Faith." Any professor who refuses to publicly acknowledge his fealty to Catholic Faith is not a professor, he is a usurper. Any bishop who does not warn his flock against such men and women is failing in his duty as bishop. The college exists to assist the parents. The presence or absence of the mandatum must be made known to parents. They have a right to know who can be trusted to approach their children and who cannot. For centuries, the Church recognized this right by requiring a license to teach from all who would teach. From the Third Plenary Council to Vatican II, America's bishops contracepted parents by actively interfering in the operation of the graces of marriage. From Vatican II to the present, many bishops have contracepted parents by refusing to support the graces of marriage as the parents seek safe educational haven for their children at the university level. Bishops must do their work so parents can accomplish their own.[25]

---

25 Tim Drake's award-winning 2004 series on the mandatum in *The National Catholic Register* reports fourteen colleges/universities have the mandatum: Aquinas College, Nashville, TN, Ave Maria College, Ypsilanti, MI, Ave Maria University, Naples, FL, Belmont Abbey College, Belmont, NC, Benedictine College, Atchison, KS, Our Lady of Corpus Christi, Corpus Christi, TX, Creighton University, Omaha, NE, DeSales University, Center Valley, PA, Franciscan University of Steubenville, Steubenville, OH, Magdalen College, Warner, NH, Our Lady of Holy Cross College, New Orleans, LA, St. Gregory's University, Shawnee, OK, University of Dallas, Dallas, TX, University of St. Thomas, Houston, TX. Two institutions take an oath of fidelity because their bishops have not seen fit to offer the mandatum: Christendom College, Front Royal, VA, Thomas Aquinas College, Santa Paula, CA.

Support Orthodox Newman Centers

Newman Centers are found on the campus of nearly every major secular college and university in the nation. These centers of Catholic teaching and Faith life are of inestimable value in bringing the adult understanding of Jesus Christ and His Church to the young men and women who have entered into fully mature adult life. An outstanding Newman Center, such as the incomparable center on the campus of the University of Illinois, Urbana-Champaign, can transform the lives of college students, regardless of their creed.

Sadly, these centers are often on the tail end of the diocesan funding train. Typically, the diocesan funding for all the Newman Centers combined is lower than the annual budget of many individual parish grade schools in that same diocese. Indeed, a study of any of the myriad diocesan funding drives would quickly demonstrate that very few bishops make adult formation at either the parish or the college level "a priority."

If the reader does not believe it, he is encouraged to look for himself. Study the numbers in the annual diocesan appeal. Add up the money invested in natural family planning, family programs, adult formation and Newman Centers. Compare this to the amount given to the Religious Education office and "young adult" ministry.[26] If a bishop's priorities are "borne out in... staffing decisions, job descriptions, budgets, and [diocesan] expectations," then we can confidently say the hopes of adults in most dioceses are cruelly dashed.

Change the Diocese

The changes described here must be implemented throughout the diocese, or parents in larger cities will simply retreat to the crutches they know best, the welfare state still present in a less "burdensome" parish. Pastors will receive many complaints and may well find cause to complain themselves. Bishops must stand firm as Pope Pius IX did. The American bishops forced the schools on parents and parishes a century ago. Now they must clean up the wreckage their schools created.

---

26 "Young adult ministry" is generally a euphemism for ministry to high school students. Contrast this to the Vatican's World Youth Days, whose audience is explicitly those 18 to 35 year old. Participation by those under 18 is discouraged.

No matter how much the parents (or the pastors) complain, bishops must remember that they are meant to enable these parents to use the power sacramental grace infuses in them. Parents will learn the Faith at an adult level. They will have been given the incentive that drives them to learn the Faith. Catechists know full well that parents will do anything to get their children through the sacraments. Instead of using this fact to strip the parents of grace, it must be used to empower them in their grace. Parents must do the formation themselves. As they do it, parents will find that they are bonding more closely with their child. Children will grow in obedience and their family will grow in harmony. The life of the parish will again be the liturgy.

Mission schools are a noble thing and have a long tradition in the Church, but mixed instruction between baptized and unbaptized violates the ontology of both groups. The parochial school might be transformed into a mission school if necessary, but Catholic parents must be formed first and foremost.

Catholics have undergone double taxation for over a century, supporting both state and private schools out of their own pockets. The money saved by not paying Catholic school tuition might be sufficient for one of the parents to actually return home to educate the children. If the parents don't feel adequate to this task, then let the natural association of families assist. Let them be parents. Help them be parents.

Yes, the public schools are terrible. Yes, Catholic children in those ravenous public schools – and they are ravenous – might get crucified for their beliefs. This is why we were baptized.

We must rediscover how to produce twelve-year olds who could command ships, how to produce saints like Katherine Drexel, who built real Catholic universities. If we want to make a difference in this country, if we want the Catholic ethos to permeate every corner of this country, then Catholics must be educated as leaders, not schooled as slaves.

Chapter 14: Recommendations for Parents

Learn the Faith

No one can explain what they don't know. Illiterate people cannot teach others to read. People who only know how to add and subtract cannot teach much math. Even when they try to teach what they know, they will hit roadblocks. Let a child ask, "Isn't there a faster way to find the answer to 4+4+4+4+4?" A parent who knows nothing of multiplication will have to reply, "I don't know of any other way, dear."

For that reason, parents who don't know the Faith at an adult level will not be able to explain the Faith to a child. They may have the grace, the power, but they won't know how to use that grace. We are all familiar with people who have power but have no idea how to use it. We have all worked for a clueless boss; the Dilbert comic strip is built around characters with this problem. Knowledge is power, as the old saying goes, and if parents want to be powerful, they have to know something.

Instruct Your Children in the Sacraments

If you do nothing else described here, do this. It is critical to your marriage and to your salvation. And don't be afraid. It isn't really difficult to learn enough to teach a seven-year old. That's the beauty of being an adult – we always know more than they think we do. Remember, sacramental preparation requires only that the child (1) knows what the sacrament does, (2) wants that to happen to him, and (3) knows how to move through the liturgy well enough to receive it. That's all.

If you have been going to Mass and confession regularly, then you already know how to teach step (3). Just help your child understand how to do what you already understand how to do. If you don't understand something, go find out. Step (2) is likewise a snap. When a sacrament is properly explained, the child always wants it. So all that leaves is (1).

Now, we could go through what needs to be known in these pages, but one of the points of this book is to help parents begin to do what they are supposed to do. One of the things Catholic parents are supposed to do is help each other raise Catholic children. So, get on the phone. Get together with other Catholic parents, perhaps in the company of an orthodox priest, and gather in someone's house to discuss this. If you invite a priest, let him know that he's there mostly for moral support and to answer questions that none of the parents can answer. You are the parents, so hash this out.

Get a *Catechism of the Catholic Church*. Read through the section on the sacrament in question. If you can't stand to read it yourself, have another parent read and summarize the passage for the group. Then discuss what the Catechism says. Do you see those footnotes with Scripture passages listed down at the bottom of the page? Look those Scripture passages up in your Bible. Read them. Figure out how they apply to the sacrament under study. You are an adult. You can do this.

The contents of the Catechism are the minimum necessary for adult understanding. If you can accurately summarize to another parent in the room what the CCC says, using at least one of the Scripture footnotes in your explanation, you have a basic adult understanding. There is more you could learn, but that is enough to get you through teaching your child.

Once you understand the sacrament at an adult level, you will be able to explain it to your child. Think about the teaching, pray on it, weigh the various aspects of it and consider how best to bring your children to understand it. Some children will learn best through books, others through discussion, others through examples, most through a combination of all three. You are the parent, you are the one who knows your child best. You figure out how to introduce it to him. Get ideas from other parents, ask the priest for suggestions, but do it. You are parents, so use the graces your own confirmation and marriage gave you, and *teach*! If He gave the words to His apostles when they stood before kings and princes, He will give the words to you when you stand before your little princess. God will send the grace, He will send the power. He always does.

Create Family Associations

This is alluded to in the previous answer, but it is given its own section here in order to flesh out the point. You've heard of the college of bishops. It is all the bishops who have ever lived and taught in union with the Pope. When the college of bishops teach in this kind of unity, it is infallible.

Parents, you are priests of the domestic Church. When you, as parents, teach in union with the Pope and your bishop, you are infallible. Don't believe me? Watch – I will now make an infallible statement. Stand back (deep breath). Here I go...(drum roll please)

"God is one God in Three Persons."

See? That statement is infallibly true. I made an infallible statement. You can do it too. It's easy. As long as you teach what the Church has always taught, you are infallibly right. In fact, that's pretty much all there is to what the Pope does. When Catholic parents together teach in union with the Pope and the bishops, they become a kind of college. In this sense, when the orthodox lay faithful teach this way, that teaching is infallible. There's even a name for this collegiality and infallibility of the lay faithful: the *sensus fidelium*, or sense of the faithful. Through the graces of baptism, when we have formed our consciences according to the Church and teach always and only what the Church teaches, we have a constant sense of what is right.

Now, this doesn't mean I am right about something just because I thought it up. I have to consciously try to follow what the Church teaches, understand it in my bones, live it. That's what it means to form your conscience. In order to develop good instincts for what is true, I have to know and accept what the Church teaches. That means I have to pray, read, think, study Scripture, study Church documents and Church history.

It also means I have to be humble enough to realize that I can be wrong. I might have to change my opinions on some subjects. Do this for even a little while and you will be amazed at how ineffective even a solidly orthodox Catholic elementary school education was in transmitting the Faith to you. There's a reason it didn't work all that well.

The Catholic Faith is for adults. As the beginning of this book pointed out, most children really don't get what it means to be Catholic, and they can't get it. They don't have the context. As an example of the difference between a child's understanding and an adult's understanding, let us consider the Eucharist from an adult perspective, the perspective Pope John Paul II called the "Theology of the Body."

You know from your second grade instruction that the Eucharist is the Body, Blood, Soul and Divinity of Jesus Christ, it is the Flesh of God. That is a second-grader's understanding – the ability to correctly identify a thing or person. But now let's put that sacrament into an adult context.

We know the Mass is called the Wedding Feast or the Nuptial Feast. We know the Church is called the Bride of Christ. In fact, we are each made a spouse of Christ at our baptism because we become part of the Bride. That is why Christ is called the Bridegroom, right? We also know that Jesus insisted we had to eat His Flesh and drink His blood if we are to have life within us.

So, let's put all of that together. When we participate in the Nuptial Feast, the flesh of the Bridegroom enters the flesh of the Bride and we are given new life. Now, when I say that being Catholic is about being married to Jesus Christ and that children don't really get it, do you see what I mean? This is one example. There are literally dozens of others like it. We are meant to walk through the world seeing Christ the Bridegroom in everything we do, in every person we meet. You may have heard this before, but does it have a different context for you now, a richer context than it did five minutes ago? It should. Would you like to learn more about this? Study.[1]

Give Your Child Adult Responsibility

Children should be constantly exposed to adult conversation, adult work, adult ways of doing things. Dependency is created by preventing a person from ever engaging in real work. If a child never does real work, he will never know what he is capable of doing. As a result, he is easily controlled through intimidation and criticism. But, give him real work that materially contributes to the well-being of the family and/or the community, and he becomes much less susceptible to baneful influences. He now has a standard of personal accomplishment which the world will not easily or artificially debase.[2]

Work is important. The Internet provides enormous opportunity in this direction. No one knows who is on the other side of that web

---

1   This whole theme is part of a concise little 100-page book written a few years ago called *Sex and the Sacred City*. It is easy to read and it is available through Bridegroom Press (www.bridegroompress.com).

2   This is the point of becoming an Eagle Scout.

page, nor do they really care, as long as their product or service arrives as described. Start your child in a business through which he can learn adult responsibility. Better yet, get him to volunteer at the local soup kitchen, food pantry or homeless shelter. The more he is working side-by-side with adults, the more adult he will be. The purpose of childhood is to grow into adulthood. Adults depend on each other. When adults regularly depend on him, he has become an adult.

This doesn't mean the home should be turned into a sweatshop, of course, but the principles of the agrarian society, in which each member of the family contributes his share for the good of the whole, should be emulated. Children learn to act like adults by... acting like adults. They have to live it, not just study it, read about it or write about it.

The child labor laws were pointless for an agrarian society. They became useful to a certain extent for an industrial society. They are again pointless in our post-industrial society. Even a child wants to feel useful. By insisting on extending childhood, we are simply extending the period in their lives in which they do not feel they have a purpose. This is not kindness.

Keep your child in an adult world. Expose your children to classic literature and classical music early and they will not stray far from it. Do this during the year they learn to read, and they will hunger for it. I have told many a bedtime story that was simply an expurgated version of the Greek myths – the three- and five-year-olds love it. They prefer those stories to the animated "educational" figures so prominent on the television and computer screens. They want to be adults. They love to hear about what adults do and how adults think. Don't deprive them. Inundate them. This is why they are children. They are meant to be exposed to adult life so that they might imitate it.[3]

Build a Sanctuary of Life

Consider a wildlife sanctuary. Rules are strict about what and who may enter, when they may enter, where they may walk, how

---

3   For a good discussion of the 1930's origin of the modern teen subculture and its anti-Catholic structure, see Chapter 13 of Charles DeNunzio's *Variations on a Theme Op. 45*, unpublished manuscript available at: http://www.charlesdenunzio.com/op45/Chapter13.pdf.

long they may stay. Look at the sanctuary in your church. Consider the atmosphere, what is there, what is not. This is the meaning of sanctuary: a certain atmosphere of peace, a respite from the assaults of the world.

As Pope John Paul II pointed out in *The Gospel of Life*, your family is a sanctuary of life. If someone asks why your home has no broadcast or cable television, why your children's bedrooms have no electronic devices besides a clock and a few battery-driven toys, why the computer is either off-limits to children or only used under close adult supervision in a very public space, tell them. The family is the sanctuary of life.

They will undoubtedly berate you, "What are you trying to do? You can't protect your children from the world!" The answer is clear. "If the Forest Service can build a sanctuary for wildlife, if we build a sanctuary for the Eucharist, why can't I build a sanctuary for my children here in my home? Are you saying my children are less worthy of protection from the world than the spotted owl? Are not my children images of the God who resides in the tabernacle?"

The world is with us always. To encounter it, we have but to step out the front door. But where can one go to rest from its incessant demands? That is the purpose of the family. It allows the young ones to rest, to recuperate, to build up strength for another foray out into the jungle of the world. To argue against such a concept is to embrace the sixth point in the heresy of Americanism – the exaltation of active virtues over angelical virtues.

God revealed Himself to us by slow degrees. Abraham knew less than Jacob, Jacob knew less than Moses, Moses knew less than John the Baptist. John the Baptist knew less than Mary. Just as God reveals Himself to us slowly so that we may become accustomed to Him, so we reveal the world to our children slowly, allowing them to retreat to the home and rest between forays into the adult world. For Christians, the world is a battlefield. We have a right to a little rest and relaxation within the bosom of the sanctuary that is our family.

So, get rid of your TV. Throw it out. What? Why yes, EWTN has quite a good set of programs. Oh, certainly I agree, the sports channel is mostly innocuous. Yes, it is absolutely wonderful that you have blocked MTV. I applaud the fact that you have restricted broadcast television viewing.

That's great. I'm proud of you.

Now throw it out.

Television advertisements teach one thing: you don't have enough. Whatever "enough" might be, you don't have it and you won't be happy until you get it, so you must go out and buy it. That is television's only lesson, it is the lesson that runs through every other lesson. Just as the curriculum of the compulsory school is contraception, so the television curriculum is the curriculum of the needy, the incomplete, the whining child. You wouldn't let a used car salesman live rent-free in the spare bedroom. Why let this thing live rent-free in your living room?[4]

If you must have it, cut the cable, rip off the antennas and operate solely on the DVD and VCR players. Don't permit your children to even be aware that broadcast or cable television exists until they have at least received the sacraments of Reconciliation, Confirmation and First Eucharist. They need grace to handle the stuff broadcast and cable have in store for them.

The same is true of the Internet. Television and computers should never be allowed in a child's bedroom, nor should a private telephone. These machines occupy public family spaces only. The sanctuary must be kept clear of such things. Clear out the magazines too – *Cosmo, Seventeen, Redbook* and the like have to leave. So does *Sports Illustrated* and other magazines that have a habit of less than savory issues during the year. Much good may be found in books, of magazines and newspaper content much less can be said and of television almost nothing at all. We seek to build good judgement, solidity, stability in our children. Newspapers, television and magazines are ephemera. You don't need them except, perhaps, as examples of content whose importance passes quickly away.

Instead of concentrating on things that pass away, give yourselves and your children a chance to live out things eternal. Concentrate on living the seasons of Advent, Christmas, Lent and Easter, focus on living the holy days, the feast days, the anniversaries of baptism, Confirmation, and First Eucharist. Try to implement the traditions as they were lived before the technology of adolescence, the technology of enforced uselessness, destroyed them. Find out when Michaelmas, Candlemas and Passiontide fall, learn the feasts and prayers of the Church, then pray them. Spend time learning how to do the various

---

4   For a wonderful analysis of the problem posed by television, see Neil Postman's *Amusing Ourselves to Death*, Viking Press, 1986.

plenary indulgences scattered through the days of the liturgical year, then do them. It will bring grace into your home and your life.

Beware of Homeschooling

If you decide you would like to try full-blown homeschooling, God bless you and I hope it works out. It is undeniably more difficult to accomplish today than it was two centuries ago. In the early eighteenth century, the culture expected homeschooling, it expected children to have adult abilities by age twelve, it actively supported the family in accomplishing its task of education.

In the early twenty-first century, the situation is quite different. The culture actively opposes homeschooling, it opposes the transformation of any child into a stable, knowledgeable adult, it works to extend childhood as long as possible. In 1805, the point was to integrate the child into society as soon as was practicable. Today, the point is to protect your child from society until he has the tools and strength to combat its skewed expectations on his own. Homeschoolers may use ancient methods, but the purpose and the context are entirely different. No matter how hard a parent tries to replicate the agrarian experience, he or she is not doing what the parents of John Chrysostom or Ben Franklin did. The only Americans who even get close are the Amish, and they manage it only by building an entirely self-contained monastic community.

The agrarian culture concentrated on instilling the life of virtue first. It assumed in-depth knowledge of any particular subject was a mere technical matter which any reasonably intelligent person could acquire on his own as he needed. Today, expectations are precisely reversed. We are expected to instill knowledge of purely technical matters first, with the assumption that the life of virtue will come later. This emphasis on the technique of being virtuous instead of the substance of virtue is called situational ethics. It is neither ethical nor virtuous.

Because the emphasis on creating technicians is so great and because it requires a significant grasp of relatively obscure knowledge to accomplish, many parents are simply not called to or capable of schooling children according to the modern expectation. Homeschooling today is generally an odd amalgam of modern content and ancient but poorly understood methodology. As a result, it is not surprising to find that some children do not respond well to being homeschooled in every subject. There are a lot of things working against today's homeschoolers, things that were simply not present in colonial America or medieval Europe. It is not an easy road.

Now, homeschooling has a lot of advantages. We have heard many Catholic adults lament the loss of consecrated religious in the schools. Well, consecrated religious are still with us in large numbers. Today's Catholic homeschooling parents constitute the religious order that oversees the home school.[5] Like the nuns, monks, sisters, brothers and priests of previous generations, homeschooling parents live a consecrated life of community under strict vows, only the members of this *ordo* live under marriage vows, not vows of celibacy. Other than that small difference, there is little to choose between marriage and monastic life. Ironically, homeschooling establishes what the Second Plenary Council decreed – adults under religious vows teach the children.

Unfortunately, while we may have the religious order of marriage ready at hand to instruct, the flawed curriculum is still with us. Because of the emphasis on technical knowledge, many modern homeschool curricula simply have the parents re-create the Prussian system in their homes. This is better only in the sense that the teacher (you) is a lot more interested in the welfare of your children than anyone at the public or private elementary school is. Still, parental love and zeal is often more than enough to make up for the deficiencies in the curriculum. In most cases, the parent transmits at least as much technical knowledge as the public or parochial school would. Even better, because the parent is the teacher, the curriculum is not built on a substructure of contraception.

Still, homeschoolers spend quite a lot of their time in museums, zoos, parks, nature conservancies, and interacting with other homeschooling families. It is quite a rigorous day, properly done; not everyone is up for the whirl of events. If you know you cannot mentally or physically support that particularly taxing lifestyle, if you decide to send your children to parochial or public school or Catholic college, there is nothing wrong with that choice. As with homeschooling, we must simply keep a few things in mind.

---

5   It is important to remember that sisters, brothers, monks and nuns are nothing more than lay people living under special lay vows. Holy Orders and Holy Matrimony are sacraments, lay vows are not. While celibacy is the higher way, properly lived marriage is most definitely religious life.

First, the word "Catholic" over the door means very little today. It is certainly no guarantee that the school is actually Catholic. Study the school first. Volunteer as a teacher's aide, in the cafeteria or as a playground supervisor for a day or two. That way, you see what the school is really like. This is often quite different from the glowing image painted in the principal's office or during the carefully controlled school tour. If you can't manage that, find out what percentage of teachers are Catholic, what percentage of students are Catholic, examine the textbooks, find out if the religion teacher is Catholic, discover how they instill Catholic culture.

If your child is already attending a "Catholic" school and it is not delivering a fully orthodox Catholic education, approach the teacher, the principal and the pastor, in that order. Try to get the situation fixed.

It is a great pity that such institutions cannot be sued for malpractice and fraud. You have a right to get what you paid for. You paid for an orthodox Catholic education. You didn't get it. You gave them a chance to fix it. They didn't. Sadly, secular courts will not allow us to treat them like adults. We cannot hold Catholic schools legally liable, as we would hold accountable any other business to which we paid thousands of dollars and which failed to provide what the contract promised. The courts refuse to rule on what constitutes the proper parts of any faith.

The tragedy at the college and university level is even greater. Institutes of higher learning are many times more expensive than parochial schools. Worse, they are the most egregious violators of Catholic Faith. As we have seen, at least one USCCB committee has testified that these universities are failing to do what they are contracted to do – provide a Catholic Faith environment or provide orthodox Catholic theological training. Sadly, lawsuits seem to be the only things many Catholic university corporate boards pay attention to. Christian charity requires that we speak to people in a language they understand, but, while leveling a lawsuit against such institutions would be an act of extraordinary charity, an act which inculturates the Gospels by explaining the problems to the relevant leaders using a medium they understand and value, it is not a course that is open to us.

Pope Pius IX lost the Papal States because he would not allow the education of a single Christian child to be ruined. The American bishops are losing the Catholic school system because it generally fails to provide Christian education to children. The system as it is currently structured will disappear in another generation or two. At this point, it isn't a question of "if," it is just a question of "when." But even as we watch the schools close, it is important for us to remember one thing. Losing a school that calls itself Catholic is not the same as losing a Catholic school. We now know the history of the parochial school system. Despite the hundreds of school closings that we have seen in the last several decades, it is hard to argue that the Catholic Church in America has ever closed a single Catholic school.

In that sense, the American Catholic parochial school system is like the Berlin Wall. The Wall was an imposing edifice constructed in order to keep two cultures apart. It became a part of the landscape, an impregnable artifice so well-known that no one could imagine a world without it. Nevertheless, in a single night it became a useless anachronism. The Catholic parochial school system, as it is currently constituted, serves exactly the same purpose as that wall and it will suffer a similar fall.

Conclusion

Every problem the Church has ever faced has come down to a problem of adult catechesis. Every heresy, every rebellion, every attack upon the individual results either from a lack of Catholic knowledge or a lack in the human will necessary to put that Catholic knowledge to use.

As this history shows, the long argument over Vatican II is essentially pointless. Vatican II was not the problem. The constant failure to emphasize or provide adult catechesis to every adult Catholic is the problem. This particular problem existed in the Church well before the Council of Trent. It continued in the American colonies due in no small part to circumstances of geography and population that were completely outside the control of America's consecrated men. In America, the problem was exacerbated by world events and by a peculiarly Protestant cultural mindset. This mindset led directly to the creation of the United States as a world leader in the eugenics movement.

Due to the pressure of the American secular culture, this eugenic mindset became the model upon which the Catholic school system was inadvertently built. Secular forces actively attempted to shape the Catholic schools into their own image. While the bishops fought to keep their flock safe from the ravages of anti-Catholic philosophies, they ultimately lost. As with the Council of Trent, the Second Vatican Council was called too late to prevent the destruction. The bishops and their flocks were swallowed up by the twin heresies of eugenics and Americanism.

As this study shows, the history of Catholic education in America is a history of the undermining of Catholic Faith. American Catholics were intentionally led astray by the Protestant culture they were marinated in. American industrialists deceived men of Christian Faith, both Catholic and non-Catholic. Catholic bishops inadvertently copied a system designed to fail by failing to act within the proper relationship between themselves, Catholic parents and Catholic children. Parents were in turn rendered unable to live out their proper role towards their own children. The Catholic parochial school structure was built on a lie.

Thus, those who want to re-establish the Catholic parochial schools of the early 1900's are not just chasing a phantom, but a falsehood. The problem with the parochial schools was not, as some assert, that these schools provided a "hothouse environment" where Catholics were kept from encountering the culture. Rather, the problem lay in the fact that the schools *embodied* the basic philosophy of the Protestant culture. Worse, Catholic schools attempted to create a space for children that was extrinsic to the family, actively undermining the sanctuary that is only properly built within the family. These schools concentrated on the wrong population, the children, and consequently took over the function of the parents. The Catholic family was, as a direct result, unable to create itself as a sanctuary of life. As the family goes, so goes the nation. As the family goes, so goes the Church.

The schools cannot replace the work of the parents. They were not, are not, and will never be up to the task. Every school built on this model has already been -- or will eventually be -- destroyed. We Catholics have depended far too heavily on schools and religious orders to transmit the Faith, and far too little on parents. We have permitted our children to be children far longer than is good for us or for society. Worst of all, we have permitted our parents to be adolescents in regards to their responsibilities towards Christ.

Today, the bishops of America know the solution, but they are afraid to implement it. They fear the backlash that we, the laity, will inflict upon them if they attempt it. Christ sweated blood in the garden. Parents, given our own attitudes towards the problem, can we really chastise His bishops for preferring sleep to crucifixion? Can we chastise them for being exactly like us?

Ladies and gentlemen, fellow parents, we may decry the passivity of the bishops all we like, we may describe the failures of our bishops with an accuracy painful for all involved, but let us not forget *why* they are passive. They are passive because we insist on being blind to what happened. We insist on an absurd solution - the reform of schools that cannot be reformed - because we do not wish to shoulder the burden of the real solution: we parents must learn the Faith and transmit it to our children ourselves. We must complete our apprenticeship for heaven.

Parents, do we want the schools reformed? Fine. We must stop asking those schools to do what only we are ordained to do. We must reform the schools by giving the parish the resources to form *us*. We must insist that the parish put more resources into our formation than it puts into our children's formation. We must insist on orthodoxy. If we aren't willing to insist that adults come first in our parishes, then we don't have an adult grasp of the Faith. If we don't have an adult grasp of the Faith, our children won't get any grasp of the Faith at all. Parents, it is not the job of the parish to form the children. It is our job.

Stop worrying about the parochial schools. Start worrying about us parents. It is said that a husband loves his children best by loving his wife first. Similarly, if we really want the children to grasp the Faith, then we must first teach the parents an adult grasp of the Faith. Arguing for anything else merely attempts to implement a solution already designed to fail.

Sex and the Sacred City

Named one of the Best Books of 2005 by Dr. Peter Kreeft!

The Critically-Acclaimed Basis for *Designed to Fail*

Beautifully written. A clear exposition of Catholic teaching in language intelligible to all readers. Before attempting to understand the meaning of human sexuality, one needs to study Church teaching concerning the Holy Trinity, the Creation, the Fall, the Incarnation, the Sacraments, Married Life, Celibacy, and Family Life. It is a down-to-earth study of John Paul II's Theology of the Body. Highly recommended for catechetical teachers. God bless you for your wonderful work!

– Father John Harvey, OSFS
Founder and Director of *Courage*

THANK YOU for *Sex and the Sacred City.* I LOVE IT! I have been using it with some patients and have been promoting it in my speaking. You did a great job making the Theology of the Body applicable to everyday life. What a gift you are to the Church. May God bless you.

– Lisa Klewicki, Ph.D.
Institute for Psychological Sciences, Arlington, VA

Steve Kellmeyer is the author of *Sex and the Sacred City*, a great little book on John Paul's Theology of the Body. He is the pre-eminent expert I know of on issues of sexuality, marriage and the Church.

– Tim Johnson
Editor, *Catholic Maniacs*

In just a hundred pages Steve Kellmeyer distills the rich and complex 'Theology of the Body.' *Sex and the Sacred City* is a masterpiece of clarity. It's size, stylistic grace as well as it's logic should guarantee this book wide readership. Rarely is such a dense topic so delightfully explained and for adults as well as adolescents at that!

– Al Kresta
President-CEO, Ave Maria Radio

Resources

Finding orthodox resources is often difficult. The authors listed below are reliable and recommended.

Every Catholic household should have a copy of the *Catechism of the Catholic Church* and a book of Holy Scripture. Avoid translations of Holy Scripture with gender-neutral language. Check to see if your translation has been neutered by looking at Psalm 8:4. It should say "What is man that thou are mindful of him, the son of man that thou carest for him?" If the masculine pronouns are missing, the translation is poor. Also, be aware that the footnotes in the New American Bible are unreliable.

Authors	Suggested reading list (in order)
Frank Sheed	*A Map of Life*
Fulton Sheen	*Life of Christ*
Frank Sheed	*Theology for Beginners*
Scott Hahn	*A Father Who Keeps His Promises*
Steve Kellmeyer	*Sex and the Sacred City*
Karl Keating	*Catholicism and Fundamentalism*
Steve Kellmeyer	*Bible Basics*
Patrick Madrid	*Surprised by Truth*
HW Crocker III	*Triumph*
Thomas E Woods	*How The Catholic Church Built Western Civilization*

Magazines
First Things • *The Catholic Answer* • *This Rock*
Lay Witness • *Celebrate Life* • *Human Life Review*
Homiletics and Pastoral Review

Early Christians
Become acquainted with the writings of the earliest Christians. Join the free email list that provides their commentary on the upcoming Sunday Gospel readings in a short, easily-read, accessible format. It is available at www.bridegroompress.com.

About the Author

Steve Kellmeyer is a popular Catholic author and lecturer who has written hundreds of articles for Catholic websites, newspapers and magazines. His work has appeared in *National Catholic Register*, *This Rock*, *Envoy*, *Lay Witness*, *Homiletics & Pastoral Review*, *The Catholic Answer*, *Social Justice Review* and *The New Oxford Review*. He has also appeared on *The Total Living Network with Jerry Rose* and the Pax TV special, *Breaking the Da Vinci Code*.

Designed to Fail is his seventh book. Earlier titles include works like *Fact and Fiction in The Da Vinci Code*, the most thorough refutation of Dan Brown's book on the market today, *Sex and the Sacred City*, a clear, concise commentary on the Theology of the Body, and *Bible Basics*, the most thorough Scriptural defense of Catholic Faith available.

With an MA in catechetical theology from Franciscan University, Steubenville and an MA in modern European history from Southern Illinois University, Edwardsville, he also has undergraduate degrees in computer science, medical laboratory technology and math education. He has worked or published in every field in which he holds a degree.

An outstanding speaker who skillfully shows how theology applies to today's headlines, he appears frequently in lecture halls and on radio and television stations both nationally and internationally. He resides in Plano, Texas with his bride, Veronica, and their children.

Author Endorsements

"Thanks again for taking the time to talk to Peter Boyles. I just tell you that in the years I have worked with Peter, I have never een a listener reaction quite like the one we have gotten from your radio interview. It has been HUGE! I have answered more calls than I can count about you, your book and your website. You really made an impact on Peter's audience. Much appreciated!"

– Kris Berard
Producer, *The Peter Boyles' Show*

"I am very impressed with your wide range of knowledge of the faith and your ability to express the truth so concisely yet with so much depth. You are providing a great service to the Church. We are grateful to you for helping make our conference a success."

– Catherine Mianecki
Michigan Homeschool Conference

Steve Kellmeyer's presentations on a variety of Catholic teachings and current issues affecting the Church are well argued and presented. Steve's presentation style is energetic and entertaining. He is also not afraid of engaging with the audience in an open dialogue. I recommend Steve as a speaker."

– Diana Bes
Office of Evangelization, Peoria Diocese

"I would like to extend my sincere thanks and gratitude, on behalf of the Catholic Radio Association and all participating stations… We were honored and blessed to have you as an interview guest."

– Steve Gajdosik
President, Catholic Radio Association

Bibliography

Magisterial Documents
Congregation for Catholic Education, *Lay Catholics in Schools.* 1982.
Congregation for the Clergy, *General Catechetical Directory.* 1971.
Congregation for the Clergy, *General Directory of Catechesis.* 1997.
Congregation for Evangelization of Peoples, *Guide for Catechists*, 1993.
Leo XIII, *On the Nature of Human Liberty (Libertas)*, 1888.
John Paul II, *On Catholic Universities (Ex Cordae Ecclesia)*, 1990.
John Paul II, *The Hundredth Year (Centesimus Annus)*, 1991.
John Paul II, *Catechesis in Our Time (Catechesi Tradendae)*, 1979.
John Paul II, *Family in the Modern World (Familiaris Consortio)*, 1981.
John Paul II, General audience, July 4, 1984.
Paul VI, *On Human Life, (Humanae Vitae)*, 1968.
Pius XI, *The Fortieth Year (Quadragesimo Anno)*, 1931.
Pius XI, *On Christian Education (Rappresentanti in Terra)*, 1929.
Piux X, *On Teaching Christian Doctrine (Acerbo Nimis)*, 1905.
Pius XII, Address to newly installed cardinals, 20 February 1946.
Pius XII, Address to Lay Apostolates, October 5, 1957.
Rite of Confirmation, Sacred Congregation for Divine Worship, Aug 22 ,1971.
Second Vatican Council, *Gravissimum Educationis,* 28 Oct 1965.
Catechism of the Catholic Church, 1997.

Other Church Documents
NCCB, *Human Life in Our Day,* 15 November 1968.
USCCB, *Our Hearts Were Burning Within Us*, 17 November 1999.
World Synod Document on Bishops and The Ministry of the Word, 2001.

Books
DeNuncio, Charles. *Variations on a Theme Op. 45* (1988), unpublished manuscript.
Gatto, John Taylor. *An Underground History of American Education.* Oxford Village Press, New York, (2003).
Gower, Joseph F. and Richard M. Leliaert, ed., *The Brownson-Hecker Correspondence*, University of Notre Dame Press, Notre Dame (1979).
Hartmann, Thom. *Unequal Protection: The Rise of Corporate Dominance and the Theft of Human Rights.* Rodale Books (2002).
MacLaren, Angus. *A History of Contraception from Antiquity to the Present Day,* Oxford, Blackwell Publishers (1992).
Maignen, Charles. *Father Hecker, Is He A Saint?* London, Burns & Oates (1898).
Postman, Neil. *Amusing Ourselves to Death*, Viking Press, New York (1986).

Richman, Sheldon, *Separating School & State: How to Liberate America's Families*, Future of Freedom Foundation, Fairfax, VA (1994).

Rothman, David. *Discovery of the Asylum*, Little, Brown and Company, New York (1971).

Rumble and Carty. *Radio Replies*, Tan Press, Rockford, IL (1979).

Tyack, David. *The One Best System*, Harvard University Press, Cambridge, MA (1974).

Taylor, James. *Poetic Knowledge: The Recovery of Education*, State University of New York Press, New York (1998).

Vitz, Paul. *Faith of the Fatherless*, Spence Publishing, Dallas (1999).

Newspapers, Magazines, Internet and Encyclopedia articles

Califano, Joseph. "How I Squared Church and State," *Washington Post*, Sunday, June 24, 2001, B-1.

Diogenes, "Personally Opposed, But..." *Catholic World News*, December, 2003. http://www.catholicworldnews.com/news/viewstory. cfm?recnum=26364.

Laugesen, Wayne. "New Study Calls Abuse an Epidemic", *National Catholic Register*, Jan 30-Feb 5, 2005, p. 1, 3.

Gary, Bruce L. *A New Time-Scale for Placing Human Events, Derivation of Per Capita Rate of Innovation and a Speculation on the Timing of the Demise of Humanity*, August 9, 1993. http://reductionism.net.seanic. net/brucegary3/Speculations/innovations(t).html.

"Mums, Dads Key to the Future," *The Sunday Times*, 10 April 2005, http://www.sundaytimes.news.com.au/common/story_page/ 0,7034,12803677%255E950,00.html.

Noguera, Pedro, "Preventing Violence in Schools Through the Production of Docile Bodies," *In Motion Magazine*, Jan 12, 1997, http://www. inmotionmagazine.com/pedro31.html.

Reilly, Patrick J. "Are Catholic Colleges Leading Students Astray?" *Catholic World Report*, March 2003, http://www.cardinalnewmansociety.org/ Publications/News/CatholicWorldReportArticle.pdf.

"Schools," *Catholic Encyclopedia* (1913), http://www.newadvent.org.

Smith, Janet. "A Mistaken Church?" *Catholic Dossier*, Volume 6, No 3, May-June 2000, http://www.catholic.net/rcc/Periodicals/Dossier/2000-5-6/ column.html.

Spiller, Christopher, *Church and State: The Sacred, the Profane, and the First Amendment*, Duquesne University 11th Annual *GSO Conference: The Academy and the Polis* (2005).

"When Catholic Catechetical Works Don't Teach the Faith", *Zenit*, December 4, 2003, http://www.zenit.org/english/visualizza.phtml?sid=46752.

Wojtyla, Karol. *Love and Responsibility*, Ignatius Press. San Francisco, 1993.

Index

Printed in the United States
64791LVS00007B/19-24